CASEBOOKS PUBLISHED

Austen: *Emma*   DAVID LODGE
Austen: *'Northanger Abbey' & 'Persuasi...*
Austen: *'Sense and Sensibility', 'Pride an...*   ...AM
Blake: *Songs of Innocence and Experience...*

...ok is to be r...

...wning: *Men and Wom...*   ...

...an: *Pilgrim's Progress*   ROGER SHARROCK
...: *'Childe Harold's Pilgrimage' & 'Don Juan'*   JOHN JUMP
...ucer: *Canterbury Tales*   J. J. ANDERSON
...eridge: *'The Ancient Mariner' & Other Poems*   ALUN R. JONES & WILLIAM TYDEMAN
...greve: *Comedies*   PATRICK LYONS
...ed: *'Heart of Darkness', 'Nostromo' & 'Under Western Eyes'*   C. B. COX
...ad: *The Secret Agent*   IAN WATT
...ens: *Bleak House*   A. E. DYSON
...kens: *'Dombey and Son' & 'Little Dorrit'*   ALAN SHELSTON
...kens: *'Hard Times', 'Great Expectations' & 'Our Mutual Friend'*   NORMAN PAGE
...ne: *Songs and Sonets*   JULIAN LOVELOCK
...orge Eliot: *Middlemarch*   PATRICK SWINDEN
...orge Eliot: *'The Mill on the Floss' & 'Silas Marner'*   R. P. DRAPER
...S. Eliot: *Plays*   ARNOLD P. HINCHLIFFE
...S. Eliot: *Four Quartets*   BERNARD BERGONZI
...S. Eliot: *'Prufrock', 'Gerontion', 'Ash Wednesday' & Other Shorter Poems*   B. C. SOUTHAM
...S. Eliot: *The Waste Land*   C. B. COX & ARNOLD P. HINCHLIFFE
...quhar: *'The Recruiting Officer' & 'The Beaux' Stratagem'*   RAYMOND A. ANSELMENT
...lding: *Tom Jones*   NEIL COMPTON
...ter: *A Passage to India*   MALCOLM BRADBURY
...y: *Poems*   JAMES GIBSON & TREVOR JOHNSON
...y: *The Tragic Novels*   R. P. DRAPER
...ns: *Poems*   MARGARET BOTTRALL
...s: *'Washington Square' & 'The Portrait of a Lady'*   ALAN SHELSTON
...on: *'Every Man in his Humour' & 'The Alchemist'*   R. V. HOLDSWORTH
...on: *Volpone*   JONAS A. BARISH
...: *'Dubliners' & 'The Portrait of the Artist as a Young Man'*   MORRIS BEJA
...s: *Narrative Poems*   JOHN SPENCER HILL
...s: *Odes*   G. S. FRASER
...Lawrence: *Sons and Lovers*   GAMINI SALGADO
...Lawrence: *'The Rainbow' & 'Women in Love'*   COLIN CLARKE
...owe: *Doctor Faustus*   JOHN JUMP
...owe: *'Tamburlaine the Great', 'Edward the Second' & 'The Jew of Malta'*
...N RUSSELL BROWN
...ell: *Poems*   ARTHUR POLLARD
...ilton: *'Comus' & 'Samson Agonistes'*   JULIAN LOVELOCK
Milton: *Paradise Lost*   A. E. DYSON & JULIAN LOVELOCK
...y: *The Dublin Trilogy*   RONALD AYLING
...e: *Look Back in Anger*   JOHN RUSSELL TAYLOR
...   *The Satirical Novels*   LORNA SAGE
...*The Rape of the Lock*   JOHN DIXON HUNT
...speare: *A Midsummer Night's Dream*   ANTONY W. PRICE
...akespeare: *Antony and Cleopatra*   JOHN RUSSELL BROWN
...akespeare: *Coriolanus*   B. A. BROCKMAN

Shakespeare: *Hamlet*  JOHN JUMP
Shakespeare: *Henry IV Parts 1 and 2*  G. K. HUNTER
Shakespeare: *Henry V*  MICHAEL QUINN
Shakespeare: *Julius Caesar*  PETER URE
Shakespeare: *King Lear*  FRANK KERMODE
Shakespeare: *Macbeth*  JOHN WAIN
Shakespeare: *Measure for Measure*  G. K. STEAD
Shakespeare: *The Merchant of Venice*  JOHN WILDERS
Shakespeare: *'Much Ado About Nothing' & 'As You Like It'*  JOHN RUSSELL BROWN
Shakespeare: *Othello*  JOHN WAIN
Shakespeare: *Richard II*  NICHOLAS BROOKE
Shakespeare: *The Sonnets*  PETER JONES
Shakespeare: *The Tempest*  D. J. PALMER
Shakespeare: *Troilus and Cressida*  PRISCILLA MARTIN
Shakespeare: *Twelfth Night*  D. J. PALMER
Shakespeare: *The Winter's Tale*  KENNETH MUIR
Shelley: *Shorter Poems & Lyrics*  PATRICK SWINDEN
Spenser: *The Faerie Queene*  PETER BAYLEY
Swift: *Gulliver's Travels*  RICHARD GRAVIL
Tennyson: *In Memoriam*  JOHN DIXON HUNT
Thackeray: *Vanity Fair*  ARTHUR POLLARD
Trollope: *The Barsetshire Novels*  T. BAREHAM
Webster: *'The White Devil' & 'The Duchess of Malfi'*  R. V. HOLDSWORTH
Wilde: *Comedies*  WILLIAM TYDEMAN
Woolf: *To the Lighthouse*  MORRIS BEJA
Wordsworth: *Lyrical Ballads*  ALUN R. JONES & WILLIAM TYDEMAN
Wordsworth: *The Prelude*  W. J. HARVEY & RICHARD GRAVIL
Yeats: *Poems, 1919–35*  ELIZABETH CULLINGFORD
Yeats: *Last Poems*  JON STALLWORTHY

*Medieval English Drama*  PETER HAPPÉ
*Elizabethan Poetry: Lyrical & Narrative*  GERALD HAMMOND
*The Metaphysical Poets*  GERALD HAMMOND
*Poetry of the First World War*  DOMINIC HIBBERD
*Thirties Poets: 'The Auden Group'*  RONALD CARTER
*Comedy: Developments in Criticism*  D. J. PALMER
*Drama Criticism: Developments since Ibsen*  ARNOLD P. HINCHLIFFE
*Tragedy: Developments in Criticism*  R. P. DRAPER
*The English Novel: Developments in Criticism since Henry James*  STEPHEN HAZELL
*The Language of Literature*  NORMAN PAGE
*The Pastoral Mode*  BRYAN LOUGHREY
*The Romantic Imagination*  JOHN SPENCER HILL

CASEBOOKS IN PREPARATION INCLUDE

Beckett: *'Waiting for Godot' & Other Plays*  JOHN RUSSELL BROWN
Defoe: *'Robinson Crusoe' & 'Moll Flanders'*  PATRICK LYONS
Pinter: *'The Caretaker' & Other Plays*  MICHAEL SCOTT
Sheridan: *Comedies*  PETER DAVISON

*Poetry Criticism: Developments since the Symbolists*  A. E. DYSON
*Post-Fifties Poets: Gunn, Hughes, Larkin & R. S. Thomas*  A. E. DYSON
*Shakespeare: Approaches in Criticism*  JOHN RUSSELL BROWN
*The Gothick Novel*  VICTOR SAGE

# T. S. Eliot

## Plays

### Sweeney Agonistes
### The Rock
### Murder in the Cathedral
### The Family Reunion
### The Cocktail Party
### The Confidential Clerk
### The Elder Statesman

A CASEBOOK

EDITED BY

ARNOLD P. HINCHLIFFE

MACMILLAN

First published 1985

Published by
Higher and Further Education Division
MACMILLAN PUBLISHERS LTD
Houndmills, Basingstoke, Hampshire RG21 2XS
and London
Companies and representatives
throughout the world

Typeset by
Wessex Typesetters
Frome, Somerset

Printed in Hong Kong

British Library Cataloguing in Publication Data
T. S. Eliot: plays: a casebook.—(Casebook series)
1. Eliot, T. S.—Criticism and interpretation
I. Hinchliffe, Arnold P.   II. Series
822′. 912   PS3509.L43
ISBN 0–333–33012–9
ISBN 0–333–33013–7 Pbk

# CONTENTS

*General Editor's Preface*                                              7
*Introduction*                                                         8

Part One: *Eliot and the Drama*

1 Eliot on Drama
  Excerpts from Essays, Lectures, Interviews &
    Correspondence                                                    19
2 Eliot's Aims and Achievements
  MURIEL C. BRADBROOK:  Eliot as Dramatist  (1965)                    31
  HELEN GARDNER:  The Comedies of T. S. Eliot  (1965)                 42
  KATHARINE J. WORTH:  'Precursor and Model Maker'
    (1972)                                                            60

Part Two: *Early Stages*

1 *Sweeney Agonistes*
  CAROL H. SMITH:  'An Alliance of Levity and Seriousness'
    (1963)                                                            73
  BERNARD BERGONZI:  'Language, Theatre and Belief'
    (1972)                                                            77
  ANDREW KENNEDY:  'Ritual and Dramatic Speech Effects'
    (1975)                                                            79
  RONALD HAYMAN:  'The Timid Pioneer'  (1979)                         81
2 *The Rock: A Pageant Play*
  T. S. ELIOT:  Two Comments  (1933, 1953)                            83
  ROGER KOJECKÝ:  'Team-Work and a Social Aim'  (1971)                84
  HELEN GARDNER:  'Experiment in Choric Verse'  (1949)                86
3 *Murder in the Cathedral*
  T. S. ELIOT:  Comment  (1951)                                       88
  CONRAD AIKEN:  A Trip to Canterbury  (1935)                         90
  HERBERT HOWARTH:  'Theatrical Ingenuity and Tact'
    (1965)                                                            92
  HELEN GARDNER:  'Sanctity versus Self-Consciousness'
    (1949)                                                            94
  STEPHEN SPENDER:  'Martyrdom and Motive'  (1975)                    96
  MICHAEL GOLDMAN:  'Dramatic Effectiveness'  (1973)                 101
  HUGH KENNER:  'The Archbishop Murder Case'  (1960)                 104
  FRANCIS FERGUSSON:  'Ritual Form of Ancient Tragedy'
    (1954)                                                           106

GARETH LLOYD EVANS:   The Dramatist in Search of a
     Language   (1977)                                          108
RAYMOND WILLIAMS: 'Dramatic Pattern'   (1968)                   115

          Part Three: *Plays for the Theatre*

1 *The Family Reunion*
  T. S. ELIOT:   Comment   (1951)                               121
  HUGH KENNER:   'The Play's Poetical Context'   (1960)         123
  JOHN PETER:   'An Artistic Failure'   (1949)                  125
  RAYMOND WILLIAMS:   'The Drawing-Room of Naturalism'
     (1968)                                                     133
  RONALD GASKELL:   'Dramatic Anguish'   (1972)                 137

2 *The Cocktail Party*
  T. S. ELIOT:   Comment   (1951)                               143
  RAYMOND WILLIAMS:   'A Theatrical Compromise'   (1968)        144
  JOHN PETER:   Sin and Soda   (1950)                           150
  STEPHEN SPENDER:   'The Search for Religious Vocation'
     (1975)                                                     156
  MICHAEL GOLDMAN:   'Eliot's Most Successful Play'
     (1973)                                                     159
  HERBERT HOWARTH:   'The Supreme Result'   (1965)              162
  HUGH KENNER:   'Something Happens At Last'   (1960);
     and 'Private Agonies'   (1975)                             165
  ROGER KOJECKÝ:   'The Role of the Guardians'   (1971)         168

3 *The Confidential Clerk*
  E. MARTIN BROWNE:   'A Producer's Retrospect'   (1981)        171
  NORTHROP FRYE:   'Atmosphere of Demure Farce'   (1963)        172
  CAROL H. SMITH:   'Christian Implications and Greek
     Myth'   (1963)                                             173

4 *The Elder Statesman*
  RAYMOND WILLIAMS:   'Spectres of a Dying Theatre'
     (1968)                                                     176
  MICHAEL GOLDMAN:   'Acceptance of Loss and Limitation'
     (1973)                                                     177
  CAROL H. SMITH:   'Love and Self-Knowledge – Badgley
     Court and Colonus'   (1963)                                179

*Select Bibliography*                                           184

*Notes on Contributors*                                         185

*Acknowledgements*                                              187

*Index*                                                         189

# GENERAL EDITOR'S PREFACE

The Casebook series, launched in 1968, has become a well-regarded library of critical studies. The central concern of the series remains the 'single-author' volume, but suggestions from the academic community have led to an extension of the original plan, to include occasional volumes on such general themes as literary 'schools' and genres.

Each volume in the central category deals either with one well-known and influential work by an individual author, or with closely related works by one writer. The main section consists of critical readings, mostly modern, collected from books and journals. A selection of reviews and comments by the author's contemporaries is also included, and sometimes comment from the author himself. The Editor's Introduction charts the reputation of the work or works from the first appearance to the present time.

Volumes in the 'general themes' category are variable in structure but follow the basic purpose of the series in presenting an integrated selection of readings, with an Introduction which explores the theme and discusses the literary and critical issues involved.

A single volume can represent no more than a small selection of critical opinions. Some critics are excluded for reasons of space, and it is hoped that readers will pursue the suggestions for further reading in the Select Bibliography. Other contributions are severed from their original context, to which some readers may wish to turn. Indeed, if they take a hint from the critics represented here, they certainly will.

A. E. DYSON

# INTRODUCTION

In his reviews of both *The Family Reunion* and *The Confidential Clerk*, Kenneth Tynan noted that Eliot could always lower the dramatic temperature but never raise it: 'and this is why the theatre, an impure assembly that loves strong emotions, must ultimately reject him. He is glacial, a theatrical Jack Frost; at the first breath of warmth, he melts and vanishes'.[1] Even when that warmth appeared in *The Elder Statesman*, a play written by an Eliot whom Tynan recognised as having now 'majored in the Humanities as well as the Eumenides', it was not enough to make 'good theatre' – for with the new simplicity had come 'simplicity's half-wit brother, banality'. This viewpoint is far from being shared by all critics – or indeed, theatre-goers. But it is one with a strong basis and influence, and it is a necessary element in forming a judgement of Eliot's work for the theatre. E. Martin Browne has described, in great and loving detail (see Select Bibliography) how the poet was translated into the theatre. But the question remains as to whether Eliot became a poet of the theatre, or remained merely a poet in the theatre.

Since most of Eliot's mature work is in drama, it is an important question. How important it is may not be immediately apparent to us, for the volumes of verse come easily to hand, for reading and discussion, but experiencing performance of the plays is not readily vouchsafed. Yet poetry of the order of *Four Quartets* possibly came into being only because of the 1939–45 war – not simply in the sense of being connected with the personal and public 'crisis' of wartime but in the very basic sense of changed circumstances for literary creativity. 'Burnt Norton' used up bits of *Murder in the Cathedral* that Eliot thought too good to waste; it was published in 1935 as the last poem in *Collected Poems, 1900–1935*. Thereafter Eliot was largely preoccupied with writing *The Family Reunion* (1939), which was far from being regarded by him as a sole venture in verse drama for the commercial theatre. It was to have been followed by another play; but the outbreak of war prevented this: theatres were closed and the outlook for theatrical life in London seemed uncertain. Eliot later considered this as a good thing – in that it prevented him from writing another play too soon – but in fact there was no point in writing a play at all at that time. Another poem in the style and mood of 'Burnt Norton' seemed appropriate – and 'East Coker' was published in

1940. While writing that second poem he realised that there should be four; and so in 1941 appeared 'The Dry Salvages' and in 1942 'Little Gidding'. The energy and inspiration which created them were, in a sense, diverted by circumstances from a theatrical intention.

Yet why should so eminent a poet and critic strive so earnestly to move into the theatre? Peter Ackroyd in his biography of Eliot (see Select Bibliography concluding this volume) suggests that drama helped to release the 'block' on poetry – as previously had been achieved for him by writing in French or medical ·treatment at Lausanne. But Eliot neither had his own theatrical sense nor, more importantly, had he found a literary context for such writing 'from which to draw energy or inspiration'. Ackroyd sees Eliot's imagination as working to receive the full force of other writing, which is then assimilated into his own design. He wanted to get away from *The Waste Land* but feared that he might have come to the end of his poetic life. Religious faith helped in the writing of *Ash Wednesday* (1930), but after finishing that he felt once more that he might not be able to write 'pure poetry' again. His attempt at a poetic sequence – 'Coriolan' – had failed. And then came the commission for choral verse which spurred him into creative activity from which emerged *The Rock* (1934).

Drama as therapy, however, cannot be the whole story. His poetry from the beginning had been called 'dramatic', and *personae* like Prufrock and Gerontion are memorable characters. Yet Eliot's remarks on Browning in 'The Three Voices of Poetry' (see excerpt IX, below)* show that he was aware of the danger of confusing the dramatic poet with the dramatist. Moreover, he was theoretically well qualified to write for the stage. As early as May 1920, the poet of *The Waste Land* (1922) was writing – in a review of Middleton Murry's *Cinnamon and Angelica: A Play* – that the composition of a poetic drama in modern times was 'the most difficult, the most exhausting task that a poet can set himself'. His first article for the *Dial* was on 'The Possibility of a Poetic Drama' (see excerpt I), and his articles in that magazine on contemporary London (1921–22) look forward to *Sweeney*. His essay on 'Four Elizabethan Dramatists' appeared in 1924, at a time when he was writing on theatrical matters to Arnold Bennett. The latter records in his journal (10 Sept. 1924) that Eliot

had definitely given up that form of writing [Wastelands as Bennett calls it] and was now centred on dramatic writing. He wanted to write a drama of

* Here and elsewhere, 'excerpt' numbering relates to the elements in section 1 ('Eliot on Drama') in Part One, below.

modern life (furnished flat sort of people) in a rhythmic prose 'perhaps with
certain things in it accentuated by drum-beats'. And he wanted my advice.
We arranged that he should do the scenario and some sample pages of
dialogue.[2]

Eliot had explored the importance of rhythm and ritual in performance in 'The Beating of a Drum' (Nation and Athenaeum, 6 Oct. 1923).
He had also looked at the usefulness of myth as a method of ordering
experience in his review 'Ulysses, Order and Myth' in the Dial (LXXV,
Nov. 1923), which looked back to The Waste Land and forward to the
plays – for Jessie Weston and J. G. Frazer were connected with
Gilbert Murray, Francis M. Cornford and Jane Ellen Harrison.
Myth, anthropology, ritual and Greek drama: these were areas that
he was exploring in Sweeney Agonistes.

'Fragments of a Prologue' appeared in the New Criterion for October
1926 and 'Fragment of an Agon' in its issue for January 1927. Both
figured under the general title of 'Wanna Go Home, Baby?', and did
not appear in book form until 1932, with a change of title to Sweeney
Agonistes: Fragments of an Aristophanic Melodrama. In Sweeney we can find
virtually all of Eliot's major dramatic ideas – a chorus, colloquial
speech rhythms, Greek conventions and sources, the use of myth and
various levels of meaning integrated into one action. In 1926, too,
when he published his mother's dramatic poem Savonarola, Eliot
noted in his introduction that the next form of drama would have to be
verse drama – 'but in new verse forms' (see excerpt II).

After Sweeney he wrote the choruses for The Rock (1934). He was
commissioned to write these by E. Martin Browne for a religious
dramatic venture, and The Rock in turn led to a commission to write
the next play for the Canterbury Festival, Murder in the Cathedral
(1935). Eliot's first play for the commercial theatre, The Family
Reunion, was staged in 1939. Ten years elapsed before The Cocktail
Party (commissioned in 1947 by E. Martin Browne) opened in 1949 at
the Edinburgh Festival. His later plays – The Confidential Clerk (1953)
and The Elder Statesman (1958) – also had their first performance at
Edinburgh. Between these two plays British theatre-goers were
presented with Beckett's Waiting for Godot (1955) and John Osborne's
Look Back in Anger (1956). Eliot's ideas about the aims and techniques
of 'serious' drama were now to share the scene with other, very
different, ideas (see E. Martin Browne's retrospective comment in
section 3 of Part Three, below).

The Rock and Murder in the Cathedral suggest certain reasons for
Eliot's move into the theatre: social usefulness, a wider audience and
a religious purpose (though in his case dramatic interest precedes

conversion). He was baptised into the Church of England in 1927, and his plays are vehicles for Christian values. His religious sincerity cannot be doubted (he would not allow John Gielgud to play Harry Monchensey because he thought the actor not religious enough to understand the motivation of the character), but it is no less true that, after *The Rock*, Eliot was stage-struck because he had seen a popular audience moved by something he had written. The venture into commercial theatre was a recognition that his first two dramatic works were limited by being religious 'events' for a particular kind of audience. He now sought to convey his Christian message to a wider audience. (See his comment of 1933, in section 2 of Part Two, below.) Conveying the message convincingly to his audience's understanding is the prime aim. Thus, as his subsequent assessments included in our selection reveal, he becomes his own severest critic: *Murder in the Cathedral* comes to be seen by him as a 'dead end' and *The Family Reunion* as 'a failure as a play'. His plays brought him fame and honour, and money too; but he got the Nobel prize for his poetry.

Eliot unquestionably was a great poet and a wise critic, but was he defeated by his move into commercial theatre and stage-presentation of aspects of modern life? His concern with an audience – get its attention and never lose it (see excerpt VI) – was probably misplaced. As Hugh Kenner points out:

It leads to plays written for an audience who will swallow the poetry if they get their Noel Coward; it leads to the West End stage and Mr Martin Browne; it leads to plays more dignified, literate and intelligent than the West End stage has supported in its time, or than Broadway has commonly occasion to mount; but not to that 'new drama . . . which was to owe something to the music halls and the ballet and the invention of a new form elevating contemporary life into something rich and strange . . .'.[3]

Eliot may have decided in the 1940s that drawing-room comedy was such a form, but if so he was betrayed – for drawing-room comedy is not so much a form as a series of devices for holding the attention of an audience. He also seems (naturally, perhaps, for a poet) to have adopted the view that speech alone gives a play its force, and that the rest can be left to the director (see excerpt X).

Nowhere is Eliot's belief in language clearer than in the passage in 'Poetry and Drama' where he is surprised to find what Ibsen and Chekhov can do in prose. Yet, he insists, they are nevertheless hampered by writing in prose! Verse grows very thin in Eliot's play-writing (whereas his more exuberant rival Christopher Fry shows that audiences do not mind poetry), and Tynan had a point when he argued, in 'Prose and the Playwrights' (1954), that we have only just made prose respectable in the theatre, and a vogue for poetic drama would only be agreeable if the theatre were not already besieged by cinema and television.

★

The critical response to a career with so many facets is, of course, vast and varied. Eliot, in the introduction to *The Sacred Wood* (1920), regretted that Matthew Arnold was tempted into social and political criticism (work that lesser men could have done, he opined), but he himself was to succumb to the same temptation.

Thus Roger Kojecký, in his study of 1971, deals with Eliot the Anglo-Catholic whose later prose was dominated by his concern over Church and State. Only a short chapter, unfortunately, is devoted by Kojecký to Eliot as poet and dramatist, but this critic usefully notes the social views in *The Rock* and Eliot's awareness of the plight of the unemployed in Britain [*], and points out that the Guardians in *The Cocktail Party* resemble the Community of Christians described in *The Idea of a Christian Society* (1939) [*]. An alternative view of that mysterious group is registered by William Arrowsmith, who sees what they do as an 'undisclosed conspiracy of conversion'.[4]

*Murder in the Cathedral* is by any standards a special case, but criticism – from both admirers and detractors – has tended to stress its ritual qualities and the problem of martyrdom, forgetting that it is first and foremost a play. And even when literary questions are asked, these tend to turn back to religion: not, is it a tragedy?; but, can there be such a thing as Christian tragedy? Robert H. Canary reminds us: 'When such discussions translate the poetry into dogma and the drama into doctrine, they stand between us and the work.'[5] Thus Francis Fergusson's approach is useful because, while admitting liturgical and Greek conventions, he recognises that the play produces an imitation of human action – like a Shakespearean tragedy [*].

There is obviously a close relation between *Four Quartets* and the plays, as has been mentioned earlier. Hugh Kenner writes of *The Family Reunion* as the next poem after 'Burnt Norton' [*]; and many critics refer to Eliot's 'John Marston' essay of 1934 with his observation on a 'doublesness of action' (see excerpt IV), and explore the use of Greek

[*] An asterisk within square brackets indicates that the viewpoint so signalised is excerpted in this Casebook's selection of criticism by the author concerned.

sources. But it should be remembered that, if Aeschylus was the dominant influence for *The Family Reunion*, Eliot also read the plays of Ibsen consecutively 'to work myself up'.[6] And when *The Cocktail Party* appeared, he was delighted that no one recognised his source in the *Alcestis* of Euripides (see his comment of 1951, in section 2 of Part Three, below).

A critic such as Carol H. Smith, for example, argues that all the plays are 'intended to lead the audience to a sense of religious awareness by demonstrating the presence of the supernatural order in the natural world' [*]; and certainly, since Eliot is concerned with spiritual values and uses the mythic method, his plays are not vulnerable to criticism in naturalistic terms. Yet his plays are static enough without this further reduction into ritual re-enactments and slogans from heaven. The Greek sources are explored in some detail by such critics as D. E. Jones and Grover Smith (see Select Bibliography), but Hugh Dickinson observes that Eliot uses these sources as a kind of private guide, subduing them to his Christian vision to such an extent that they are no longer recognisable in the theatre. What resemblances remain are more a matter for literary exegesis than for apprehending in performance.[7] Dickinson is almost certainly correct in suggesting that knowledge – or ignorance – of them does little to affect our understanding in performance. Many critics, let it be said, get by without too much involvement in myth or Greek tragedy, or even in Eliot's obsessive concern with language.

Indeed, stressing religious themes, double actions, poetic drama and the problems of creating and sustaining it, all this keeps Eliot's plays in what Katharine J. Worth (1970) calls the 'not very jolly corner labelled "verse and religious drama" '.

It cannot quite be avoided, however, and Stephen Spender has a point when, in writing about *The Cocktail Party*, he suggests that for Eliot the choice of eternity was so preferable to life on earth 'that it is difficult for him not to make actual living seem second-rate' [*]. In another perspective on the same play, Raymond Williams feels that Eliot was so anxious about the surface (drawing-room comedy) that the surface became the substance and dramatic tension was turned into theatrical compromise [*]. D. E. Jones (see Select Bibliography) approves the indirection with which Eliot presents the religious themes to secular audiences (while admitting this may be a source of weakness in them); but since he sees *Sweeney* as a dead end, has little time for *The Rock* and judges *Murder in the Cathedral* as a special case (albeit the finest modern religious play) he has to see the modern plays – in spite of the thinness of verse and flatness of character – as part of a steady advance.

Eliot's achievement is best summed up by studies like those of Muriel C. Bradbrook – who notes only a faint resonance from the Greek myths [*] – and Helen Gardner, who relates the plays to the comic tradition in the English theatre and suggests that they explore the classic subject of comedy: 'our almost unlimited powers of self-deception' [*]. Katherine J. Worth, writing in 1972, sees Eliot as an inventive dramatist and notes the possibilities of *Sweeney* [*] – which Eliot himself believed to be the most original of his compositions.[8] His plays explore subjects that fascinate modern theatre-goers, deploying techniques that foreshadow those of Albee and Pinter. For Worth, *The Cocktail Party* has some claim to be the first black comedy in post-war English theatre. Even Noel Coward in this perspective is seen in a more honest (that is to say, less dismissive) light than Hugh Kenner would view him by, as we have earlier noted. All of which brings us firmly back to the testing ground of the theatre.

If we can accept that Eliot prepared the way for the dramatists of our own day, it nonetheless remains unquestionable that *The Elder Statesman* – however moving as a personal document – was a good deal more than two years' belated after *Look Back in Anger*; and it was a long, long way distant from that new drama 'which was to owe something to the music halls and the ballet and the invention of a new form elevating contemporary life into something rich and strange . . .'. But, with that said, not everything has yet been said in relation to Eliot's significance for the theatre. In 1981, *Cats* – a musical version of *Old Possum's Book of Practical Cats* (1939) – was staged. This award-winning and immensely *popular* fusion of words, music, song and dance about low-life in feline London would seem to recapture that 'new form' envisaged by the poet-dramatist. It would, I am sure, have delighted him.

NOTES

1. Kenneth Tynan, review in *Observer* (10 June 1956), reproduced in *Tynan on Theatre* (Harmondsworth, 1964), p. 44.
2. Newman Flower (ed.), *The Journals of Arnold Bennett*, vol. 3, *1921–29* (London, 1933), p. 52.
3. Hugh Kenner, *The Invisible Poet: T. S. Eliot* (London and New York, 1965), p. 188.

4. William Arrowsmith, 'The Comedy of T. S. Eliot', in W. K. Wimsatt (ed.), *English Institute Essays: English Stage Comedy* (New York, 1954).

5. Robert H. Canary, *T. S. Eliot: The Poet and His Critics* (Chicago, 1982), p. 245.

6. Peter Ackroyd, *T. S. Eliot* (London, 1984), pp. 38, 244.

7. Hugh Dickinson, *Myth on the Modern Stage* (Evanston, Ill., 1969), ch. VII.

8. Ackroyd, op. cit., p. 146. Ezra Pound felt that Eliot's 'fragments of an Agon are worth all his stage successes': cf. R. Murray Schafer (ed.), *Ezra Pound and Music* (London, 1978), p. 439.

# PART ONE

# Eliot and the Drama

1. Eliot on Drama: Excerpts
2. Eliot's Aims and Achievements

# 1. ELIOT ON DRAMA: EXCERPTS FROM ESSAYS, LECTURES, INTERVIEWS AND CORRESPONDENCE

I

[*1920*]

The questions – why there is no poetic drama today, how the stage has lost all hold on literary art, why so many poetic plays are written which can only be read, and read, if at all, without pleasure – have become insipid, almost academic. The usual conclusion is either that 'conditions' are too much for us, or that we really prefer other types of literature, or simply that we are uninspired. As for the last alternative, it is not to be entertained; as for the second, what type do we prefer?; and as for the first, no one has ever shown me 'conditions', except of the most superficial. The reasons for raising the question again are first that the majority, perhaps, certainly a large number, of poets hanker for the stage; and second, that a not negligible public appears to want verse plays. Surely there is some legitimate craving, not restricted to a few persons, which only the verse play can satisfy. And surely the critical attitude is to attempt to analyse the conditions and the other data. If there comes to light some conclusive obstacle, the investigation should at least help us to turn our thoughts to more profitable pursuits; and if there is not, we may hope to arrive eventually at some statement of conditions which might be altered. Possibly we shall find that our incapacity has a deeper source: the arts have at times flourished when there was no drama; possibly we are incompetent altogether; in that case the stage will be, not the seat, but at all events a symptom, of the malady.

From the point of view of literature, the drama is only one among several poetic forms. The epic, the ballad, the chanson de geste, the forms of Provence and of Tuscany, all found their perfection by serving particular societies. The forms of Ovid, Catullus, Propertius, served a society different, and in some respects more civilized, than any of these; and in the society of Ovid the drama as a form of art was comparatively insignificant. Nevertheless, the drama is perhaps the most permanent, is capable of greater variation and of expressing more varied types of society, than any other. . . .

The essential is not, of course, that drama should be written in verse, or that we should be able to extenuate our appreciation of broad farce by occasionally attending a performance of a play of Euripides where Professor Murray's translation is sold at the door. The essential is to get upon the stage this precise statement of life which is at the same time a point of view, a world – a world which the author's mind has subjected to a complete process of simplification. I do not find that any drama which 'embodies a philosophy' of the author's (like *Faust*) or which illustrates any social theory (like Shaw's) can possibly fulfil the requirements – though a place might be left for Shaw if not for Goethe. And the world of Ibsen and the world of Tchehov are not enough simplified, universal.

Finally, we must take into account the instability of any art – the drama, music, dancing – which depends upon representation by performers. The intervention of performers introduces a complication of economic conditions which is in itself likely to be injurious. A struggle, more or less unconscious, between the creator and the interpreter is almost inevitable. The interest of a performer is almost certain to be centred in himself: a very slight acquaintance with actors and musicians will testify. The performer is interested not in form but in opportunities for virtuosity or in the communication of his 'personality'; the formlessness, the lack of intellectual clarity and distinction in modern music, the great physical stamina and physical training which it often requires, are perhaps signs of the triumph of the performer. The consummation of the triumph of the actor over the play is perhaps the productions of the Guitry.

The conflict is one which certainly cannot be terminated by the utter rout of the actor profession. For one thing, the stage appeals to too many demands besides the demand for art for that to be possible; and also we need, unfortunately, something more than refined automatons. Occasionally attempts have been made to 'get around' the actor, to envelop him in masks, to set up a few 'conventions' for him to stumble over, or even to develop little breeds of actors for some special Art drama. This meddling with nature seldom succeeds; nature usually overcomes these obstacles. Possibly the majority of attempts to confect a poetic drama have begun at the wrong end; they have aimed at the small public which wants 'poetry'. ('Novices', says Aristotle, 'in the art attain to finish of diction and precision of portraiture before they can construct the plot.') The Elizabethan drama was aimed at a public which wanted *entertainment* of a crude sort, but would *stand* a good deal of poetry; our problem should be to take a form of entertainment, and subject it to the process which would leave it a form of art. Perhaps the music-hall comedian is the best material. I am aware that this is a dangerous suggestion to make. For every person who is likely to consider it seriously there are a dozen toymakers who would leap to tickle aesthetic society into one more quiver and giggle of art debauch. Very few treat art seriously. There are those who treat it solemnly, and will continue to write poetic pastiches of Euripides and Shakespeare; and there are others who treat it as a joke.

SOURCE: extracts from 'The Possibility of a Poetic Drama', in *The Sacred Wood* (London, 1920), pp. 60–1, 68–70.

II

[*1926*]
. . . The next form of drama will have to be a verse drama but in new verse forms. Perhaps the conditions of modern life (think how large a part is now played in our sensory life by the internal combustion engine!) have altered our perception of rhythm. At any rate, the recognized forms of speech-verse are not as efficient as they should be; probably a new form will be devised out of colloquial speech. . . .

SOURCE: extract from Eliot's Introduction to Charlotte Eliot's *Savonarola: A Dramatic Poem* (London, 1926), p. *xi*.

III

[*1928*]
. . . People have tended to think of verse as a restriction upon drama. They think that the emotional range, and the realistic truth, of drama is limited and circumscribed by verse. People were once content with verse in drama, they say, because they were content with a restricted and artificial range of emotion. Only prose can give the full gamut of modern feeling, can correspond to actuality. But is not every dramatic representation artificial? And are we not merely deceiving ourselves with appearances, instead of insisting upon fundamentals? Has human feeling altered much from Aeschylus to ourselves? I maintain

the contrary. I say that prose drama is merely a slight by-product of verse drama. The human soul, in intense emotion, strives to express itself in verse. It is not for me, but for neurologists, to discover why this is so, and why and how feeling and rhythm are related. The tendency, at any rate, of prose drama is to emphasise the ephemeral and superficial; if we want to get at the permanent and universal we tend to express ourselves in verse. . . .

SOURCE: extract from 'A Dialogue on Dramatic Poetry' (1928); reproduced in *Selected Essays* (London, 1932; 3rd edn 1951), p. 46.


IV

[*1934*]
. . . It is possible that what distinguishes poetic drama from prosaic drama is a kind of doubleness in the action, as if it took place on two planes at once. In this it is different from allegory, in which the abstraction is something conceived, not something differently felt, and from symbolism (as in the plays of Maeterlinck) in which the tangible world is deliberately diminished – both symbolism and allegory being operations of the conscious planning mind. In poetic drama a certain apparent irrelevance may be the symptom of this doubleness; or the drama has an under-pattern, less manifest than the theatrical one. . . .

SOURCE: extract from 'John Marston' (1934); reproduced in *Selected Essays*, op. cit. (3rd edn), p. 229.


V

[*1936*]
. . . Furthermore, in the desire to emphasize those essentials of drama which have tended to be forgotten – the permanent struggles and conflicts of human beings – we wish to remind the audience that what they are seeing is a play, and not a photograph. The theatre, in the effort to get greater and greater realism – that is, greater illusion – and thereby attempting to do what the cinema can do better, has tended to

depart so far from poetry as to depart from prose too; and to give us people on the stage who are so extremely lifelike that they do not even talk prose, but merely make human noises. So we want to take the opposite direction, and not let the audience forget that what they are hearing is verse. Blank verse can too easily be made to sound as if it were bad prose, and the more regular the verse the more easily it can be maltreated in this way. So we introduce rhyme, even doggerel, as a constant reminder that it *is* verse and not a compromise with prose. . . .

SOURCE: extract from 'The Need for Poetic Drama', *Listener* (25 Nov. 1936).

VI

[*1938*]   *Five Points on Dramatic Writing*
. . . 1. You got to keep the audience's attention all the time.
   2. If you lose it you got to get it back QUICK.
   3. Everything about plot and character and all else what Aristotle and others say is secondary to the forgoin.
   4. But IF you can keep the bloody audience's attention engaged, then you can perform any monkey tricks you like when they ain't looking, and it's what you do behind the audience's back so to speak that makes your play IMMORTAL for a while.
   If the audience get its strip tease it will swallow poetry.
   5. If you write a play in verse, then the verse ought to be a medium to look THROUGH and not a pretty decoration to look AT. . . .

SOURCE: extract from letter to Ezra Pound, reproduced as 'Five Points on Dramatic Writing', *Townsman*, 1/3 (July 1938), p. 10.

VII

[*1944*]
. . . A verse play is not a play done into verse, but a different kind of play; in a way more realistic than 'naturalistic' drama, because, instead of clothing nature in poetry, it should remove the surface of

things, expose the underneath, or the inside, of the natural surface appearance. It may allow the characters to behave inconsistently, but only with respect to a deeper consistency. It may use any device to show their real feelings and volitions, instead of just what, in actual life, they would normally profess or be conscious of; it must reveal, underneath the vacillating or infirm character, the indomitable unconscious will; and underneath the resolute purpose of the planning animal, the victim of circumstance and the doomed or sanctified being. So the poet with ambitions of the theatre must discover the laws, both of another kind of verse and of another kind of drama. . . .

SOURCE: extract from Eliot's Introduction to S. L. Bethell, *Shakespeare and the Popular Dramatic Tradition* (London, 1944).

VIII

[*1951*]
Reviewing my critical output for the last thirty-odd years, I am surprised to find how constantly I have returned to the drama, whether by examining the work of the contemporaries of Shakespeare, or by reflecting on the possibilities of the future. It may even be that people are weary of hearing me on this subject. But, while I find that I have been composing variations on this theme all my life, my views have been continually modified and renewed by increasing experience; so that I am impelled to take stock of the situation afresh at every stage of my own experimentation.

As I have gradually learned more about the problems of poetic drama, and the conditions which it must fulfil if it is to justify itself, I have made a little clearer to myself, not only my own reasons for wanting to write in this form, but the more general reasons for wanting to see it restored to its place. And I think that if I say something about these problems and conditions, it should make clearer to other people whether and if so why poetic drama has anything potentially to offer the playgoer, that prose drama cannot. For I start with the assumption that if poetry is merely a decoration, an added embellishment, if it merely gives people of literary tastes the pleasure of listening to poetry at the same time that they are witnessing a play, then it is superfluous. It must justify itself dramatically, and not merely be fine poetry shaped into a dramatic form. From this it follows that no play should be written in verse for which prose is *dramatically* adequate. And from this it follows, again, that the audience, its attention held by the dramatic action, its emotions stirred by the situation between the characters, should be too intent upon the play to be wholly conscious of the medium.

Whether we use prose or verse on the stage, they are both but means to an end. The difference, from one point of view, is not so great as we might think. In those prose plays which survive, which are read and produced on the stage by later generations, the prose in which the characters speak is as remote, for the best part, from the vocabulary, syntax, and rhythm of our ordinary speech – with its fumbling for words, its constant recourse to approximation, its disorder, and its unfinished sentences – as verse is. Like verse, it has been written, and rewritten. Our two greatest prose stylists in the drama – apart from Shakespeare and the other Elizabethans who mixed prose and verse in the same play – are, I believe, Congreve and Bernard Shaw. A speech by a character of Congreve or of Shaw has – however clearly the characters may be differentiated – that unmistakable personal rhythm which is the mark of a prose style, and of which only the most accomplished conversationalists – who are for that matter usually monologuists – show any trace in their talk. We have all heard (too often!) of Molière's character who expressed surprise when told that he spoke prose. But it was M. Jourdain who was right, and not his mentor or his creator: he did not speak prose – he only talked. For I mean to draw a triple distinction: between prose, and verse, and our ordinary speech which is mostly below the level of either verse or prose. So if you look at it in this way, it will appear that prose, on the stage, is as artificial as verse: or alternatively, that verse can be as natural as prose.

But while the sensitive member of the audience will appreciate, when he hears fine prose spoken in a play, that this is something better than ordinary conversation, he does not regard it as a wholly different language from that which he himself speaks, for that would interpose a barrier between himself and the imaginary characters on the stage. Too many people, on the other hand, approach a play which they know to be in verse, with the consciousness of the difference. It is unfortunate when they are repelled by verse, but can also be deplorable when they are attracted by it – if that means that they are prepared to enjoy the play and the language of the play as two separate things. The chief effect of style and rhythm in dramatic speech, whether in prose or verse, should be unconscious.

From this it follows that a mixture of prose and verse in the same play is generally to be avoided: each transition makes the auditor aware, with a jolt, of the medium. It is, we may say, justifiable when the author wishes to produce this jolt: when, that is, he wishes to transport the audience violently from one plane of reality to another. I suspect that this kind of transition was easily acceptable to an Elizabethan audience, to whose ears both prose and verse came naturally; who liked high-falutin and low comedy in the same play; and to whom it seemed perhaps proper that the more humble and rustic characters should speak in a homely language, and that those of more exalted rank should rant in verse. But even in the plays of Shakespeare some of the prose passages seem to be designed for an effect of contrast which, when achieved, is something that can never become old-fashioned. The knocking at the gate in *Macbeth* is an example that comes to everyone's mind; but it has long seemed to me that the alternation of scenes in prose with scenes in verse in *Henry IV* points an ironic contrast between the world of high politics and the world of common life. The audience probably thought they were getting their accustomed chronicle play garnished with amusing scenes of low life; yet the prose scenes of both Part I and Part II provide a sardonic comment upon the bustling ambitions of the chiefs of the parties in the insurrection of the Percys.

To-day, however, because of the handicap under which verse drama suffers, I believe that in verse drama prose should be used very sparingly indeed; that we should aim at a form of verse in which everything can be said that has to be said; and that when we find some situation which is intractable in verse, it is merely because our form of verse is inelastic. And if there prove to be scenes which we cannot put in verse, we must either develop our verse, or avoid having to introduce such scenes. For we have to accustom our audiences to verse to the point at which they will cease to be conscious of it; and to introduce prose dialogue would only be to distract their attention from the play itself to the medium of its expression. But if our verse is to have so wide a range that it can say anything that has to be said, it follows that it will not be 'poetry' all the time. It will only be 'poetry' when the dramatic situation has reached such a point of intensity that poetry becomes the natural utterance, because then it is the only language in which the emotions can be expressed at all. . . .

Source: extract from 'Poetry and Drama' – the first Theodore Spencer Memorial Lecture, delivered at Harvard University, 1950

(Cambridge, Mass., and London, 1951); reproduced in *On Poetry and Poets* (London, 1957), pp. 72–4.


IX

*[1953]    Three Voices of Poetry*

The first voice is the voice of the poet talking to himself – or to nobody. The second is the voice of the poet addressing an audience, whether large or small. The third is the voice of the poet when he attempts to create a dramatic character speaking in verse; when he is saying, not what he would say in his own person, but only what he can say within the limits of one imaginary character addressing another imaginary character. The distinction between the first and the second voice, between the poet speaking to himself and the poet speaking to other people, points to the problem of poetic communication; the distinction between the poet addressing other people in either his own voice or an assumed voice, and the poet inventing speech in which imaginary characters address each other, points to the problem of the difference between dramatic, quasi-dramatic, and non-dramatic verse. . . .

In a verse play, you will probably have to find words for several characters differing widely from each other in background, temperament, education, and intelligence. You cannot afford to identify one of these characters with yourself, and give him (or her) all the 'poetry' to speak. The poetry (I mean, the language at those dramatic moments when it reaches intensity) must be as widely distributed as characterization permits; and each of your characters, when he has words to speak which are poetry and not merely verse, must be given lines appropriate to himself. When the poetry comes, the personage on the stage must not give the impression of being merely a mouthpiece for the author. Hence the author is limited by the kind of poetry, and the degree of intensity in its kind, which can be plausibly attributed to each character in his play. And these lines of poetry must also justify themselves by their development of the situation in which they are spoken. Even if a burst of magnificent poetry is suitable enough for the character to which it is assigned, it must also convince us that it is necessary to the action; that it is helping to extract the utmost emotional intensity out of the situation. The poet writing for the theatre may, as I have found, make two mistakes: that of assigning to a personage lines of poetry not suitable to be spoken by that

personage, and that of assigning lines which, however suitable to the
personage, yet fail to forward the action of the play. There are, in
some of the minor Elizabethan dramatists, passages of magnificent
poetry which are in both respects out of place – fine enough to
preserve the play for ever as literature, but yet so inappropriate as to
prevent the play from being a dramatic masterpiece. The best-known
instances occur in Marlowe's *Tamburlaine*. . . .

The peculiarity of my third voice, the voice of poetic drama, is
brought out in another way by comparing it with the voice of the poet
in non-dramatic poetry which has a dramatic element in it – and
conspicuously in the dramatic monologue. Browning, in an uncritical
moment, addressed himself as 'Robert Browning, you writer of plays'.
How many of us have read a play by Browning more than once; and, if
we have read it more than once, was our motive the expectation of
enjoyment? What personage, in a play by Browning, remains living in
our mind? On the other hand, who can forget Fra Lippo Lippi, or
Andrea del Sarto, or Bishop Blougram, or the other bishop who
ordered his tomb? It would seem without further examination, from
Browning's mastery of the dramatic monologue, and his very
moderate achievement in the drama, that the two forms must be
essentially different. Is there, perhaps, another voice which I have
failed to hear, the voice of the dramatic poet whose dramatic gifts are
best exercised outside of the theatre? And certainly, if any poetry, not of
the stage, deserves to be characterized as 'dramatic', it is Browning's.

In a play, as I have said, an author must have divided loyalties; he
must sympathize with characters who may be in no way sympathetic
to each other. And he must allocate the 'poetry' as widely as the
limitations of each imaginary character permit. This necessity to
divide the poetry implies some variation of the style of the poetry
according to the character to whom it is given. The fact that a number
of characters in a play have claims upon the author, for their
allotment of poetic speech, compels him to try to extract the poetry
from the character, rather than impose his poetry upon it. Now, in the
dramatic monologue we have no such check. The author is just as
likely to identify the character with himself, as himself with the
character: for the check is missing that will prevent him from doing so
– and that check is the necessity for identifying himself with some
other character replying to the first. What we normally hear, in fact,
in the dramatic monologue, is the voice of the poet, who has put on the
costume and make-up either of some historical character, or of one
out of fiction. His personage must be identified to us – as an
individual, or at least as a type – before he begins to speak. If, as

frequently with Browning, the poet is speaking in the role of an historical personage, like Lippo Lippi, or in the role of a known character of fiction, like Caliban, he has taken possession of that character. And the difference is most evident in his 'Caliban upon Setebos'. In *The Tempest*, it is Caliban who speaks; in 'Caliban upon Setebos', it is Browning's voice that we hear, Browning talking aloud through Caliban. It was Browning's greatest disciple, Mr Ezra Pound, who adopted the term 'persona' to indicate the several historical characters through whom he spoke: and the term is just....

SOURCE: extracts from 'The Three Voices of Poetry' – eleventh annual lecture of the National Book League (Cambridge, 1953); reproduced in *On Poetry and Poets*, op. cit., pp. 89, 92–3, 94–5.


x

[*1963*]

INTERVIEWER: Do you still hold to the theory of levels in poetic drama (plot, character, diction, rhythm, meaning) which you put forward in 1932?

ELIOT: I am no longer very much interested in my own theories about poetic drama, especially those put forward before 1934. I have thought less about theories since I have given more time to writing for the theatre.

INTERVIEWER: How does the writing of a play differ from the writing of poems?

ELIOT: I feel that they take quite different approaches. There is all the difference in the world between writing a play for an audience and writing a poem, in which you're writing primarily for yourself – although obviously you wouldn't be satisfied if the poem didn't mean something to other people afterwards. With a poem you can say, 'I got my feeling into words for myself. I now have the equivalent in words for that much of what I have felt.' Also in a poem you're writing for your own voice, which is very important. You're thinking in terms of your own voice, whereas in a play from the beginning you have to realize that you're preparing something which is going into the hands of other people, unknown at the time you're writing it. Of course I won't say there aren't moments in a play when the two approaches may not converge, when I think ideally they *should*. Very often in

Shakespeare they do, when he is writing a poem and thinking in terms of the theatre and the actors and the audience all at once. And the two things are one. That's wonderful when you can get that. With me it only happens at odd moments.

INTERVIEWER: Have you tried at all to control the speaking of your verse by the actors? To make it seem more like verse?

ELIOT: I leave that primarily to the producer. The important thing is to have a producer who has the feeling of verse and who can guide them in just how emphatic to make the verse, just how far to depart from prose or how far to approach it. I only guide the actors if they ask me questions directly. Otherwise I think that they should get their advice through the producer. The important thing is to arrive at an agreement with him first, and then leave it to him. . . .

SOURCE: extract from *Writers at Work*, The *Paris Review* Interviews, 2nd series (London, 1963), p. 87.

XI

. . . Reflecting on rehearsals, Eliot said, 'I come to them prepared to question lines – rewrite some and cut others. The actors are very helpful. They say to the director, "This line is impossible to say", or "I don't know what this means", and practically all of the time they are right, and I rewrite the lines to suit them. Playwriting is not something you can complete in a study; it is a communal enterprise. After all, a play belongs to the performing arts. It is not something to be read; it is meant to be seen on the stage. One has to accept this responsibility if one writes a play. It *is* a communal enterprise.' . . .

SOURCE: extract from William Turner Levy and Victor Scherle, *Affectionately T. S. Eliot: The Story of a Friendship, 1947–1965* (London, 1968), pp. 40–1.

# 2.  ELIOT'S AIMS AND ACHIEVEMENTS

*Muriel C. Bradbrook*        Eliot as Dramatist
(1965)

### I THE NIGHTMARE DREAM

... Although he had made his reputation as a poet for the few, Eliot's first notion for the theatre was to revive music hall. *Sweeney Agonistes*, though but a fragment, is perhaps his most modern play. Returning to the London stage by way of pageants and festival drama, he 'aspired to Shaftesbury Avenue' and in at least one play, *The Cocktail Party*, achieved this kind of success. Eliot asked that all his plays should be judged as experiments, and has expressed his dissatisfaction with all; but his influence, example and prestige were vital at a certain period – roughly the twenty years between 1935 and 1955 – for the development of English imaginative drama. He has been more influential as a propagandist for drama than as a dramatist; his dramatic ideas, which provided, with those of Yeats, the only attempt since Dryden to construct a theory of the drama in England, have undergone radical changes as a result of his practice.

From the early 1920s Eliot wrote on the Elizabethan dramatists and on classical drama, but it was not till his religious and social preoccupations of the Thirties gave him the necessary drive towards public statement that he produced *Murder in the Cathedral* (1935), a play designed for those who go to religious festivals and expect to be patiently bored but who are 'prepared to put up with poetry'. It may be that Eliot's mastery of the dramatic monologue was a handicap in his search for a full dramatic form; in his first play, as he has admitted, there was only one dramatic character, the hero. (Angus Wilson once remarked that the Puritan mentality tends to see a central character who is very large, surrounded by much smaller characters; in Eliot the doctrinal Anglo-Catholic does not succeed in overlaying completely the temperamental Puritan.)

*Murder in the Cathedral* gratified Eliot's ten-year-old ambition; it is also a landmark in English dramatic history; for it proved that

English verse drama could still succeed, and Eliot's younger contemporaries hastened to follow him. A number of verse plays came out in the later Thirties, though none of these has maintained itself as *Murder in the Cathedral* has done. His first play may well turn out to be Eliot's most enduring stage success, for though not often professionally performed it can be successfully played by amateurs.

The formal simplicity of the character groups, the contrast between the crisp verse of the Hero or his enemies, and the nightmare dreams of the Chorus, or its lyrical hymns, achieve a consistent simplification. It is a classically severe style.

I once saw a performance of a play of Euripides in the theatre of Herodas Atticus under the Acropolis. The main characters were formal and hieratic, as they stood in their masks; they might have been reciting an old ballad, worn smooth with familiarity. The Chorus of women, supple, responsive in mood, moving in a slow dance of fear or joy, evoked an immediate response, and carried all the emotional significance of the story.

Something like this may be felt in *Murder in the Cathedral*. Thomas à Becket's story is known, to him, to the tempters, to the audience; death and what comes after death is already settled; the fine point of decision is all the finer. This play exists as a moment in time, a moment of choice which brings in something outside time. 'The point of the intersection of Time with the Timeless' is the point of Incarnation, and Thomas, after surmounting the temptation of the senses, of power, of private revenge and 'the last temptation' of pride makes his decision, on behalf of all. He is the one who sees, who has the responsibility of making the choice. By this decision he crosses an internal boundary line, after which he is 'not in danger; only near to death'. The actual murder is a ritual performance by the Knights, who then are rapidly transformed into modern demagogues and address the audience rather than the Chorus in their ingenious justifications. By his death, Thomas has released new spiritual forces into the world, as the Chorus see in the end.

The Chorus, those who 'do not wish anything to happen', the humble women of Canterbury, acknowledge their share of the guilt. For them, there is still hope and fear, pleading and remorse, new assaults from the powers of darkness whose presence they scent upon the air. In a sense although Thomas is the Hero, the Chorus remains the chief actor. Eliot has said that he wrote the play as a protest against totalitarianism in Europe, and the final speeches of the Knights now bear only too familiar a sound. Thomas is not to be allowed the glory of being a martyr; the verdict is that his death was self-provoked, 'suicide while of unsound mind'.

The poets of the 1930s took up such political themes; and within the last few years the story of Beckett has been used by other playwrights. Anouilh's Beckett chooses the honour of God, and thus is bound to ignore the honour of the King. Like Antigone, he says:

> I shan't try to convince you. I shall only say no.

The severity and simplicity of Eliot's medieval pageant play are at the opposite extreme to the complexity of *The Family Reunion* (1939). There is a close relation between the plot and that of *Sweeney Agonistes*, written in 1926. A 'nightmare dream' of a drowned murdered woman, interspersed with ominous songs, and the cheap clichés of the uncomprehending Chorus, build up a comedy of menace. In the one story, the murderer 'does a girl in' and keeps her in a bath; in the other, she is lost in the Atlantic Ocean, but the remorse and isolation of the 'murderers' are the same.

Sweeney came from Eliot's own personal mythology. The author was perhaps influenced to some extent by Cocteau in choosing the rhythms of the music hall for *Sweeney Agonistes*, but he based the fragment on Pound's Noh, and Yeats's adaptations; expecting the primitive drum-beat to be maintained throughout. He wrote with the idea that the spectators, like the characters, would be graded in degrees of understanding; that only a few would understand the hero. For the rest, since he hoped for a popular audience, he depended on 'doing monkey tricks behind the audience's back'.

This is a play full of gaps in communication, and Sweeney cannot hope to explain.

> I gotta use words when I talk to you.
> But if you understand me or if you don't,
> That's nothing to me and nothing to you.

The three main phases of Eliot's dramatic writing show him moving from the idea of a rhetorical, 'distanced' presentation – that of *Sweeney Agonistes* and the critical writings of the Twenties – to a theatre that would be socially useful – his view in the early Thirties. Finally he became preoccupied with the technique of making effects indirectly. Concealed and unobtrusive rhythm replaced the drum beat, and like 'concealed lighting' on a picture, made its effect without being noticed. By this means, Eliot hoped to cut across all stratifications of public taste.

One of his chief difficulties has always been the method by which the superhuman may be presented. In *Murder in the Cathedral* he was able to write from Christian presuppositions, but in other plays the problem has produced some very eccentric solutions. An unpublished ending for *Sweeney Agonistes* introduced (to the sound of the Angelus) a figure resembling Father Christmas, who bore a champagne bottle (empty) and an alarm clock; he wore evening dress with a carnation in the buttonhole

> THE OLD GENTLEMAN: *Good evening. My name is Time. . . . I wait for the lost trains*
> *that bring in the last souls after midnight. The time by the exchange clock is now*
> *9.46.*
> SWEENEY: *Have you nothing else to say?*
> OLD GENTLEMAN: *Have you nothing to ask me?*
> SWEENEY: *Yes.*
> OLD GENTLEMAN: *Good.*
> SWEENEY: *When will the barnfowl fly before morning?*
> *When will the owl be operated on for cataract?*
> *When will the eagle get out of his barrel-roll?*
> OLD GENTLEMAN: *When the camel is too tired to walk further,*
> *Then shall the pigeon pie blossom in the desert*
> *At the wedding breakfast of life and death . . . .*

It was perhaps as well that Eliot suppressed this ending; but the wedding breakfast of life and death concludes *The Family Reunion* (1939), in the bizarre ritual of blowing out candles on the birthday cake. ('Out, out, brief candle'.)

This drama, which appeared less than six months after Yeats's *Purgatory*, includes in its houseparty a troupe of family ghosts; like Yeats's beggar man, Lord Monchensey inhabits 'the past that is always present'. The core of Eliot's third tragic monodrama is played out among dead shadows and live puppets. Harry Monchensey, who is 'rather psychic, as they say', endures his inner solitude without hope of release or of understanding. He is one of the Hollow Men. His dead father's wish to kill his mother produced the fearful waking dream in which he saw himself as the murderer of his wife; the misery of the dead threw a shadow of remorse on the living. Agatha, who exorcises the dead, had loved his father, and prevented the murder to save the unborn child – himself. She is therefore his true mother, and he, in accepting a vicarious suffering and continuing to endure it, becomes momentarily both her lover and her child.

> You are the consciousness of your unhappy family,
> Its bird sent flying through the purgatorial flame.

The exchange of 'death's dream kingdom' for enlightenment frees him from his invisible chains, and from the rôle that his original mother would impose; his election takes him away on an unknown quest, for 'liberty is a different kind of pain from prison'. This act of choice kills his mother, since she has maintained herself by the trivialities of routine and now 'the clock has stopped in the dark'.

The most innocent is he who suffers most; Harry's ruthlessness, which appears as shock or discontinuity, marks his escape from 'the war of phantoms'. The question of responsibility or 'punishment', which has misled some literal-minded critics, has been handled with sure insight by D. W. Harding,[1] who sees the play as a study in separation experience, or psychological weaning – the final parting of Harry and his mother. Like Thomas crossing an internal boundary line, Harry enters into a new relation with everyone and passes to a state 'on the other side of despair'. The Furies become transformed to 'the bright angels'; instead of fleeing, he must follow.

For the moment of enlightenment, Eliot took as immediate model Jean Cocteau's *The Infernal Machine* (1934), a play on the story of Oedipus. Agatha, enlightening Harry, like the Sphinx enlightening Oedipus, holds the threads of fate, steps into the place left vacant by the furies between the windows, assumes the goddess.[2] The flashback in time enlarges the scene.

The Sphinx, as Nemesis, says:

I weave, I winnow, I wind, I knit, I plait, I cross, I go over it again and again, I tie and untie again and again, retaining the smallest knots.

And Agatha, as Athena:

> A curse comes to birth
> As a child is formed. . . .
> According to the phase
> Of the determined moon . . .
> The knot shall be unknotted,
> And the crooked made straight.

The Infernal Machine, 'one of the most perfect ever constructed by the infernal gods for the destruction of a mortal', is the vehicle of a determinist ethic. It gives a grand and cosmic assertion of a purely negative kind. Cocteau, 'the first of his generation, even before Giraudoux, to reinterpret Greek tragedy, because the new era needed a Racine,' reinterpreted it in the light of *Phèdre*. This return to tradition, when used as a basis for 'Freudian' studies of character, gave grandeur to statements of cosmic unbelief and defiance.

It was natural that Eliot should take this determinist pattern and adapt it to 'play tricks behind the audience's back'. Much earlier, he had defined the uses of myth, and praised the method of Yeats's Plays for Dancers:

Myth . . . is simply a way of controlling, ordering, of giving shape and significance to the great panorama of futility and anarchy which is contemporary history. . . . Instead of narrative method we may now use mythical method. It is, I believe, a step towards making the modern world possible for art . . . towards form.[3]

The form was not clearly established, but I would think that the story is not only one of separation, but of initiation. Harry sets out on a quest, the goal being unknown, while the Chorus, who have 'lost their way in the dark', regain their unreal trivial existence; they recoil from the possibility of initiation

> as if the earth should open
> Right to the centre, as I was about to cross Pall Mall.

There are large and deliberate gaps in knowledge here; there are also mistakes. Eliot acknowledged the injudiciousness of presenting the Furies visually. He has also said that his sympathy is now with the mother, and Harry seems an insufferable prig. This perhaps only proves the completeness with which he has dissociated himself from the limitations of his hero.

Harry's ironic wit, his torments, the nature of his relations with his mother are reminiscent not only of Orestes, but of Hamlet. There is no way in which Harry can communicate the nature of his inner suffering, or even recognise it, and Eliot noted this as a characteristic of *Hamlet*. 'Loathing diffused' when he is inside his waking dream, dissociated obsession when he is outside, are represented dramatically for the audience by the gaps or jumps between different dramatic levels; and these in turn are represented by different kinds of verse. Characters engaged in ordinary conversation suddenly enter a trancelike state, in which they utter prophecies, while the Chorus of uncles and aunts occasionally emerge from their satisfied triviality to utter a general confession of fear or discomfort.

> And the past is about to happen, and the future was long since
>     settled.
> And the wings of the future darken the past, the beak and claws
>     have desecrated . . .

>   . . .                                              Have torn
> The roof from the house, or perhaps it was never there.

In all three plays, Eliot presents on the dramatic level a contrast between the Hero who bears the burden of guilt and insight, and the Chorus, who can respond, if at all, only by intuition. In *Sweeney Agonistes*, the ominous pounding rhythm, the echoes and repetitions,

sustain an atmosphere of menace. In *Murder in the Cathedral*, the crisp
astringent dialogue of Thomas with his enemies or his uncomprehending friends alternates with the poetic rhythms of the Chorus
and with the prose of Thomas's sermon or the address of the
murderers. These are spoken directly to the audience – for this, of
course, Eliot had precedent in his medieval model, since *Everyman*
concludes with a sermon on pride. The technical problems involved
in presenting different dramatic levels of speech, including the most
familiar and banal, have been treated by Eliot as the most important
aspect of his work. Earlier poets who wrote for the stage were content
to produce lines that 'could not have been spoken by anyone but a
poetry reciter'. To maintain a certain level of artifice and yet to avoid
the limitations of the consciously 'poetic' posed a problem which Eliot
succeeded in solving for himself, but which he could not solve for
others.

Gradually the ghosts and choruses of the Greek models are
dispensed with, until, in his last three plays, Eliot confines himself to
the flat speech of everyday. To have taken the superficial talk of the
drawing room and exposed what lies beneath is perhaps not an
unexpected thing for the author of *Prufrock* and *Portrait of a Lady* to
have done. The drawing room at least has the advantage that its
range of tone and inflection is restricted. For one of the chief
difficulties which Eliot had to meet was the strong individuality of his
own poetic accent. When 'the author and character are speaking in
unison' the lines become powerful and memorable. Ironic wit or the
lyric cry are within Eliot's compass; but he cannot present Doris and
Dusty, Eggerson or Mrs Piggott except sardonically. 'May I pour a
drop of oil on these troubled waters?' or 'She'll come back to tell us
more about the peace and quiet' hit off a type, almost too neatly.

The difficulty of integrating a deep and central vision with alien
trivialities has been met by applying a great deal of theory, a great
deal of reading and taking a great deal of pains. In this Eliot resembles
that Elizabethan dramatist whose achievement he once brilliantly
summarised – Ben Jonson. Much of his art, like Jonson's, is an art of
caricature; it is judicious, and passionate at the core, but it remains an
art for the few. These few, however, include his fellow-writers, who do
not imitate him directly but have been stimulated by his work to
develop on quite different lines of their own. His drama has worked
like yeast, not upon the stage, but upon the writers. He should not be
held responsible for Christopher Fry – who would probably have
written in any case – but seen rather as an indirect influence behind
the very different work of Pinter or Albee.

## II  LATER PLAYS: THE ICONS

In Eliot's last three plays, the themes of Initiation, Adoption and the Quest are pursued, with some faint resonance from the Greek myths of Alcestis, Ion and Oedipus at Colonus. By now, the dramatic theory that poetry 'should be put on a thin diet' had evolved; the rhythm had become almost imperceptible, for to Eliot his first necessity was to accept the language of ordinary speech, even its deterioration. The poet should be prepared to lay down a tradition which he could not hope to perfect, to submit himself to the language available, in the available dramatic forms.

Eliot therefore took the shabby professional form of drawing room comedy – a much less promising medium than the music hall. It remained stiffly detachable from what he chose to put into it. The sets for *The Cocktail Party* were carefully commonplace, the cigarettes by Abdulla and the stockings by Kayser Bondor. So strict was the purging of ornament that Eliot said: 'It is perhaps an open question whether there is any poetry in the play at all.'

From time to time, however, the façade of social banality rolls away to reveal some deliberate piece of mystification. Gaps in knowledge remain around the hero and the sacrificial victim. The mysterious sanatorium recalls that

> The whole world is our hospital
> Endowed by the ruined millionaire
>
> ('Little Gidding')

The Libations are vaguely religious, Sir Henry dismisses his patients with the adjuration of Buddha to his disciples and the leading lady is crucified offstage (for which reason, I have been told, the play cannot be staged in France, as no leading lady will forgo her appearance in the last act). Except for Sir Henry's brief assumption of the role of Hercules when he first appears (including a bawdy song), and his quotation of *Prometheus Unbound* at the end, to describe his psychic vision, there is not much in the way of supernatural shock for the audience. Flat mystification, seen from the outside, does not extend the boundaries of the play; on the contrary, it merely blocks the spectator's way to inserting his own cosmic views. The Initiates, who know the way of illumination, are gradually revealed, but their peculiar ritual is bound to seem trivial; perhaps if it were in a really unknown language, like the Sanscrit benediction at the end of *The Waste Land*, the effect would be less disturbing. The Unknown Guest, who turns out to be the Unknown God of modern secular society, the analyst, carries his burden of insight, leads the novices to make their choices, and sends them on their several quests. One after another, the puppets admit their private, vulnerable, secret life; in the end, all are saved and the play is called a Comedy.

Although Eliot's model has not been directly copied, yet the younger playwrights have worked upon principles which he was the first to point out. They have used broken, repetitive, almost inarticulate speech, charged with the ominous power that Eliot sought in his underlying rhythm, the 'hidden' drumbeat. In particular, Harold Pinter's earlier comedy seems to reflect Eliot indirectly. *The Birthday Party*, whose very title is reminiscent, shows the unlucky hero being abducted, after a scene of mystification, by two diabolical Guardians, to be treated at an unknown destination by a sinister and powerful character, Monty (who may be either military or sartorial or diabolic). The hero's inability to communicate is crucial.

Eliot has made the point that a major writer deserves to be read as a whole, and his last three plays offer a special kind of interest for the light they throw on each other and on the themes of his earlier work. The images of the various characters in these plays have acquired an identity that persists from one play to the next. For example, Gomez and Mrs Cargill, the man of affairs and the prying chatterbox, seem dark refashionings of Alex and Julia from *The Cocktail Party*. Given the peculiar flatness of character and the brief, abrupt, nature of the action, it is particularly tempting to trace such patterns, derived presumably from Eliot's Internal Society.

The most persistent, I think, is the Imaginary Murder, which can be found also in the lyrics. In *Sweeney Agonistes* and *The Family Reunion*, it is murder of a woman, wife or mistress; in *The Elder Statesman*, of an old man. There are two real murders, which are both martyrdoms, Thomas's and Celia's; two offstage deaths of parents caused by the son's defection. External action culminates in Initiation; to the martyrs by death; to Harry, by the divine Agatha, as Athena; to Colby, by another incarnation of Athena, Mrs Guzzard; to Lord Claverton and his son, by his 'ghosts'. Ghosts and messengers from another world appear everywhere – Pereira on the telephone, an ominous threatening visitant; Thomas's tempters, from his past life; Harry's Furies; Celia, and by way of parody, Lavinia's aunt; Mrs Guzzard, with the news of Colby's dead father: Gomez and Maisie.

The sacrament of Initiation is penance or confession, which admits to the divine Adoption; with adoption a new identity is acquired and a new kind of suffering, which is purgatorial.

The symmetry of the plot is always so obvious that careful

impressions of spontaneity have to be created by parties, reunions, conferences and sessions. Eliot has evolved for himself a sort of personal and idiosyncratic comedy of masks.

The taking up and dropping of rôles is of great importance. In the family patterns sisters are nearly always good, and brothers bad; women can be simply divided into goddesses and tarts, though they may assume disguises. Men take up public rôles and cower behind them; sons reject their parents at great cost, but if parents repudiate children, they are most severely punished. Men in public life are usually better than artists, who tend to be mediocre. Relations with the dead are as important as relations with the living. There is no such thing as accident; every act is part of a cosmic design.

The chief embarassment continues to be the supernatural. The cosmic jokes of *The Cocktail Party* and *The Confidential Clerk* are almost as unfortunate as Father Time; the religious games of the Libation and the descent of Mrs Guzzard show traces of misplaced facetiousness. The position is recovered in *The Elder Statesman*, where Mrs Piggott's stagey briskness conveys the insufferable patronage that is one of the humiliations reserved for decrepitude. The diabolic visitants here employ a crisp astringent accent, which seems to record that 'the character and the author are speaking in unison'. Even the music hall star, since she knows her man, can rise to epigram:

> Your conscience was clear!
> I've very seldom heard people mention their consciences
> Except to observe that their conscience was clear. . . .

The transparent valedictory quality of this play gives it a distinction which is not that of a work for the stage; all the characters are disembodied from the start. Monica, the only one to achieve a complete absolution of solitude, a complete capacity for love, finds that in her the 'obstinate silent self' who is the unspeaking director of ordinary persons has been replaced by 'a love that's lived in, but not looked at'; and 'this love is silent'.

Monica is the only character permitted to reach the emotional level of poetry; Mrs Cargill defines Lord Claverton as one of the Hollow Men ('Or did she say "yellow"? I'm not quite sure.') He, who had become an idol to his daughter, is permitted at last to walk off the stage, after he has confessed himself and stripped off all his public rôles. The 'broken-down actor' can then change into his own clothes and speak as himself; Monica, too, released from the deep possessiveness that holds her back, can acknowledge her love. 'The dead has poured out a blessing on the living.'

The force of this play is concentrated in the last act. Claverton has to learn to live with his ghosts; 'what he has to pass beyond are not the faults but the savagely unforgiving judge within him'.[4]

Ordinary human love is the subject of initiation in this play, and no extraordinary vocation or distant quest.

In all the plays, what has been sought is the release from solitude, and from a sense of guilt that goes with it. For Harry it is 'the solitude in the crowded desert', when the self is reduced to an eye, watching. For Celia, too, it is an 'awareness of solitude':

> a revelation about my relationship
> With everybody

Colby, who does not seem to need people, needs yet to know his own identity – what he has it in him to be. Lord Claverton cannot bear company, but neither can he bear to be alone; he is afraid of 'the private self' that may be met in solitude.

For the characters of the earlier plays, solitude is only to be overcome at great cost, and in the pursuit of a difficult quest. Edward and Lavinia come together in humility, knowing that they do not understand each other, but what they achieve is limited. They can

> choose, whether to put on proper costumes
> Or huddle quickly into new disguises;
> They have, for the first time, somewhere to start from.

The loneliness of the individual, which had been the theme of much of Eliot's lyric, is in itself a paradoxical subject for dramatic communication. The direct appeal to introspection is strong. Eliot's plays, even more thoroughly than Yeats's, reveal a solitary man essaying a public art and for his purpose evolving a doctrine of masks. His plays consist of a single action, the distinctive act of choice; as such they offer a deep, incisive judgement with which the spectator may concur. It is as definition and judgement, rather than experience, that they are valid.

Eliot's dramas of responsibility and choice, based upon classical myth, have clearly much in common with the French theatre of Cocteau and Giraudoux, Sartre and Camus. The choice of the hero is an existentialist's choice. The drama is a drama of crisis. If it involves such depths of the self as can hardly be described, only recalled, it also involves the public world. Edward and Lavinia end by giving another Cocktail Party.

This attempt to retain an accepted structure goes with Eliot's experiments in verse, with his determined use of the traditional materials to hand. In the precarious and uncertain period during which he wrote, these explorations were needed. But for the last decade [written in 1965 – Ed.] the theatre has been in revolt. Quite suddenly a breakthrough was achieved, and already Eliot's dramatic achievement has become a part of history.

SOURCE: ch. 9 ('Eliot as Dramatist') of *English Dramatic Form* (London, 1965), pp. 162–77.

### NOTES

[Reorganised and renumbered from the original – Ed.]

1. D. W. Harding, 'Regressional Theme in Eliot's Modern Plays', in *Experience into Words* (London, 1963).

2. Agatha's position as head of a women's college points to her role as Athene, the presiding goddess in the *Oresteia*'s final movement on which the story is based. Eliot also described Mrs Guzzard of *The Confidential Clerk* as 'a cross between Pallas Athene and a suburban housewife'.

3. This is part of a review of Joyce's *Ulysses*, published in 1923. The comparison with Yeats's plays for dancers occurs in the course of the review.

4. D. W. Harding, op. cit., p. 160. The connection between the use of the Icon and the possession of a strong conscience (or superego) is very clear in Eliot's plays.

## *Helen Gardner*     The Comedies of T. S. Eliot
## (1965)

*The Cocktail Party*, *The Confidential Clerk* and *The Elder Statesman* are distinguished from Eliot's earlier plays by their author's obvious desire to accommodate himself to the conventions of the stage at their most conventional level. In the earlier plays, *Sweeney Agonistes*, *Murder in the Cathedral*, and *The Family Reunion*, Eliot was working in the experimental theatre of the Thirties, using such devices as the chorus, the direct appeal to the audience, soliloquy, lyrical solos and duets, and ritual and symbolic acts. In these last plays he deliberately wrote within the limits of what has been contemptuously called the 'West End Play', or what Mr Terence Rattigan called 'Plays for Aunt Edna'. He used the picture-frame stage, with a conventional setting: the modern flat, the library, the consulting-room, the terraces of an expensive rest-home. He made no use of chorus, soliloquy or aside, and employed for his machines the telephone and front-door bell. It has recently been said that Eliot was unfortunate in choosing to model his plays on a type of drama that was dying or dead by the time he came to imitate it, and that to the theatre-going public of the 1960s (and, these critics assume, of the future) these plays are merely exercises in an effete tradition. I cannot take very seriously a criticism that assumes that what is temporarily unfashionable is permanently out-of-date. The tradition of social comedy which Eliot took up is a very tough tradition. It has broken out again and again in the course of the last two thousand and more years. At the moment these plays are dated, but as they recede into history their social verisimilitude will be as much a source of strength as is the social truth of Restoration Comedy. The fact that they belong so clearly to the early Fifties makes them seem obsolescent in the Sixties. They will look, I imagine, very different in the Eighties and Nineties. To catch the tone of an age is one of the merits of high comedy; and these plays catch the accents and the moral tone of what one may call 'polite society' in the post-war decade.

Eliot's desire to write plays that would be commercially successful was wholly in accord with his ideals as a writer. He always declared that a writer must use what lies to hand: that the poet's task is to make poetry out of the living speech of his day. Conditions may be unpropitious but they must be accepted. A poet cannot choose his linguistic environment; even more, a dramatist must use the theatre of his day. The poet, said Wordsworth, works under the single restriction of giving immediate pleasure to a human being. The dramatist works under a much severer restriction. He has to give immediate pleasure to an audience, a mass of individuals who must feel that pleasure simultaneously; for the presence in an audience of large numbers of persons who are not enjoying the play is fatal to the enjoyment of others. A dramatist's success is measured by his power to convert a heterogeneous collection of persons into an audience, stirred to a common hilarity, shocked by a common apprehension, or raised to a common sense of awe and wonder. The dramatist cannot give pleasure to the discerning few unless he is also giving pleasure to the less discerning many. Further he must give his audiences what they want, because otherwise he will have no audiences and so cannot discover what demands he can make of them. It is now, I think, clear that the experimental poetic theatre of the 1930s struck no real roots. The great mass of the theatre-going public stayed away. Eliot was surely right to feel that plays acted to an audience of like-minded

persons in small half-empty theatres or converted drill-halls were not
really plays. If they could not draw an audience, and a mixed
audience at that, they had failed artistically as well as socially. And
Eliot was always deeply interested in the drama as the most socially
relevant of the arts.

The three plays differ from Eliot's earlier plays not only in their
acceptance of the banalities of the well-made commercial play of the
first half of the twentieth century, but also in being, in some sense or
other, comedies. *Sweeney Agonistes* was a fragment of an Aristophanic
melodrama, *Murder in the Cathedral* a religious tragedy, and *The Family
Reunion* a psychological tragedy. Eliot's first plays, like the greatest of
his earlier poems, are informed by the tragic sense of human solitude.
For his first full-length play he took a heroic subject, martyrdom; for
his second, the story of Orestes the mother-murderer, the scapegoat
hero, scourge and saviour of his family. The earlier plays, like the
earlier poetry, communicate a sense that life is agonisingly trivial and
meaningless, unless some power from without breaks in to create a
gleam of meaning. It creates it within the individual heroic soul – in
Thomas, the martyr, or Harry, the conscience of his unhappy family.
But in the course of *Four Quartets* a change of mood is clearly apparent.
There is a progress towards acceptance of the conditions of life in this
world, the kind of acceptance that underlies the comic writer's
realism, sympathy, human compassion and moral concern. 'East
Coker' has the tragic sense of human loneliness and of the irrelevance
of human achievement. It is a poem about loneliness and suffering,
ending with the tragic urge towards exploration: 'Old men ought to
be explorers.' 'We must be still and still moving/Into another
intensity.' But even in 'East Coker':

> There is a time for the evening under starlight,
> A time for the evening under lamplight
> (The evening with the photograph album)

And moving through 'The Dry Salvages' to 'Little Gidding' we pass
beyond the tragic sense to a mood that transcends and includes both
the tragic and the comic vision of life, the mood expressed by the
saying of Julian of Norwich that Eliot put at the heart and at the close
of his poem: 'Sin is Behovely but all shall be well, and all manner of
thing shall be well.' It is out of this mood that the last plays spring,
and they may in one way be regarded as footnotes or *exempla* to *Four
Quartets*. But in another sense their roots lie much further back.
Tragedy deals with man in solitude, or forced into solitude. Comedy
with man in society; not with man discovering his own fate, but with

man discovering how to live with his fellows. Eliot's serious concern with the nature of the good society is apparent in his criticism and his prose writing long before it flowers in his poetry. In his last plays he attempted to embody in works of art problems he had revolved and conclusions he had arrived at in his editorship of *The Criterion*, and in his *The Idea of a Christian Society* and his *Notes towards the Definition of Culture*.

Comedy is often regarded as less serious than tragedy. Whether this is so or not, its proper seriousness is reached by the opposite route. Plot, which is the soul of all drama, must in tragedy have a rigid logic. The wild improbabilities of comedy, its coincidences and preposterous assumptions, are improper in tragedy, which must convince us of its essential truth to the course of human life as we know it. Abandoning fidelity to the audible and visible surfaces of life, dealing with those better than ourselves and with terrible and exceptional events, tragedy must not strain our credulity. But comedy, if it is to be serious in its own way, must turn to fantasy for its plot. Dealing as it does with men and women like ourselves, or worse in one thing, 'the ridiculous', which is a species of the ugly; showing us not archetypal characters but characters we can hardly think of apart from their setting in place and time; entertaining us by its mimicry of social habits, fashions, and our neighbours' follies, it must, if it is to reach beyond mimicry and give us a true *imago vitae*, reach from truth local and particular to truth general and universal, call on fantasy and fictions to shape its plot. This distinction, that the comic writer *invents* but the tragic writer *finds* his plot, is as old as the fourth century. Sentimental or domestic comedy is as much an offence against the nature of the comic kind as is sentimental or bourgeois tragedy against the nature of the tragic kind. Both are products of the destruction of the drama by the growth of the novel. Eliot saw this clearly, and with his sense of classic tradition did not attempt to give us dramatised novels, but to write comedies that would express through fictions and fables truths about man as a social being: not the discoveries that the tragic writer makes but the convictions out of which the comic writer writes. For if the tragic writer finds his story and discovers what pattern he can within it, the comic writer begins from assumptions already clarified in his mind and shapes his fable to express them. Comedy tends naturally towards the didactic, which is destructive of tragic feeling. Eliot's three comedies are naturally and unashamedly didactic, within plots artificially constructed to produce the maximum of comic surprise and comic encounter. The weakness of the third and last of the plays, *The Elder Statesman*,

compared with *The Cocktail Party* and *The Confidential Clerk*, lies in its
author's failure to invent sufficient complications of plot, and so
incorporate his message in an artefact.

The plot of *The Cocktail Party* has a double origin. The central situation
is taken from the *Alcestis*. In the Greek play a dead wife, who has died
in place of her husband, is restored by the intervention of the
semi-divine Heracles. Here a runaway wife is brought back, as if from
the dead. In each case a marriage that had ended has to begin again.
This, as Eliot said, was where he began from: 'the return of a dead
wife'. But the *Alcestis* provided only the germ of the play, which in its
final form owes very little to its primary source. Its only direct
influence on the conduct of the plot is in the initial situation, where the
husband disguises his domestic calamity in order to fulfil the duties of
hospitality – and even here the motives of Edward are quite different
from those of Admetus – and in the unconventional behaviour of the
stranger at the party and after. Like Heracles, Reilly appears at first
in the role of a badly-behaved guest. There is a reminiscence of the
return of Heracles leading the veiled stranger in Reilly's insistence
that Lavinia, when she returns, will be a stranger and must be greeted
as a stranger; and his condition – that Edward is to ask her no
questions – reminds us of the three days' silence imposed on Alcestis
by her consecration to the Gods below. But what in the *Alcestis* is a
part of the machinery of the plot and a tribute to Greek religious
sentiment becomes in *The Cocktail Party* a comment on human
relationships: 'At every meeting we are meeting a stranger'; and a
piece of good moral advice: 'Don't strangle each other with knotted
memories.' At one moment in the last scene, there seems to be a
reference to the sacrifice of Alcestis. Euripides's play suggests that
there was a cult of Alcestis at Athens. The cult of the dead Celia, to
whom the natives had 'erected a sort of shrine', seems a parallel to the
prayer of the chorus in the Greek play: 'Let her grave not be
accounted the resting-place of one of the departed dead, but let her be
honoured as a god and receive the worship of the passers-by. Let the
traveller turn aside from the road and say, "She gave her life for her
husband and now she is a blessed spirit. Hail Lady, and be gracious to
me".' The reminiscence, if it is one, underlines one difference between
the two plays. Death is not cheated of his claim in *The Cocktail Party*.
Edward's wife is restored to him; but another woman dies in his and
her place. But although the *Alcestis* is only a remote source for *The
Cocktail Party*, reference to it is of value. It helps us to get our focus
right. *The Cocktail Party* began as a play about a marriage, and Edward

and Lavinia are the central characters in its design. Also the memory of the Euripidean Heracles may help us not to take Eliot's saviour more portentously than we need to do.

The second source of the plot is no one work but the general tradition of high comedy. To the original triangle of husband, wife, and semi-divine saviour have been added the amorous entanglements that have been the stock in trade of social comedy since Dryden's *Marriage à la Mode*. The central pair are flanked by two younger single persons, Celia, Edward's mistress, and Peter, who was once Lavinia's lover but is now in love with Celia. To balance this and preserve the symmetry of the plot, the original demi-god has been provided with two assistant doubtful deities: an elderly lady, a kind of fairy-godmother, and a young man who is a kind of modern Mercury. The re-interpretation of Greek myths in modern terms is very popular in this century, particularly on the French stage. But Eliot went further than a rendering of the *Alcestis* in terms of modern life. The world of drawing-room comedy engaged his imagination as much as the story of the *Alcestis*. *The Cocktail Party* has a double inspiration.

High comedy, like high tragedy, excludes all aspects of life irrelevant to its concern. Tragedy, in order to display the flaw in the universe that sets a man at odds with his environment and seems to suggest that this world is inimical to the nobility to which it gives birth, paints a world remote from ours. Its heroes are placed above daily annoyances and pains that they may suffer enormous griefs and be undistracted in their experience of them. High comedy, which like all comedy shows a world that is friendly to man if he will only learn how to live in it, is similarly exclusive. Its characters are relieved of the ordinary anxieties of life in order that they may give their whole attention to those anxieties that, for the mass of men, are mingled with the anxieties of earning a living, succeeding in a business or profession, preserving one's health, and fulfilling the duties of one's station. They inhabit a material paradise, free from want and fear of want. They are dowered with good looks and perfect health, and have ample leisure to devote themselves to the pursuit of personal satisfaction. They have no duty except the duty of being happy.

Restoration Comedy took happiness to be success in love; and by success it meant the achievement of satisfaction in love without the forfeiting of other satisfactions. Love was shown as a dangerous game requiring high skill from its players, in which both man and woman ran the risk of social humiliation. The woman's stake was the higher; her triumph when she secured an accomplished gallant on her own terms – marriage – was consequently the higher. The man's task was to secure the lady without losing her own or his fortune. The butts of Restoration Comedy are those who cannot play this game, who can neither win by skill, nor, when defeated, take their defeat with grace. The well-mannered hero and the witty heroine shine by contrast with the fops whom any woman of sense can put down, the rejected mistresses who cannot hide their wounds, and such ghastly figures as Lady Wishfort grotesquely refusing to acknowledge defeat at the hands of implacable Time. Its ruthlessness towards the old, the defeated and the inept gives Restoration Comedy a bitter flavour. If love is a game, then, as one of Congreve's heroines [Cynthia] observes, 'consequently one of us must be a loser'; and the dénouement of a Restoration Comedy shows too many losers for us to feel much confidence in the permanence of the heroine's triumph. All we can be confident of is that she will preserve her dignity, good manners and good temper. If her marriage turns out a failure, at least the world will not know it from her.

Comedy reflects the morality of its age. Restoration Comedy is the product of a society in which the current serious philosophy did not rank sexual satisfaction very high in the scale of human values, and in which marriage was, in general, indissoluble in law. The comedy arises from the conflict between man's wayward passions and the stable structure of society. The satire is turned against social failures, not against society itself. Human inconstancy is taken for granted: 'Our love is frail as is our life and full as little in our power; and are you sure you shall outlive this day?' [Emilia, in *The Man of Mode*]. Anything so unstable as human desire cannot be expected to give more than 'fun while it lasts'; the skilful can so manage their affairs that their 'fun' does not cost them the more enduring satisfactions represented by a settlement and social respectability. Our age gives sexual satisfaction a much higher place in the hierarchy of human values than the seventeenth century did; or indeed, I would say, than any previous age in Western Europe has. It also allows the unhappily married to obtain their freedom without loss of social standing. In our comedy love cannot be treated as a game, and marriage is not sufficiently stable to be mocked at. Social convention is not powerful enough to provide the context for a true comedy of manners. High comedy today must either be sentimental and satirical, exalting love and satirising the frivolity of the wealthy, giving to its audience the pleasure of a romantic day-dream along with the pleasure of disapproving of those one envies; or it must be ethical, and use the limitations of the comedy of manners for a serious exploration of what personal happiness means. *The Cocktail Party* was born of a fusion

between ancient myth and the assumption that underlies most
modern social comedy: that the *summum bonum* for men and women in
this world is the fulfilment of their personalities in love.

The *Alcestis* belongs to a world where the idea of duty reigns. In the
world of modern comedy this conception has no place. Admetus lies
to his guest to fulfil the duty of hospitality. Edward carries on with his
party because to tell his guests that his wife has run away would be to
expose himself to ridicule. Alcestis dies in obedience to a code by
which a wife must put her husband's and children's welfare before her
own. She dies that he may live and that their children may not be
fatherless, the worst of fates in the ancient world. The childless
Lavinia 'dies', or leaves her husband, in obedience to no such settled
standards of behaviour; nor does she return to him from any sense of
loyalty to her marriage vow. Celia's death, though a consequence of
her remaining at her post, is not the result of any sense of duty to her
fellowmen. 'Fay ce que vouldras' is the motto of all the four main
characters of *The Cocktail Party*. But the author confronts his
characters with the necessity of discovering what it is then that they
want. Accepting as a hypothesis the assumption that man's moral
duty is the fulfilment of his personality, the play asks us to
contemplate what this generalisation means in terms of four individuals. The discovery of what one wants means discovering what one
is. The play is concerned with choices; but in the end there is only one
choice. Choose to be yourself or choose not to be. There are a lot of
possible sub-choices under the heading 'Choose not to be'; but this is
the main choice.

Edward and Lavinia have to learn they are not what they think
they are. Edward is not a passionate man married to a cold wife;
Lavinia is not an attractive woman whose husband does not
appreciate her. Both are sentimentalists. Edward is an egoist hardly
capable of loving at all. Lavinia, sharp-tongued and socially ambiti-
ous, is extremely unlovable. They are, as Reilly points out, admirably
suited to each other. Edward needs to be loved; his weakness and
vanity need support. Lavinia needs someone to love. Each has a root
of virtue: Edward the knowledge of his own mediocrity; Lavinia the
habit of taking responsibility for others. She may be bossy, but at least
she is aware that her husband needs clean shirts. If Edward will
accept being loved he may become loving, and if Lavinia will try to
love she may become lovable.

Celia's lesson is different. She was not mistaken about herself. She
is passionate. But she was mistaken in the object of her passion. What
she has to give is a total gift, something Edward does not want. The

offer terrifies him. It is perhaps something no human being wants or should be offered, unlimited devotion. She has to find a proper object for her passion. Whatever the pain, terror, and ignominy of her death, it is the consequence of her choice. Her offering is accepted. She is taken at her word. When she chose this life she chose death. For Peter who loved her, the 'naturally good man', who is to succeed by his own and the world's standards, and go far in his career as an artist, it is something he must come to terms with, something he has to learn to understand. The 'thought of Celia' is to be with him all his life, which will remain under the judgement of her life and death. It will save him from pretence, reminding him that 'another race hath been and other palms are won'.

The element of fantasy which removes the play from drawing-room comedy is provided by the Guardians, the comic engineers of the plot, who are responsible for its surprises. At first they are apparently distinct and unconnected with each other, and resented for their interference, but at the close it is clear they have been in collusion all along and their interference is accepted. They are comic Furies who are in the end seen to be Kindly Ones. But although there would be no play without them and they seem to have worked things, fundamentally they do not. They bring the horses to the water; they do not make them drink, and at the end it is seen that the horses were asking to be brought to the water. The true Guardians are inner ones: Edward's 'stronger partner', who like Socrates's daemon says 'No'; Celia's 'sense of sin'; Lavinia's non-existent aunt, invented by Edward to explain what made her run away. Edward's own self-knowledge makes him reject Celia and want his wife back. Celia's knowledge that the ecstasy was real, even though she and Edward were not real to each other, is what makes her reject ordinary life and choose the road that leads to martyrdom. Lavinia, the least self-analytical, though extremely shrewd in analysis of the weakness of others, sets everything in motion. Something tells her she must break away and on Julia's advice she seeks out Reilly. Lavinia's aunt is therefore rightly the first and the last toast of the play. The Guardians are not at the centre of the action. At the true centre there is an unnamed Power who speaks within the heart and conscience of every man.

The underlying conception of the play as expressed in its plot is related to the conception of *The Family Reunion*, in which Harry has to discover his role in the drama of his family.[1] But here it is generalised. All four characters have to find their roles. Living is like acting in a play whose plot we do not know, in parts we have not chosen. Our choice is whether we will play those parts or invent parts for ourselves. We are helped by an innate sense that tells us we are going wrong, which says: 'You are not cast for the leading lady; your part is the comic nurse.' There are some people we know who are able, like experienced actors acting with amateurs, to guide us, get us on to the right part of the stage at the right moment, and cover up our mistakes. They may even make us realise that we have a great role to play, that we must stop being charming, civilised and popular, and commit ourselves to the extreme. These persons have some detachment and seem to have some insight into the obscure intentions of the author of the play. But they cannot make us act well, or even at all, and we can always decide that we will not act in this play but in another drama of our own making, in which we can hold the centre of the stage and act to ourselves to our own rapturous applause. All the same, we need not take these persons too seriously. If deities, they are comic deities; if angels, they are charged with folly: the one-eyed Reilly, the psychiatrist who has to lie down on his own couch, Julia, always losing her spectacles, and Alec, whose cooking 'is absolutely deadly'. They can be laughed at. There is only one thing that is beyond laughter: heroism. The heroic, von Hügel said, is the clear revelation of the supernatural. Heroism is absolute: all wisdom is partial.

The distinction on which the play turns is between love, the exchange of tenderness, forgiveness and loving-kindness between separate and ultimately solitary persons only partially understanding each other, and passion, which seeks to lose itself in its object, desiring ecstasy and a union that can only be perfectly attained in death, and which seeks to obliterate distinction of personalities in union. This conception may owe something to Denis de Rougemont's attack on the whole conception of romantic love in *L'Amour et l'Occident*, called in its English translation *Passion and Society*. De Rougemont saw romantic love, embodied in the Tristan story, as destructive of all social values and ultimately of life itself, a quest for death, something sterile and perverse; and he linked the origins of the concept of romantic love in Provence with the Catharist heresy, with its contempt for the created world. *The Cocktail Party* is built on the distinction between passion and love, *eros* and *agape*, and it is possible that de Rougemont's description of the organisation of the Cathari, an invisible Church within society, may have suggested the handling of the Guardians. In Celia, the romantic quest for union is directed to its true object and consummated in death. *Causa diligendi Deum Deus est; modus est sine modo.* It is a happy ending for her, for we see the alternative in her first savage reaction to Edward's cowardice and rejection of her. Too fastidious for a plunge into sexual experiments, she will become a devourer, destroying the unfortunate men who disappoint her. But we misinterpret the play if we find its meaning solely in Celia. Its concern is with a concept of society, where in different ways men and women can work out their salvation with diligence. A cocktail party is not one of the higher forms of hospitality. It is not a meal, but a prelude to a meal. The Symposium, the banquet of love, will come after. And at the Great Supper, in the house of many mansions, there will be places not only for 'the soldier saints, who row on row, burn upward each to his point of bliss', but also for those who have in various ways lived a 'good life', and learned while on earth to 'bear the beams of love' and exchange forgiveness.

The subject of any comedy of manners is always the relation between the sexes, since it is here that social conventions are most at war with human nature and manners are most required yet seem most remote from real feeling. A comedy of manners is always dominated by women and *The Cocktail Party* is a woman's play. Lavinia and Celia are 'better men' than Edward and Peter, and the apparently rattlepated Julia, not Reilly, is found to be the mastermind among the Guardians. *The Confidential Clerk* is not a comedy of manners and it is a man's play. Its subject is the relation of parents to children and of son to father rather than son to mother. Edward's profession as a barrister is irrelevant to the theme of *The Cocktail Party*. What Colby is to be, a financier or an organist, is the issue in *The Confidential Clerk*. The play has a complicated and highly entertaining plot in a very old tradition. Its source is the *Ion* of Euripides, the fountainhead of romantic comedy, the first play on the well-worn plot whose theme-song is 'Whose baby are you?' or 'Excuse me, sir, but have you by any chance a strawberry mark on your left shoulder?' As Shakespeare doubled his twins in *The Comedy of Errors* to make the fun faster, Eliot gave us two foundlings and an illegitimate daughter in place of the single foundling of the source. He used the fantastic mistakings of his plot to explore the problem of personal identity: Who am I? And for the first time he found a plot which gave him a natural dénouement in the discoveries of the third act. *The Confidential Clerk* differs from Eliot's earlier plays in having a weak and untheatrical opening but a strong third act, with a superb final curtain. Always before, the expositions raised expectations that the conclusion disappointed. Here the last act with revelation on revelation is a genuinely theatrical climax. On the other hand, the slow exposition is a price that has had to be paid for the complications of the plot and for the classic restriction of the cast.

The subject of *The Cocktail Party* was freedom and destiny, our narrow but real area of choice. *The Confidential Clerk* also turns on choice; but choice here is the recognition of choices made long ago, and not made by ourselves alone, which we have to live with. Mrs Guzzard, the mother of Colby Simpkins, the new confidential clerk to Sir Claude Mulhammer, chose long ago to be her son's aunt, not his mother, to pretend that her own child was her dead sister's illegitimate baby. She thought it would give him a better start in life to be under the patronage of that sister's wealthy lover, Sir Claude, than to be the orphan son of a poor organist. Lady Elizabeth also chose not to be a mother and let her lover farm out their illegitimate son. Then, after her lover's death, she conveniently forgot the name and address of the foster-mother and was able to grieve in perfect safety over the loss of her child. Sir Claude chose to be Colby's patron rather than his father, to keep a son as it were in cold storage or deep freeze until it was convenient to have him around, and to have a fiduciary relation with his illegitimate daughter, passing her off as the daughter of a dead friend. Sir Claude's passion in life is pottery. He was once tempted to be a potter; but he chose not to be. He decided that he would never be more than a second-rate potter and that he would follow his father's career, be a financier, and keep pottery as a hobby. Colby's passion is music. Sir Claude tries to persuade him that he will never be more than a second-rate musician and his music had better be, like Sir Claude's collection of pots, a hobby, an inner dream, a refuge.

Colby Simpkins holds the centre, a personable, intelligent, well-behaved young man whom everyone wants, the ideal son ready-made off the peg. At the beginning he is trying to adapt himself to what he conceives to be the true situation. In the second act he is claimed by both Sir Claude and Lady Elizabeth as a son. He asks for the truth and when in the last act his aunt is summoned, the Pallas Athene of the suburbs, and he is asked by her what he wants, he replies that what he wants is what he has had. The only true father he can ever have is a father who died before he was born, who did not reject him because he had no chance to do so, a father whom he may discover by report and within himself. His music is not like Sir Claude's passion for ceramics; it is something in his being, not a hobby or relaxation, but what he really likes doing. He is granted his wish and told the truth. His father was an unsuccessful organist, husband of the woman he has always known as Aunt Sarah. His mother must 'rest in peace'. She has become Aunt Sarah, whom he shows to her taxi. He will go to see her, be grateful for what she did for him as a child, and no doubt

keep her photograph in a silver frame in his sitting-room. (Living in
the suburbs, he need not trouble himself with Lady Elizabeth's
standards of social propriety.) But she can never be his mother
though he was born from her womb. And Sir Claude's fatherhood,
which was always a spiritual fraud, has now lost even its poor base in
physical fact. Colby declares that he will go the way of his true father
and live with the old clerk Eggerson in the suburb of Joshua Park,
where the church needs an organist. Like Colby, Eggerson gets his
wish, though he does not utter it. He is the only person in the play who
has had a true relationship, has really known a father's 'pains and
benefits'. He and Mrs E. had a son, born in lawful wedlock in a
bedroom, one imagines, with its walnut suite they had saved up for, in
Joshua Park; nursed through childish croup and measles; taken to the
panto at Christmas and to the sea for a fortnight in the summer; seen
through his school; and then – 'lost in action, his grave unknown'. 'To
him that hath shall be given, from him that hath not shall be taken
away even that which he thinketh he hath.' Sir Claude loses the son he
thought he had. To Eggerson, who truly had a son, a second son is
given, a son after the spirit. Mrs E. will be less low-spirited around the
'season . . . getting near the anniversary' with Colby in her dead son's
bedroom to be fussed and petted as he works, as Eggerson hints he
will, for his ordination exams.

Sir Claude is left with the wife he married for her social rank, with
the daughter he has always regarded as a nuisance – someone to be
given an allowance and have her debts paid – and with the extremely
vulgar young man she is to marry, who has turned out to be Lady
Elizabeth's long-lost son. Lady Elizabeth is left with the husband she
has always regarded as uninterested in 'higher thought', the son she
abandoned as a baby, a dreadfully common young man, and her
husband's much-disliked daughter, who is to be that son's wife.
Comedy always ends with the establishment of relationships, usually
with marriage. Here it ends with a family that has never thought of
itself as a family or tried to be a family before. Make-believe is over.
They must make the best of what they are and of what is, and accept
what cannot be undone.

The plot of *The Confidential Clerk* is preposterous and amusing. It is
given *vraisemblance* by the lifelikeness of the characters: Lady
Elizabeth, the 'seeker', at times shrewd, at times pathetic, at moments
wise; Lucasta, with her pose of the tough blonde, a frightened,
unhappy girl, embittered by the knowledge that her father is ashamed
of her and that she is ashamed of her mother; B. Kaghan, whose
brashness covers a similar need for reassurance; Sir Claude, a clever

man who talks as if he were a wise one. His house of make-believe tumbles about his ears. In the first act he is sure he is right when he explains to Colby how he chose to follow his father as a successful financier. In the third act, waiting for Mrs Guzzard, he starts to talk for the first time to his wife and wonders if he has been wrong all the time. 'Could a man be said to have a vocation to be a second-rate potter?' he asks Colby ironically. The answer lies in another question: Can one have a vocation to be first-rate? What has vocation to do with success? The play's theme is vocation and Sir Claude has persistently ignored 'callings' – the calling of his deepest nature, the calling of marriage, the calling of fatherhood. He has chosen to be a successful financier – he realises at the end he was nothing more, and that he has not really followed his father, to whom finance was a passion; he has chosen to be the unloved and unloving husband of a wife he married for her title and connections, and who he thought wanted an important husband; to give his daughter money without love; and to keep his son at a distance until he can, as it were, fit him in comfortably.

At the opposite pole from Sir Claude is the old clerk Eggerson, the Celia of *The Confidential Clerk*, who provides the test of values: good husband, good father, good servant, without ambition and without envy, whose inner and outer life are one – and, one must say outright, a crashing bore. In *The Cocktail Party*, the divine broke into the pattern of ordinary relationships in the form of the heroic. Here, we are asked to feel its presence in a life of the utmost banality, and in a personality unenriched by our highest secular values. To Mr Eggerson, whose pleasure is in pottering about in his garden, who never opens his mouth without a cliché, and thinks everyone has a heart of gold, the marvels of the human spirit, the 'monuments of unageing intellect', are, I do not doubt, meaningless. His reading is the evening paper; the power of music, I imagine, means to him 'Abide with me' and 'In a monastery garden'; and one hates to think of what pictures keep down the wallpaper, and what ornaments stand on the mantelpiece, in his home at Joshua Park. For a poet to place such a figure at the heart of his play is to declare that 'the poetry does not matter': that it is the whole conception of the play that is significant. That conception involves a more powerful reversal of worldly values than anything Eliot had written before. We bring what is within us to any work of art and we, like the characters in *The Confidential Clerk*, are shaped by life. I am a child of the London suburbs, not Joshua Park, which I locate on the Liverpool Street line,[2] and I know and knew as a child the kind of parish in which Mr Eggerson is vicar's warden and where Colby will be organist. The Christian faith first presented itself to my childish imagination not as inspiring great art and literature, nor as a great intellectual system, nor as a call to high adventures of the spirit; but as the informing grace of many obscurely faithful lives. When I came out of the theatre after seeing *The Confidential Clerk* I was haunted by memories of such 'Confidential Clerks', going about their master's business, and by some lines from a poem that Eliot once mentioned in a broadcast as one of the poems that came often to his mind: Johnson's lines on his humble and obscure friend Dr Robert Levet.

> Well tried through many a varying year,
>     See Levet to the grave descend;
> Officious, innocent, sincere,
>     Of ev'ry friendless name the friend.
>
> Yet still he fills affection's eye,
>     Obscurely wise and coarsely kind;
> Nor, letter'd arrogance, deny
>     Thy praise to merit unrefin'd. . . .
>
> His virtues walk'd their narrow round,
>     Nor made a pause, nor left a void;
> And sure th'Eternal Master found
>     The single talent well employ'd.

Spiritually Colby is to be Eggerson's son, to find happiness in doing his duty in that sphere of life to which it shall please God to call him; and by sphere of life is meant that whole complex of circumstances into which we are born, and grow up, and find ourselves. Colby is a natural solitary. His lonely childhood has shaped him for a special lot. 'When my father and my mother forsake me, the Lord taketh me up.' He is called to know more clearly than any of the others what Lady Elizabeth glimpses when she says, 'We are nearer to God than to anyone.'

I have left myself little time to speak of *The Elder Statesman*, the weakest of the three plays. Its plot is simplicity itself and I think one feels in it that Eliot's inventiveness and talent for comic surprise had failed him. Except that both are concerned with death, that Lord Claverton, like Oedipus, dies alone under a tree, that he has a devoted daughter, and that he quarrels with his son, the play bears no true relation to the *Oedipus at Colonus*. Its sources are in Eliot's own poetry: in the poem 'Difficulties of a Statesman', and particularly in the beautiful, sombre passage in 'Little Gidding' on the 'gifts reserved for age'.

Let me disclose the gifts reserved for age
  To set a crown upon your lifetime's effort.
First, the cold friction of expiring sense
Without enchantment, offering no promise
  But bitter tastelessness of shadow fruit
  As body and soul begin to fall asunder.
Second, the conscious impotence of rage
  At human folly, and the laceration
  Of laughter at what ceases to amuse.
And last, the rending pain of re-enactment
  Of all that you have done, and been; the shame
  Of motives late revealed, and the awareness
Of things ill done and done to others' harm. . . .

Lord Claverton is one of those important persons – an 'eminent man' – who, in 'East Coker', 'all go into the dark'. He has had a stroke and retired from political life, where he has had an honourable and successful career, with a reputation for probity and ability. He has never quite reached the top – still by the world's standards he is a distinguished man, 'an elder statesman'. In fact his whole life has been a fraud, a pretence, an escape from himself. Dick Ferry has spent his life creating Lord Claverton, and in the face of death Lord Claverton is only a hollow man, an old guy, a public figure without a private existence. He will be forgotten in five years – perhaps at most mentioned in a footnote by historians as 'a member of So-and-So's Cabinet'.

   Both Lord Claverton's loving daughter Monica, to whom he finally makes confession, and her lover are so shadowy as to be non-existent. The love-scenes between them are painfully unconvincing. But the central theme of the play is handled with the unsparing moral realism that is the strength of Eliot's other plays. The grim jest is that the blackmailers who come to harry the dying Lord Claverton, the ghosts of his youth, have not in one sense been ruined by him at all. They therefore cannot be bought off. And the things they know about him are not seriously discreditable. No scandal sheet would pay them for these 'secrets'. So it is impossible for him to say to them, 'Publish and be damned'. They have both done very well. Freddy Culverwell, having served his sentence for forgery, has become Gomez, a South American millionaire. Maisie Batterson, who was bought off by young Dick Ferry's father, is now Mrs Carghill, a wealthy widow. Both are apparently very well pleased with themselves. And yet, they are all the same lost souls; and they know it. They need not have been so. Freddie Culverwell, the grammar-school boy, might have got his first, and lived an honourable and useful life as a master at the kind of school from which he won his scholarship, if he hadn't been taken up by Dick Ferry and taught tastes and habits beyond his means. As for Maisie Batterson, she loved Dick Ferry and he loved her when they were both young and foolish. Though they were totally unsuited, and if they had married the marriage might have – probably would have – come to disaster, she might have been less wholly mercenary and sentimental in her middle age if he had not, like a coward, allowed his father to 'make it worth her while' to give up her lover. Why do they come back to haunt Lord Claverton on the verge of death? They are, of course, like the tempters in *Murder in the Cathedral*, objectifications of the trouble in the dying man's mind: reminders of two occasions, symbolic of his whole life, when he was a coward and shirked his responsibilities, because to have faced them would have spoilt the picture of himself which he wanted to present to the world. But they are also themselves, persons he has ruined, and for all their apparent self-satisfaction they know it and want their revenge. In their first encounters they have the upper hand because they do know it and are not, as he is, frauds. Freddie Culverwell *is* Gomez; Maisie *is* Mrs Carghill. Lord Claverton is a stuffed dummy. They want revenge on the public figure because in their hearts they are still haunted by the young Freddie and the young Maisie whom he killed. Gomez is haunted by Freddie Culverwell, the simple, clever, but weak boy he was: Mrs Carghill by Maisie, the romantic chorus girl; and both of them by the young Dick Ferry whom they had loved and admired. In their final encounters they have lost the upper hand, for their victim has abandoned the weak defence of 'Am I my brother's keeper?' and knows that he has done what cannot be undone. He is free because he has owned the truth and is now ready to die. He has attained the only wisdom:

> Do not let me hear
> Of the wisdom of old men, but rather of their folly,
> Their fear of fear and frenzy, their fear of possession,
> Of belonging to another, or to others, or to God.
> The only wisdom we can hope to acquire
> Is the wisdom of humility: humility is endless.

*The Elder Statesman* is like an unfinished picture, a sketch drawn by a master's hand with only some portions worked up. I would not be without it; but I cannot believe that it will have a future on the stage. The central subject is powerfully handled and comes home strongly to the conscience. But the weakness of the love-scenes and the facile satire on the expensive nursing-home that is not a nursing-home provide a bad frame for this sombre study of a life under the judgement of death.

And, of course, the other two plays have serious weaknesses too. Eliot himself said that the last act of *The Cocktail Party* was too much of an epilogue to the play; and, apart from this, its substance is unsatisfactory. Celia's death has to be recounted as a piece of straight narrative, like a classical messenger's speech, which is stylistically inappropriate in a naturalistic comedy. It is also awkwardly introduced. Edward and Lavinia's 'good marriage' is inevitably rather tedious in representation. Just as happy nations have no history, so happy marriages lack drama. But Eliot need not have represented their domestic concord in such banal terms. We seem to have moved into the world of the Women's Magazines: 'Take an interest, dear, in what has happened in the office,' and 'Don't forget to tell her how nice she looks in her new dress.' There is an excessive use of conversation between two persons in *The Confidential Clerk*; and the sheer weight of exposition in the first act is a heavy price to pay for the brilliance of the third. There is, perhaps, also a failure in the presentation of Eggerson, who is too much a 'character part', tempting the actor to give a plummy performance as a 'dear old man'.

But it is not the weaknesses of these plays that I would wish to dwell on. Their merits are to my mind far more conspicuous. I have left without comment one most striking merit: their 'speakability'. The unobtrusive vigour of their language modulates from chatter, gossip, or prattle to reflection and serious self-probing, without ever losing its rhythmic vitality. Eliot's desire to create a 'transpicuous language' as a vehicle for drama was fulfilled in what is best described as the 'heightened speech' of these plays. Their language would be a subject for an essay in itself. Here, I wished rather to concentrate on their reading of life. I cannot believe that *The Cocktail Party* and *The Confidential Clerk* will not find a place in the national repertory of the future. No other plays of our generation present with equal force, sympathy, wisdom and wit the classic subject of comedy: our almost, but mercifully not wholly, unlimited powers of self-deception, and the shocks and surprises that life gives to our poses and pretences.

SOURCE: a lecture ('The Comedies of T. S. Eliot') to the Royal Society of Literature (18 March 1965); reproduced in Allen Tate (ed.), *T. S. Eliot: The Man and His Work* (London, 1967), pp. 159–81.

NOTES

[Reorganised and renumbered from the original – Ed.]

1. See Helen Gardner, *The Art of T. S. Eliot* (London, 1949; new edn 1968),
pp. 142–51.

2. Mrs Eliot tells me I was wrong here, and that Joshua Park is in fact
Muswell Hill in North London. Eggerson was a reminiscence of an old clerk
in Lloyd's bank, where Eliot worked from 1917, who was always talking of his
garden.

## *Katharine J. Worth*    'Precursor and Model
## Maker'   (1972)

At first glance Eliot's progress as a playwright seems to be a
movement away from experiment. His most modern-looking piece, a
jazz melodrama, was published in 1926; his last play, produced in
1958, looks more like a piece of staid neo-Ibsenism. Many of his critics
saw the post-war plays as a regression: even Martin Browne, who
produced them all and was deeply in sympathy with his playwright,
was inclined to take that view. He thought them an unconscious
reversion to the style of theatre Eliot had known as a young man. Eliot
did jokingly say himself about some improvement suggested for *The
Cocktail Party* that every step seemed to take him nearer to Lonsdale.

But experiment of some kind is going on all the time in Eliot's
drama. He had an extraordinarily keen sense of new theatrical
possibilities. *Sweeney Agonistes*, his most radical experiment (of the
plays not written for religious occasions) was so far ahead of orthodox
theatre practice that for years it was thought of as a poem rather than
as what it now clearly looks to be, an exciting (if unfinished) piece of
theatre. *The Cocktail Party* has a claim to be considered the first black
comedy in the post-war English theatre and *The Confidential Clerk*
indicated some interesting new directions for farce. Both these plays,
and in its own way *The Elder Statesman*, explore subjects that fascinate
the modern theatre – role playing, the search for identity – with
techniques that foreshadow those of Albee and Pinter.

Eliot's central characters suffer from a troubling sense of division
between their real and their acted selves. 'Real' self is a concept that
still has force in his drama – here he separates from successors like

Pinter – but the performing self is very much in the foreground, uneasily conscious of its liability to be taken over by the 'speechless self', the mute, tough one.

Eliot finds some interesting answers to the problem of how to represent these selves, with their different voices. To a great extent, of course, he relies on the traditional means of verse drama, imagery. There is a tremendous amount of acting imagery in the plays, a fact that Martin Browne draws attention to in his absorbing account of his collaboration with Eliot; an indispensable book, this, for anyone concerned with the drama of the period as well as with Eliot's work.[1] Through all the plays runs a chain of nightmarish images to do with losing one's part, being in the wrong play, having a sense of existing only in a part.

The Chorus in *The Family Reunion* resent being summoned to 'play an unreal part in some monstrous farce, ridiculous in some nightmare pantomime'. Harry comes home prepared for one part and finds 'another one made ready – The book laid out, lines underscored, and the costume / Ready to be put on', and Lord Claverton, who describes himself as a broken-down actor, dreads the moment when he will have to walk off the stage 'without his costume and makeup. / And without his stage words'.

Other more direct methods are tried out too. In one interesting sequence from an early draft of *The Cocktail Party*, much cut down in the final version, Peter Quilpe is invited by the other characters to imagine roles for them in the film he is supposed to be making about a country house murder. 'Very few people can act the thing they are', he says, and goes on to cast accordingly. Edward can't be a lawyer in the film, though he is in the play, because he doesn't look secretive; neither does Alex, so he can be the Secret Service character; as for Reilly and Julia, they can't be in it at all: nothing about them is ordinary enough for what an 'ordinary' murder film requires. The effect of this – trying to imagine characters as characters – is unsettling. Even in the unsatisfactorily verbose form it has in the draft, the scene takes us to the edge of that phantasmagoric region where Edward exists, not sure whether he is really there, except in his role as husband to Lavinia: 'Without her, it was vacancy. / When I thought she had left me, I began to dissolve, / To cease to exist.'

The feeling of being an actor is closely related to the feeling of being spied on which Eliot's characters suffer from. Roles, false names and identities are protection against being known. The characters are terribly repressed and inhibited by the polite society they live in: the point is made in that way in *The Family Reunion*. They have to be shocked into opening up and revealing themselves. A violence comes in here which takes Eliot's drama very close to Pinter's. Characters are subjected to painful, mysterious inquisitions, the Furies appear at a window, bringing their victim near to total nervous collapse; an uninvited guest arrives at a cocktail party; with the aid of two spies he manoeuvres three of the characters to a consulting room for 'treatment'[2] which ends in the violent death of one of them; two unwanted visitors descend on an elderly man taking a 'rest cure'[3] and badger him into confessing past faults; he collapses and dies.

Of course these summaries are misleading, omitting as they do the 'bright angel' aspect of the inquisitors and the emphasis Eliot puts on conversion and reconciliation. But perhaps all the same they hint at a truth about the plays, that their greatest theatrical vitality is just in those dark and icy areas where they draw so near to Pinter's drama. *The Birthday Party* seems to take over where they leave off: it's a very live connection.

Eliot is certainly good at suggesting suppressed violence. He manages at times to look like a forerunner of the theatre of cruelty without ever allowing an act of physical violence to erupt on his stage. He can manoeuvre the audience into a worrying sense of complicity with sadism, for instance with the jokes in *The Cocktail Party* about Christians eating monkeys and pagans eating Christians. They are nasty jokes but the audience usually laughs at them, to their embarrassment when they learn that Celia was one of the victims. Martin Browne was relieved when Eliot agreed to cut out some of the horrific detail[4] that outraged the first audiences in Edinburgh. He was surely right in thinking that the emphasis on physical horror would distract attention from Celia as a person. I'm not so sure, though, that Eliot did think of Celia as a person in quite the way Browne himself did: it was he who had advised Eliot to build up sympathy for her: 'She is the character whom above all we want to love – the heroine, the play's necessary focus of sympathy.'[5] But that last scene was first written as an epilogue: the germ of the play was the marriage of Edward and Lavinia and, to my mind, it's in that Strindbergian dance of death relationship that the strongest dramatic interest lies. The prevailing mood is grotesque; masked actors in a cruel harlequinade, decidedly in tune with the modern spirit which encourages the rewriting of *The Dance of Death* in the near-farcical terms of Dürrenmatt's *Play Strindberg*.

I began by referring to the extremely modern look of Eliot's first dramatic piece, the unfinished *Sweeney Agonistes*. If he had continued to write in that vein he would have been in the front ranks of the anti-realists and I would probably have been discussing him now along with O'Casey and Arden and other makers of the alternative tradition rather than in relation to Pinter and Priestley.

Even as it is, *Sweeney Agonistes* has had some influence on the playwrights who have made the sharpest break with realism, on Auden and Isherwood, and on John Arden, who tells us that his first schoolboy attempt at dramatic writing was a play inspired by the death of Hitler written in the style of *Sweeney Agonistes*.

It's odd that this seminal piece should still be included among the poems in the collected editions of 1969, especially as it has had a number of interesting productions. In Peter Wood's 1965 production[6] – with Cleo Laine as Dusty and jazz by Dankworth – it came over as an exhilaratingly open piece of theatre, with its evocative changes of rhythm, its easy, swinging movements out of dialogue into soft shoe turns and musical comedy numbers like 'My little island girl'. Osborne seems to be recalling this in *Look Back in Anger* when he has Jimmy and Cliff go into one of their turns as T. S. Eliot and Pam, 'Bringing quips and strips to you'. There's the same feeling here that knockabout is a blessed means of breaking out from an oppressive atmosphere of sexual tension – what Pinter's characters, for instance, can't ever do – nor Eliot's own in later plays.

*Sweeney* is very much a play of breaking out and acting out rather then talking out. There's a feeling that anything could happen: it's in key for an old gentleman looking like Father Christmas to turn up, as he did in Peter Wood's production, with an alarm clock in one hand and a champagne bottle in the other, to close down the proceedings.[7] Violence is *in* the action, not just something heard about. Sweeney's tale of his friend who did a girl in and pickled the body in a bath of Lysol comes over as a kind of sleep-walking preliminary to the real thing, the murder of a woman such as Dusty by a man driven by a mysterious loathing of women: 'Any man has to, needs to, wants to,/ Once in a lifetime, do a girl in.' It's the world of Jack the Ripper or of the Grand Guignol theatre – which was active in London in the Twenties – illuminated by the understanding of a poet who is deeply involved in Sweeney's complex feelings about women and violence.

Whether because the method of *Sweeney* was too direct and physical for the subject he wanted to handle or because he saw no hope of getting the right production for this style of play in the theatre of the time – these are questions to which there are as yet no answers. Certainly there wasn't a regular theatre company in London in 1926 (the year *Sweeney* was published) geared to the style of production the play needed. Eliot knew this well: it was in these years that he was enthusing in the pages of the *Criterion* about the superior training in bodily discipline and expressiveness that ballet dancers had; the ballet was the great potential source of the truly modern drama of the future, (a remark which seems to point straight to Beckett's mimes and the ritualistic movements of *Endgame* and *Krapp's Last Tape*). The other acting qualities he admired – and aimed to bring into *Sweeney* – came from another kind of non-realist theatre, the music hall. Eliot was fascinated by the directness of entertainers like Marie Lloyd, their openness to their audience, their capacity for improvisation. His account of her 'searching in her handbag' turn[8] shows a feeling for the music hall art that makes one understand why a writer like John Arden should have been so drawn to *Sweeney*: something of that feeling got into the play.

It seems rather sad that Eliot couldn't find an outlet for these sympathies in the theatre of the Twenties and that *Sweeney* had to remain for so long a fragment on a page. When he did see it performed by the Group Theatre[9] in 1935 he apparently wasn't very enthusiastic: one can't tell whether it was because the production was poor or because his interest in the method had waned.

Perhaps the closed form of the fourth wall play better expressed his state of mind at that time. Certainly one feels that the special force of *The Family Reunion* comes from the sense of the lid being held on so tight: the moments when the repressed feelings trickle through in delicate verbal music are poignant just because the context is so stiff and anti-musical.

Eliot has, I think, a stronger interest in the 'ordinary' part of his material, the non-mystical part, than he's usually credited with. There are striking resemblances of detail between his play and the typical family plays and detective plays of the Thirties, and some interesting indications that he was aware of experiments being made with the material by contemporaries such as Priestley.

The first audiences of *The Family Reunion* had an opportunity of seeing the standard family play and Eliot's adaptation of it playing almost side by side. Dodie Smith's *Dear Octopus*, the epitome of the popular family drama, opened at the Queen's Theatre on 14 September 1938, while Eliot was finishing his play. For a time there was even the entertaining possibility that Gielgud, who was playing Nicholas Randolph in *Dear Octopus*, might take on Harry as well in matinée performances of *The Family Reunion*. Harry in the afternoon, Nicholas at night – a mind-boggling prospect, as the advertisements for *The Mousetrap* have it! Gielgud was looking forward to bringing out the contrasting treatments of 'the same characteristics, the family theme, the return of the prodigal, etc. . . .'[10] He would have had plenty to work on.

In each play, as he indicates, a prodigal returns home for a family anniversary: in *Dear Octopus* it's a daughter who, like Harry, has been kept abroad for years by an unhappy sexual relationship. Both have to come to terms with fiercely possessive mothers and with families obsessively taken up with their own past. About here the resemblances end and the obviously much more important differences begin. One wonders how Gielgud's performance as Nicholas would have survived the cold light thrown on that cosy family from the other one. Just occasionally the irony might have gone the other way, perhaps: one of Dodie Smith's child characters has a line nicely pointing out to *The Family Reunion*: 'I wish we didn't have any dead people in the family. It sort of spoils the party.' But it seems safe to assume that *Dear Octopus* would have been the play to shrivel under the comparison!

The uncanny thing about it – viewed alongside *The Family Reunion* – is its deep unselfconsciousness. The characters manage to evade real scrutiny, as they do in most of the family plays of the time, even those, like Van Druten's *After All*, which ask to be taken rather more seriously than *Dear Octopus*. Eliot seems to provide the critical focus for the whole genre, to give it full selfconsciousness for the first time.

His way of forcing his characters to examine themselves is to put them in the framework of an amateur detective play, borrowing from another popular type of Thirties drama, which was represented in the London theatre at the time he was writing by Anthony Armstrong's *Mile-Away Murder* [1937]. He sets the play up as a probe into the causes of Harry's breakdown; witnesses come forward in turn – Agatha, Mary, the family doctor, the chauffeur – even the stolid country policeman is brought into the scene, and we hear of the off-stage brother getting into trouble with the police. Some of the conventional elements – the bucolic sergeant, for instance – make an uneasy fit, but they function usefully as a means of keeping some sort of connection with the outside world – clearly important for Eliot – and of emphasising the family's dread of publicity, the strength of their will to keep everything closed and hushed. One after another of the witnesses brings out this governing principle:

WARBURTON: Harry, there's no good probing for misery.
There was enough once: but what festered
Then, has only left a cautery.
Leave it alone. . . .

and

CHORUS: Why should we stand here like guilty conspirators, waiting for some
    revelation
When the hidden shall be exposed, and the newsboy shall shout in the
    street?
When the private shall be made public, the common photographer
Flashlight for the picture papers: why do we huddle together
In a horrid amity of misfortune? why should we be implicated, brought in
    and brought together?

In applying pressure from the detective play to the 'matter' of the
family drama Eliot had hit on a technique with rich possibilities. He
was taking up where Joyce left off in *Exiles* but going much beyond
him into the area where feelings are nameless, the sense of guilt
obscure and undefined.

His true heir in this sphere is Pinter. Contemporaries seem to have
picked up hints too, though: Priestley in *An Inspector Calls* (1947) uses
the detective technique in a similar way. And Eliot in turn picks up
from Priestley, to judge from the striking similarities between *The
Family Reunion* and *I Have Been Here Before* [1937].

This particular comparison brings out interestingly, I think, how
Eliot tried to move away from the analytical, narrative methods of the
thirties novelist/playwrights into a more direct and physical kind of
drama. Priestley's play is about a moment of fatal choice on the
Yorkshire moors. An unhappily married couple, a young schoolmaster and a German doctor meet at a country inn. A love affair develops
between the wife and the schoolmaster; the husband reacts violently,
threatens to wreck his rival's career: his own suicide seems inevitable.
The German doctor intervenes: he has come to this obscure inn
simply to avert the tragic outcome which – so he claims – he has
witnessed in another dimension of time.[11] Watching now, he says, is
'like watching the performance of a play that one has first read
carefully'. The other characters are sceptical, then resentful. Are they
just marionnettes, the wife asks, with no minds and wills of their own?
No, says the doctor, now they have knowledge from the 'past', they
have freedom too: this is the 'great moment' of choice: 'In the end the
whole universe must respond to every real effort we make. We each
live a fairy tale created by ourselves.'

There are some rather remarkable anticipations already here of
Eliot's themes and situations, even his way of putting things. And
when Dr Görtler speaks of 'what seems to happen continually just
outside the edge of our attention', we are getting very close to Harry's
account of the Eumenides as something sensed, 'Here and here and
here – wherever I am not looking, / Always flickering at the corner of

my eye,/ Almost whispering just out of earshot.' Priestley's Ormund too is a haunted man: the knowledge he doesn't know he has casts its shadow:

All my life I've had a haunted sort of feeling . . . as if, just round the corner, there'd be a sudden blotting out of everything.

Dr Görtler is his mentor, as Agatha is Harry's: he offers a way out from under the 'spell':

You can return to the old dark circle of existence, dying endless deaths, or you can break the spell and swing out into new life.

It's at this point of greatest closeness that one is reminded how much more direct and physical the 'haunting' is in *The Family Reunion*. Whether the Eumenides are given some tangible shape or indicated by changes of light – Eliot's final preference – they are a real presence in the play, something that enters the action and freezes it in a moment of terror: 'Come out! Where are you? Let me see you,/ Since I know you are there, I know you are spying on me.' It is confrontation, not narrative. But yet they are not there: Mary, for instance, doesn't see them. So the audience is involved directly in the experience of being haunted without having to lose belief in the solid, ghost-free world.

These are the places where Eliot now looks so modern. It's just those experiments that seemed to cut him off from the mainstream in the Thirties theatre that bring him back into it in the theatre of the Seventies. His method of indicating 'unvoiced' thought, for instance, by changing from one rhythm and verbal style to another has been followed up by writers as diverse as Pinter and Charles Wood, Pinter keeping to prose, Wood often using a strange patterned colloquial speech which is as poetically free from normal restraints in its own way as Eliot's 'duets' and 'arias'.

In the postwar plays Eliot took over forms from the other main area of the tradition, smart drawing-room comedy. Again he darkened the material, put it into ironical focus and drew out forcefully implications that the early master, Coward, had just touched on. The rituals of the cocktail party world are given a push in a sinister direction. Reilly sipping gin and water is a Coward character poised for a leap into a Pinter scene. No wonder Eliot was appalled when he once dropped in on a performance of *The Cocktail Party* to find Rex Harrison getting an illicit laugh by sneaking an extra gin and water when he was alone on the stage; how easy to wreck the effect of machine-like inevitability in the sequence of invitation, response and refusal that makes up the gin and water ritual.

This sense of an unstoppable machine at work seems to me the strongest single impression made by the play. Behind every small move in the social game there's the shadow of a dark manoeuvre in the subconscious: every word is being registered and scrutinized by someone or something: an 'obstinate, unconscious sub-human strength' – Edward's phrase for Lavinia – is felt to be taking over the action. Of course Eliot intended his guardians to be seen as benevolent figures and the detailed working out of Celia's conversion – the nursing order, the missionary work, the crucifixion – push a Christian interpretation forward. But there's so much to undermine it; the black magic element in the consulting room ritual – the moon is invoked, Celia is to be 'fetched' at full moon and so on – and the overbearing ways of the guardian-intruders. Martin Browne speaks of the difficulty of knowing how far nosiness like Julia's could be taken without ceasing to seem comic and benevolent: for some people, he recognised, it had passed that point. That is certainly how it seems to me: what we get from Julia, I should say (and from Reilly and Alex rather less forcefully), is a perfectly chilling demonstration of what happens when the genie is loosed from the bottle, to prise and probe – like Ibsen's Rat Wife again – into the dark corners the characters want to keep hidden. Julia has some very undermining habits, including the Pinterish one of unsaying what she has just said, as when she makes a joke about Lady Klootz (opens the play with it, in fact) and a little later professes never to have heard the name: 'Who is Lady Klootz?' Her whimsies have a nightmarish tinge – that vision of the missing Lavinia being all the time in the pantry 'listening to all we say'. 'I don't want to probe', she says, and gets a laugh, almost the kind a harmless Coward gossip might get, but well on the way to being the uneasy laughter drawn out by a Mick or a Lenny.

The Coward convention is immensely useful to Eliot in his attempt to strike a balance between outer and inner reality. It's such a highly selective arrangement of material from ordinary life, instantly recognisable as 'real' and yet, as a context for living, worryingly incomplete and unreal. What sort of beings can exist only in a cocktail party context, as the guardians seem to do? When they move on to the Gunnings (poor Gunnings!) at the end of the play, it's a neat, Cowardish joke ending and at the same time a powerful reinforcement for the subterranean impression of the guardians as genie who only exist in one dimension – perhaps really inside rather than outside the self. Given the bias of the convention towards caricature and silhouette, it's remarkable that Eliot gets as much solid human interest into the play as he does: it's an indication of how committed he is to the drama of character and motive. One may not be so sure about Celia; she seems something of a dream. But Lavinia and Edward sitting side by side having their 'nervous breakdowns' diagnosed – this ludicrous and sad scene remains in one's mind as a compelling human episode, perhaps even the reason for the whole play.

The innovatory force that makes *The Cocktail Party*, like *The Family Reunion*, such a seminal play, can still be felt, though more faintly and intermittently, in Eliot's last two plays. He was still seeing possibilities in the old forms for new types of drama. In *The Confidential Clerk* he rediscovered farce – one remembers Maugham deploring its disappearance from the theatre of his time – and gave it a new, Pirandellian look that propelled it well into the future. Joe Orton is one of his (unlikely) successors in this sphere: he follows up audaciously and grotesquely in directions gently indicated by Eliot. And the trend is strongly carried forward by plays like David Mercer's *Flint*.

No doubt the idea is better than its working out in *The Confidential Clerk*, but still there are moments when the comic losing and finding of parents leads into genuinely disorientating effects and the precariousness of identity becomes an experience rather than a theme. The farcical structure sets the characters free to express their sense of being 'characters' in a spontaneous, direct way. B. Kaghan can come on saying 'Enter B. Kaghan'. Colby can be given a choice of identities: a selection from a number of possible parents and the roles that would be their legacy. He is rather a good farce hero, with a touch of the cool opportunism the type requires; 'a certain deliberate ambivalence' was Eliot's phrase for him. When he does choose from Mrs Guzzard's alternatives a 'dead obscure man' for his father, the absurd takes on a sombre, troubling quality, the kind of effect modern audiences have come to recognise and respond to; farce in a new dimension, to borrow N. F. Simpson's phrase for his own play, *One Way Pendulum*.

Even in *The Elder Statesman* which comes closest of Eliot's plays to being a piece of flat, conversational realism in Thirties style, there are interesting shadowings of new techniques for a new type of realism. Touches of farcical exaggeration in the characters of Gomez and Mrs Cargill reinforce the impression made by their name changing that they are masks or ghosts rather than solid beings. The flamboyant new identities they have acquired don't ring true, but what else are

they? They bring home with chilling persistence how close Lord
Claverton's situation is to theirs. He has had three sets of names and
identities, is almost as disconnected as they are. Names always have
magic force for Eliot's characters. The way they are used in *The Elder
Statesman* – as something to hide behind and to attack with – points, as
so much of Eliot does, to Pinter and the swoops in and out of different
names that his characters practise so alarmingly.

Although Eliot doesn't carry through his ideas with the sustained
force of successors like Pinter and Orton, he seems to me an important
precursor and model maker. His innovating instinct was so strong
that it almost took him right out of the realist tradition with *Sweeney
Agonistes*. Chiefly, though, it has operated within the tradition,
extending and enriching it to the benefit of present-day playwrights.
Apart from its intrinsic value – and *The Family Reunion* seems to me one
of the truly haunting plays of our time – his drama must surely always
have interest as the melting pot where the old forms were recast and
made new.

SOURCE: ch. IV, on T. S. Eliot, in *Revolutions in Modern English Drama*
(London, 1972), pp. 55–66.

NOTES

[Reorganised and renumbered from the original – Ed.]

1. E. M. Browne, *The Meaning of T. S. Eliot's Plays* (London, 1969).
2. M. C. Bradbrook draws attention to this anticipation of Monty's in *The
Birthday Party* in her *English Dramatic Form* (London, 1965). [Included in this
selection, above – Ed.]
3. *The Rest Cure* was Eliot's original title for *The Elder Statesman*.
4. References to Celia's body being smeared with a 'juice attractive to ants'
and to its decomposition.
5. Browne, op. cit., p. 176.
6. Globe Theatre 13 June 1965. In a memorial programme, 'Homage to
T. S. Eliot'.
7. A transcript of this scene (discarded from an early draft) was included in
the programme to the 1965 production.
8. 'Marie Lloyd', *Dial 73* (1922); rptd (rev.) in *Criterion* (1923) and in his
*Selected Essays* (1932).
9. See J. Isaacs's account in his *An Assessment of Twentieth Century Literature*
(1951), pp. 135–6.
10. See Gielgud's letter to Martin Browne, in Browne, op. cit., pp. 145–6.
11. The idea came from Ouspensky's *New Model of the Universe*, which
Priestley describes as 'an idea of modified recurrence'.

## PART TWO

# Early Stages

1.  *Sweeney Agonistes*  (1932)
2.  *The Rock*  (1934)
3.  *Murder in the Cathedral*  (1935)

# 1. *SWEENEY AGONISTES*        (1932)

## *Carol H. Smith*        'An Alliance of Levity and Seriousness'   (1963)

. . . The new title given to the fragments in 1932, *Sweeney Agonistes: Fragments of an Aristophanic Melodrama*, is an example of Eliot's use of wit to provide clues to the deeper level of meaning. In the new title a kind of ultra-sophisticated effect (for wit is basically a reliance on sophistication) is sought by coupling 'Sweeney', previously Eliot's characterisation of the natural man, with 'Agonistes', suggesting analogies with Milton's *Samson Agonistes* both with regard to Samson's spiritual dilemma and to the Greek dramatic structure used in Milton's work. Thus the audience is intended to get both a comic-ironic impression of the incongruities of Sweeney in Samson's place, while at the same time it perceives on another level the meaning of such a possibility. Samson's dilemma is that of the exile in an alien world who feels compelled by divine will to pull that world down around his own head in order to destroy its iniquities. Sweeney is another spiritual exile in an alien world, and he too must destroy part of himself in his attack on that world. Eliot was trying to achieve comic and tragic effects simultaneously, though on different levels, in an attempt to create a form which would reach through the levels of comedy and tragedy in order to explore beneath the surface of both and of all human experience. His view on this matter was clearly expressed in the following comment:

To those who have experienced the full horror of life, tragedy is still inadequate. . . . In the end, horror and laughter may be one – only when horror and laughter have become as horrible and laughable as they can be . . . then only do you perceive the aim of the comic and the tragic dramatists is the same: they are equally serious [for] there is potential comedy in Sophocles and potential tragedy in Aristophanes, and otherwise they would not be such good tragedians or comedians as they are.

Perhaps this passage also makes somewhat clearer what Eliot meant to convey by the subtitle *Fragments of an Aristophanic Melodrama*. His play is Aristophanic in that it combines a comic surface of social satire with the ritualistic celebration of death and rebirth which Cornford found to underlie comedy. Eliot's presentation is thus intended to evoke both horror and laughter in those who could see 'the potential tragedy' in Aristophanes. It is melodramatic in the older sense of the term, a play combining music and drama, because it is in the music-hall tradition, but it is also melodramatic in another sense. The elements which characterise melodrama, Eliot had said in 'Wilkie Collins and Dickens', were an emphasis on plot and situation, flat characters who suggest 'humour' characters, an atmosphere in which 'the coincidences, resemblances and surprises of life' are utilised for emotional effect, and the postponement of the dénouement – 'delaying, longer than one would conceive it possible to delay, a conclusion which is inevitable and wholly foreseen'. I believe Eliot used the term melodrama in the subtitle of *Sweeney Agonistes* to suggest the conception of a dramatic world he had enunciated in the Jonson essay, where characters were flat to fit the world they moved in. In addition, *Sweeney Agonistes* includes a postponement of the dénouement in the sense that the play is a commentary on the postponement of spiritual awakening in modern man.

The epigraphs which Eliot placed at the beginning of the fragments also hint at the spiritual theme of the work:

Orestes: You don't see them, you don't – but *I* see them: they are hunting me down, I must move on. – *Choephoroi*

Hence the soul cannot be possessed of the divine union, until it has divested itself of the love of created beings. – *St John of the Cross*

Their arrangement points out a connection between the purgation of Orestes and of St John of the Cross. The first quotation is Orestes's exit line in the *Choephoroi* when he first becomes aware of the Furies, who haunt and pursue him after his murder of his mother and her lover until he has achieved purgation. The passage from St John of the Cross is taken from *The Ascent of Mount Carmel*, which describes the mystical path to union with God. The passage is part of the instruction to the novice who wishes to pass through the first stage of the mystic path – the dark night of the senses in which purification of all human desires must occur before the next stage can be reached. In both passages purgation is the goal; and in both cases the pursuit before purgation can occur is as terrible as it is necessary. This 'witty' juxtaposition of seeming incongruities in order to suggest the hidden meanings became a typical feature of Eliot's drama and added to its esoteric effect.

The treatment of the characters in *Sweeney Agonistes* conforms to Eliot's idea of stylised surface. They are undeniably 'flat' and, with the possible exception of Sweeney, are sketched in the broad outlines of intentional caricature. Doris and Dusty (a name suggestive of *The Waste Land* imagery) are lower-class London prostitutes. They are both superstitious and superficial and are differentiated only by Sweeney's more sustained attentions to Doris. The world these characters are proportioned to fit is, on the surface level, the demimonde world of the jazz age where men want a spree with women who are willing to give it to them in return for material rewards and relief from boredom. The fact that jazz symbolised the superficial elements of a modern society of materialistic automatism at the same time that it suggested the primitive side of man's nature in its throbbing rhythms provided the kind of double-edged dramatic device that Eliot liked best. Both analogy and irony could be developed; both the most superficial and the most elemental aspects of the modern world could be suggested by the audible rhythm and the visible setting. The comic and satiric could thus be portrayed on the surface while the tragic and spiritual existed simultaneously beneath.

'Loot' Sam Wauchope, 'Cap' Horsfall, and their former war buddies, Klipstein and Krumpacker, now American business men visiting London and 'out on the town', remain types, although much of the dialogue is excellently effective and true to the types intended. Swart and Snow seem to be entertainers brought in to provide jazz song and dance routines so popular at parties in the nineteen-twenties. . . .

Sweeney's tale of murder and the awfulness of the life-in-death existence of the murderer is meant to illustrate the process that the penitent must pursue in order to achieve purgation. The tale is a grotesque version of the epigraph from St John of the Cross: 'Hence the soul cannot be possessed of the divine union, until it has divested itself of the love of created beings.' According to St John the distance between the creator and the creature is irrecoverable unless the creature is purged of all human affections, since they represent dependence on the senses and make demands which cut man off from his first duty, complete attention to God's love. Thus the murder and dissolution in a lysol bath (lysol is a cleansing agent, albeit a violent one) of the girl in Sweeney's tale represents the violent murder of human desire and dissolution of the old life of 'birth and copulation and death' in the sacramental purgatorial bath which will bring rebirth.

Sweeney's tale is another version of Eliot's use of the Lazarus theme. Sweeney returns from the dead to tell the story of his own

horrible purgation, his divestment of the love of created beings in the
form of sensual allurements and purely human attachments in order
to achieve rebirth and union. As one who has been through the ordeal
and has passed from darkness into light, he re-enacts the battle with
those still in darkness. Doris's terror is caused by her recognition that
she, who represents the old life of the senses in the battle with spiritual
forces, is due for the same murder as the girl in Sweeney's tale.

Thus Eliot sees in the death-rebirth process of the god, which is the
type of the Passion and Resurrection of Christ, a wider meaning than
the final death of the body and eternal life of the soul after death. He
sees that pattern applied to the mystic's process of killing desire in
order to bring to birth the spirit. He pictures the agon as the
representation of that struggle, since humanity living in earthly
darkness in every age, including the modern, must be brought to
awareness of another life of spiritual light. In the agon in *Sweeney
Agonistes* he reproduces a re-enactment of that struggle.

The final song sung by the 'full chorus' is a description of the
nightmare-like pursuit of the penitent by the purgatorial forces. As
the epigraph from Aeschylus suggests, the hoo-ha's serve the same
function as the relentless Furies in their pursuit of Orestes. This is
Eliot's version of the 'Hound of Heaven' theme. The meaning of the
hangman should be clear to all readers of *The Waste Land*. The
effectiveness of portraying the hanged god of Jessie Weston and
Frazer as the hangman lies in the extension of the murder analogy
which was begun in Sweeney's tale. Just as a murderer awaits the
hangman who will mete out punishment for his crime, here the
supplicant awaits the 'hanged man' who will mete out purgatorial
justice.

It is significant that the final song is sung by the 'full chorus', since
in Cornford's discussion of the chorus in Aristophanes he describes
the attempts of the opponents in the agon to woo the sympathies of the
chorus. The chorus takes one side, then the other, and finally is won
over to the side of virtue represented by the hero. In *Sweeney Agonistes*
the chorus in the beginning of the agon indicates its endorsement of
the copulation theme but in the end it too voices the final purgatorial
ode. . . .

SOURCE: extracts from *T. S. Eliot's Dramatic Theory and Practice: From
'Sweeney Agonistes' to 'The Elder Statesman'* (Princeton, N.J., 1963),
pp. 57–61, 70–2.

## *Bernard Bergonzi* 'Language, Theatre and Belief' (1972)

. . . In *Sweeney* Eliot uses a superbly rhythmic language, which though seemingly naturalistic to the point of banality, wholly embodies his aspiration, recorded in his review of *The Duchess of Malfi* in 1919, for a verse drama that would 'obtain, with verse, an effect as immediate and direct as that of the best ballet'. This was entirely in keeping with his consistent interest in the ballet as a dramatic form; Massine, he had remarked, was the best actor in London. But the ballet is a silent form, which becomes dramatic by miming pure action; and Eliot, despite his professed reverence for Aristotle's *Poetics*, and his acknowledgement that 'behind the drama of words is the drama of action, the timbre of voice and voice, the uplifting hand or tense muscle, and the particular emotion', was not able to project action in this nonverbal way. Nearly all of Eliot's critical discussion of the problems of poetic drama is concerned with the question of *language*. In *Sweeney* he developed a mode of dramatic speech that triumphantly met his demands, but he could not project an appropriate action to accompany it, which was, no doubt, why the play remained incomplete, for *Sweeney* is as essentially static as 'Prufrock' or 'Gerontion'. This, at least, is the argument of Hugh Kenner, in his brilliant and indispensable account of the play in *The Invisible Poet*. Kenner sees *Sweeney* as the first draft of *The Family Reunion*:

*Sweeney Agonistes* is a drama about a man no-one else on the stage can understand; exactly as is *The Family Reunion*. And while *The Family Reunion* is written through to its conclusion, nothing is more difficult than to explain just what revelation frees Harry and allows him to take his departure. It is, as Eliot himself said, a good first act, followed by more of the same. The original conception, which we may trace back to *Sweeney*, was radically undramatic because inactive.

More recently, another critic, Katharine Worth, has disagreed with Kenner; she found the 1965 production of *Sweeney* in London, with jazz accompaniment by John Dankworth, a very vital theatrical experience, and she quotes the opinions of reviewers that the play was 'in the same class as the Berlin classics of Brecht and Weill', and that it 'uncannily' foreshadowed the British *avant-garde* drama of the fifties. As Mrs Worth remarks, Eliot's early prescriptions about making serious theatrical use of the music hall and the minstrel show were fully developed by Beckett; having become familiar with *Waiting for*

*Godot* we may be more inclined to appreciate *Sweeney Agonistes*, since Beckett offers striking examples of the dramatic possibilities of nothing happening. The 'theatrical' is not necessarily the same as the 'dramatic', and in an expert production with appropriate music, *Sweeney Agonistes* might still be effective as spectacle and verbal play even though deficient as drama. Eliot himself, writing about Seneca in 1927, said that in the Roman dramatist's work 'the drama is all in the word, and the word has no further reality behind it . . . the characters in a play of Seneca behave more like members of a minstrel troupe sitting in a semicircle, rising in turn each to do his "number", or varying their recitations by a song or a little back-chat.' The Senecan model, as well as the popular theatre, lay behind *Sweeney*.

After he abandoned his 'jazz play' Eliot did not attempt to write again for the stage for several more years, and when he finally returned to the drama he did not persist in the immensely original manner that he had opened up in *Sweeney*.

One must remark, finally, that *Sweeney* marked thematically an important stage in Eliot's movement toward Christian belief. The Sweeney in the second fragment of the play is a more serious and philosophical person than the *homme moyen sensuel* of 'Sweeney Erect' or 'Sweeney Among the Nightingales' who is also, presumably, the Sweeney who awaited Mrs Porter in *The Waste Land*. This Sweeney is 'much possessed by death' and has dwelt on the state of not knowing whether one is alive or dead; he is aware of the cyclical hopelessness of a life lived wholly in biological terms, without the possibility of transcendence:

> That's all the facts when you come to brass tacks:
> Birth, and copulation, and death.
> I've been born, and once is enough.

The others do not know what he is talking about: in Kenner's words, Sweeney is a 'man no-one else on the stage can understand'. The play has two significant epigraphs. One is from Aeschylus: 'You don't see them, you don't – but *I* see them: they are hunting me down, I must move on.' This was enlarged on in *The Family Reunion*, and indicates that Sweeney is a superior consciousness, haunted by powers that ordinary mortals cannot perceive. The second quotation is from St John of the Cross: 'Hence the soul cannot be possessed of the divine union, until it has divested itself of the love of created beings.' Here we see Eliot, who had long been familiar with the *Bhagavad-Gita* and other major texts of Indian mysticism, publicly invoking for the first time one of the masters of Christian mysticism, who was to appear again in *Ash-Wednesday* and *Four Quartets*. St John was writing of a high and rare stage in the ascent of the mystical ladder, and not uttering everyday spiritual counsel: nevertheless, a sense of disparity between divine and human love was to haunt Eliot's cruelly bleak mode of Christian belief. Only at the end of his life does a new and more affirmative mode enter.

> SOURCE: extract from *T. S. Eliot* (London and New York, 1972), pp. 107–9.

## *Andrew Kennedy* 'Ritual and Dramatic Speech Effects' (1975)

... To read *Sweeney Agonistes: Fragments of an Aristophanic Melodrama* – taking up Eliot on the words of the subtitle – alongside [Francis M.] Cornford's *The Origin of Attic Comedy* (1914) is to gain insight into Eliot's rediscovery of the 'Ur'-ritual. For Cornford 'the tragic Myth and the comic Logos', the highly organised structure of Greek drama and the broken-down folk drama of puppets and mummers – with parallels in Punch and Judy, and St George and the Dragon – have the same underlying pattern. Such a discovery opened the way back to what Eliot took to be the primitive sources of drama: offering the hope of a revitalised dramatic language through 'imitation by means of rhythm – rhythm which admits of being applied to words, sounds, and the movement of the body'.[1] While Shakespeare's Plutarch gives us a direct understanding of how the actual words of the text were transmuted (how the description of Cleopatra's barge, for example, became dramatic speech), Eliot's Cornford gives us only the conception behind the dramatic language. It was nevertheless a generative conception. It led to the 'possibility' of ritual and liturgy. And it led to Eliot hearing, as it were simultaneously, the antique drum and the beat of the jazz drum under vulgar, contemporary, metropolitan speech: the fallen liturgy of *Sweeney*. 'This invention of language' – to apply what Eliot said of Baudelaire's intense imagery of damnation taken from the sordid life of the metropolis – 'is the nearest thing to a complete renovation that we have experienced.'[2]

*Sweeney* is, then, most successful as an experiment in speech, or more precisely, in turning speech into rhythmic sound effects. We know that Eliot intended the whole work to be accompanied by 'light drum taps to accentuate the beats (esp. the chorus which ought to have a noise like a street drill)';[3] and that emphatic modern rhythm was associated by him with the internal combustion engine. We are meant to experience the play upon our pulses. We shall see later how colloquial cross-talk is itself turned into near-abstract orchestration. Here we should recall how many of the elements in the short play are language-as-sound: the constant repetition of names, questions and greetings, for phonic play ('Good bye. Goooood bye'); the telephone bell's 'Ting a ling' and the 'knock, knock' woven into the texture of the dialogue (spelt out as fourteen lines); Sweeney's speech, about *his* unutterable experience, merging into crooning ('We're gona sit here and have a tune'); the six visitors, with the unnecessary names, forming a broken chorus even before they burst into jazz song and into the final nightmare-chorus. The spirit of the Hoo-ha's pervades this work; the toys of Dionysus, top, rattle, dice-bones,[4] have been rediscovered. But one can see why Eliot excluded *Sweeney* from the *Collected Plays*; from his point of view it was the first dead end; the experiment with popular forms drawing on the music hall and the street were left to others. The return to the 'origins' of drama resulted in a small-scale work best *heard* on record or radio – the original radio play.

SOURCE: extract from *Six Dramatists in Search of a Language* (London, 1975), pp. 100–1.

NOTES

[Reorganised and renumbered from the original – Ed.]

1. 'The Beating of a Drum'. The article opens with Darwin and ends with the view that through various rationalisations 'we have lost the drum'. Cornford too is invoked; and the two titles, 'The Origin of Species' and 'The Origin of Attic Comedy', meet the eye on the same page. The words quoted are Eliot's quotations from Aristotle: Butcher's translation, p. 139.

2. Eliot's essay 'Baudelaire' (1930), in *Selected Essays* (3rd edn), p. 426.

3. See letter to Hallie Flanigan, the producer of the play-fragment at Vassar (1933), quoted in Carol H. Smith, *T. S. Eliot's Dramatic Theory and Practice* (Princeton, N.J. 1963), p. 52. Cf. the well-known reference to the 'internal combustion engine' – Introduction to Charlotte Eliot's *Savonarola* (London, 1926) – with Eliot's appreciation of Stravinsky's *Sacre du printemps* ('it did seem to transform the rhythm of the steppes into the scream of the

motor horn, the rattle of machinery, the grind of wheels . . . and the other
barbaric cries of modern life') in 'London Letter', *Dial*, LXXI (Oct. 1921).
   4. As in Orphic Fragment 21: K. Freeman, *Ancilla to the Pre-Socratic
Philosophers* (Oxford, 1962).

## Ronald Hayman        'The Timid Pioneer'    (1979)

. . . Eliot understood that the central problem facing the serious
dramatist was the problem of language, but he might have become a
better playwright if he had not turned his back so uncompromisingly
on his first tentative attempt to solve the problem. In 1932 he had
published a work he had abandoned without thinking it had any
chance of being staged: *Sweeney Agonistes—Fragments of an Aristophanic
Melodrama.* Using the uneducated speech of low-life characters, he
imposed jazz rhythms on their repetitions, circumlocutions, and
approximations:

DORIS: I like Sam
DUSTY:            *I* like Sam
Yes and Sam's a nice boy too.
He's a funny fellow
DORIS:            He *is* a funny fellow
He's like a fellow once I knew.
*He* could make you laugh.
DUSTY:                    Sam can make you laugh:
Sam's all right
DORIS:            But Pereira won't do.
We can't have Pereira
DUSTY:                    Well what you going to do?

Today some of the dialogue may remind us of early Pinter, though the
rhythms are stronger and the characters more self-conscious about
the difficulty of communicating:

          I gotta use words when I talk to you
          But if you understand or if you don't
          That's nothing to me and nothing to you
          We all gotta do what we gotta do

Ten years earlier, using unrhymed dialogue, Eliot had written a
comparable passage in *The Waste Land* (lines 139–72). There is only

one speaker, a barmaid, and apart from shouting 'HURRY UP PLEASE
ITS TIME' five times, her monologue consists almost entirely of quoted
dialogue, and, as in *Sweeney*, the liveliness and tension of the writing
depend not so much on accurate mimicry of the character's speech as
on an intensity which derives from Eliot's mixture of fascination and
revulsion:

> You have them all out, Lil, and get a nice set,
> He said, I swear, I can't bear to look at you.

Writing about Baudelaire in a 1930 essay Eliot said: 'It is not merely
in the use of imagery of common life, not merely in the use of imagery
of the sordid life of a great metropolis, but in the elevation of such
imagery to the *first intensity* – presenting it as it is, and yet making it
represent something much more than itself – that Baudelaire has
created a mode of release and expression for other men.'[1] Among
Baudelaire's images are prostitutes, mulattoes, hermaphrodites,
corpses, shrouds, lice, and defecation, but his preoccupation, as Eliot
says, was with the possibility of redemption and with the problem of
good and evil. In the pub sequence of *The Waste Land* and in *Sweeney*,
Eliot used the cliché-ridden language of prostitutes, procuresses,
pimps, garrulous barmaids and newspaper reports on crime, and the
tawdry imagery of false teeth, fortune-telling, and pills taken to
induce abortions, but, like Baudelaire, he made squalor and evil
flower into something beautiful.

It was left for later playwrights to develop the mineral resources of
the territory Eliot had pioneered. He rejected *Sweeney*, excluding it
from the collection of his plays, making no reference to it in his
retrospective comments on his development as a playwright,[2] and
refusing to learn from his own experience. The principal characters in
his later plays may be more articulate, and he tried to make them
more complex, but they are less vivid. None of them is under-
educated or underprivileged. The choruses in *Murder in the Cathedral*
(1939) are spoken by the Women of Canterbury. But their language
has nothing to do with that of their real-life equivalents. . . .

SOURCE: extract from *British Theatre Since 1955* (London, 1979),
pp. 5–6.

NOTES

[Reorganised and renumbered from the original – Ed.]

1. 'Baudelaire' (1930), in *Selected Essays* (3rd edn), p. 426.
2. In 'Poetry and Drama' (1950) and 'The Three Voices of Poetry' (1953);
both reproduced in *On Poetry and Poets* (London, 1957).

## 2. *THE ROCK: A PAGEANT PLAY* (1934)

*T. S. Eliot* Two Comments (1933, 1953)

I

[*1933*]

. . . I believe that the poet naturally prefers to write for as large and miscellaneous an audience as possible, and that it is the half-educated and ill-educated, rather than the uneducated, who stand in his way: I myself should like an audience which could neither read nor write. The most useful poetry, socially, would be one which could cut across all the present stratifications of public taste – stratifications which are perhaps a sign of social disintegration. The ideal medium for poetry, to my mind, and the most direct means of social 'usefulness' for poetry, is the theatre. . . .

Every poet would like, I fancy, to be able to think that he had some direct social utility. By this, as I hope I have already made clear, I do not mean that he should meddle with the tasks of the theologian, the preacher, the economist, the sociologist or anybody else; that he should do anything but write poetry, poetry not defined in terms of something else. He would like to be something of a popular entertainer, and be able to think his own thoughts behind a tragic or a comic mask. He would like to convey the pleasures of poetry, not only to a larger audience, but to larger groups of people collectively; and the theatre is the best place in which to do it. There might, one fancies, be some fulfilment in exciting this communal pleasure, to give an immediate compensation for the pains of turning blood into ink. . . .

SOURCE: extract from 'Conclusion' in *The Use of Poetry and the Use of Criticism* (London, 1933); paperback edn (1975), pp. 153, 154.

II

[*1953*]

. . . Twenty years ago I was commissioned to write a pageant play to be called *The Rock*. The invitation to write the words for this spectacle – the occasion of which was an appeal for funds for church-building in new housing areas – came at a moment when I seemed to myself to have exhausted my meagre poetic gifts, and to have nothing more to say. To be, at such a moment, commissioned to write something which, good or bad, must be delivered by a certain date, may have the effect that vigorous cranking sometimes has upon a motor car when the battery is run down. The task was clearly laid out: I had only to write the words of prose dialogue for scenes of the usual historical pageant pattern, for which I had been given a scenario. I had also to provide a number of choral passages in verse, the content of which was left to my own devices: except for the reasonable stipulation that all the choruses were expected to have some relevance to the purpose of the pageant, and that each chorus was to occupy a precise number of minutes of stage time. But in carrying out this second part of my task, there was nothing to call my attention to the third, or dramatic voice: it was the second voice, that of myself addressing – indeed haranguing – an audience, that was most distinctly audible. Apart from the obvious fact that writing to order is not the same thing as writing to please oneself, I learnt only that verse to be spoken by a choir should be different from verse to be spoken by one person; and that the more voices you have in your choir, the simpler and more direct the vocabulary, the syntax, and the content of your lines must be. This chorus of *The Rock* was not a dramatic voice; though many lines were distributed, the personages were unindividuated. Its members were speaking *for me*, not uttering words that really represented any supposed character of their own. . . .

SOURCE: extract from 'The Three Voices of Poetry' (1953); reproduced in *On Poetry and Poets* (London, 1957), p. 91.


*Roger Kojecký*          'Team-work and a Social Aim'
(1971)


. . . *The Rock* was performed at Sadler's Wells for a fortnight in May and June 1934. Eliot insisted that it was not really a play at all, only a pageant. 'My only seriously dramatic aim was to show that there is a

possible role for the Chorus.' A prefatory note to the published work
made it clear that although the 'book of words' was described as by
Eliot, it was the joint effort of a team. Eliot wrote only one of the
scenes, together with the choruses which were to be reprinted in the
*Collected Poems*. Elsewhere his ideas were altered and adapted with the
help of E. Martin Browne, the Rev. R. Webb-Odell, Bonamy Dobrée,
Frank Morley and the Rev. Vincent Howson, who played the part of
Bert.

The action involves the building of a London church by some
workmen, of whom Ethelbert is foreman. They meet both difficulties
and encouragements, and the opportunity is taken to illustrate the
enduring nature of the Church, and the temporal limitedness of
opposition past and present. The chorus, representing the voice of
wisdom, prophecy and prayer, has the role of illuminating the
different scenes. Modern social ideas and political movements are
brought in. There are, for instance, some Fascist blackshirts who
boast of upholding the rule of law. But when they are asked whether
they consider themselves under the law of God they merely sneer at
their questioners:

> . . . This being the case we must firmly refuse
> To descend to palaver with anthropoid Jews.

And the chorus comments upon Communists and Fascists inclu-
sively:

> There seems no hope from those who march in step,
> We have no hope from those with new evangels.

Political systems and parties alike come under criticism. A plutocrat
appears who claims to stand for 'Church and State and Liberty', but
he gives himself away as one whose 'new solution' is a golden calf
called Power. Already the chorus has exposed him and his kind:

> There is no help in parties, none in interests,
> There is no help in those whose souls are choked and swaddled
> In the old winding sheets of place and power
> Or the new winding sheets of man-made thought.

Our policy, however, is given a more sympathetic airing, Social
Credit:

> ETHELBERT. I knew you ad'ered to some antiquated theory of money. So you
>    think that buildin' more churches means buildin' fewer 'ouses and flats,
>    does you?
> AGITATOR. O' course it does.

ETHELBERT. Now, wait a minute. I'm telling you, mate. Deny if you can as there's enough clay and lime and tools and men to build all the 'ouses that's needed in this country, and all the churches too? Well that bein' the case, I say, *to 'ell with money*! You can arrange the convenience o' money so's to get these things.

Whether or not Eliot wrote this, the idea seems to have been sympathetic to him. In *After Strange Gods* he wrote that 'when anything is generally accepted as desirable economic laws can be upset in order to achieve it'. *The Rock* in fact, for all its crudities, displayed a lively awareness of the plight of Britain's large numbers of unemployed. . . .

SOURCE: *T. S. Eliot's Social Criticism* (New York, 1971), pp. 103–5.

## *Helen Gardner*     'Experiment in Choric Verse'
## (1949)

. . . Although *Sweeney Agonistes* looks back in its subject-matter, it looks forward in its style. The pageant-play *The Rock*, to an even greater degree, should not be thought of as a dramatic experiment, but as having provided Mr Eliot with an opportunity for writing another kind of dramatic verse: choric verse. The traditional distinction between the metres of dialogue and the metres of the choruses of a play is also a practical one. Choric speaking must be emphatic or the sense is lost: it must keep time, and cannot indulge in much variation of speed and tone. Many voices speaking together are incapable of the subtle modulations of a single voice, and of the innumerable variations from a regular metrical base that make up the music of poetry. If the metre is regular, choral speaking will soon reduce it to the monotony of sing-song. Anyone knows this who has had to listen to classes of children reciting in unison verse not written for this method of delivery. Choric verse must therefore be itself written in free metres; the necessary variety must be inherent in the metrical structure, in variation in the length of line, and the length of the breath units. Where dialogue approximates to speech, choric verse must approximate to chant. The choruses of *The Rock*, which owe

much to the rhythms of the Authorised Version, and to the
Prayer-Book Psalms, have the simplicity of syntax, the emphatic
repetitions, the rhythmical variety which choric verse must possess.
These experiments culminate in *Murder in the Cathedral.* . . .

SOURCE: extract from *The Art of T. S. Eliot* (London, 1949; new edn
1968), pp. 132–3.

# 3. *MURDER IN THE CATHEDRAL* (1935)

*T. S. Eliot* Comment (1951)

... When I wrote *Murder in the Cathedral* I had the advantage, for a beginner, of an occasion which called for a subject generally admitted to be suitable for verse. Verse plays, it has been generally held, should either take their subject matter from some mythology, or else should be about some remote historical period, far enough away from the present for the characters not to need to be recognizable as human beings, and therefore for them to be licensed to talk in verse. Picturesque period costume renders verse much more acceptable. Furthermore, my play was to be produced for a rather special kind of audience – an audience of those serious people who go to 'festivals' and expect to have to put up with poetry – though perhaps on this occasion some of them were not quite prepared for what they got. And finally it was a religious play, and people who go deliberately to a religious play at a religious festival expect to be patiently bored and to satisfy themselves with the feeling that they have done something meritorious. So the path was made easy.

It was only when I put my mind to thinking what sort of play I wanted to do next, that I realized that in *Murder in the Cathedral* I had not solved any general problem; but that from my point of view the play was a dead end. For one thing, the problem of language which that play had presented to me was a special problem. Fortunately, I did not have to write in the idiom of the twelfth century, because that idiom, even if I knew Norman French and Anglo-Saxon, would have been unintelligible. But the vocabulary and style could not be exactly those of modern conversation – as in some modern French plays using the plot and personages of Greek drama – because I had to take my audience back to an historical event; and they could not afford to be archaic, first because archaism would only have suggested the wrong period, and second because I wanted to bring home to the audience the contemporary relevance of the situation. The style therefore had to be *neutral*, committed neither to the present nor to the past. As for the versification, I was only aware at this stage that the essential was to avoid any echo of Shakespeare, for I was persuaded that the

primary failure of nineteenth-century poets when they wrote for the
theatre (and most of the greatest English poets had tried their hand at
drama) was not in their theatrical technique, but in their dramatic
language; and that this was due largely to their limitation to a strict
blank verse which, after extensive use for non-dramatic poetry, had
lost the flexibility which blank verse must have if it is to give the effect
of conversation. The rhythm of regular blank verse had become too
remote from the movement of modern speech. Therefore what I kept
in mind was the versification of *Everyman*, hoping that anything
unusual in the sound of it would be, on the whole, advantageous. An
avoidance of too much iambic, some use of alliteration, and
occasional unexpected rhyme, helped to distinguish the versification
from that of the nineteenth century.

The versification of the dialogue in *Murder in the Cathedral* has
therefore, in my opinion, only a *negative* merit: it succeeded in avoiding
what had to be avoided, but it arrived at no positive novelty: in short,
in so far as it solved the problem of speech in verse for writing to-day,
it solved it for this play only, and provided me with no clue to the verse
I should use in another kind of play. Here, then, were two problems
left unsolved: that of the idiom and that of the metric (it is really one
and the same problem), for general use in any play I might want to
write in future. I next became aware of my reasons for depending, in
that play, so heavily upon the assistance of the chorus. There were
two reasons for this, which in the circumstances justified it. The first
was that the essential action of the play – both the historical facts and
the matter which I invented – was somewhat limited. A man comes
home, foreseeing that he will be killed, and he is killed. I did not want
to increase the number of characters, I did not want to write a
chronicle of twelfth-century politics, nor did I want to tamper
unscrupulously with the meagre records as Tennyson did (in
introducing Fair Rosamund, and in suggesting that Becket had been
crossed in love in early youth). I wanted to concentrate on death and
martyrdom. The introduction of a chorus of excited and sometimes
hysterical women, reflecting in their emotion the significance of the
action, helped wonderfully. The second reason was this: that a poet
writing for the first time for the stage, is much more at home in choral
verse than in dramatic dialogue. This, I felt sure, was something I
could do, and perhaps the dramatic weaknesses would be somewhat
covered up by the cries of the women. The use of a chorus
strengthened the power, and concealed the defects of my theatrical
technique. For this reason I decided that next time I would try to
integrate the chorus more closely into the play.

I wanted to find out also, whether I could learn to dispense altogether with the use of prose. The two prose passages in *Murder in the Cathedral* could not have been written in verse. Certainly, with the kind of dialogue verse which I used in that play, the audience would have been uncomfortably aware that it was verse they were hearing. A sermon cast in verse is too unusual an experience for even the most regular churchgoers: nobody could have responded to it as a sermon at all. And in the speeches of the knights, who are quite aware that they are addressing an audience of people living eight hundred years after they themselves are dead, the use of platform prose is intended of course to have a special effect: to shock the audience out of their complacency. But this is a kind of trick: that is, a device tolerable only in one play and of no use for any other. I may, for aught I know, have been slightly under the influence of *St. Joan.* . . .

SOURCE: extract from 'Poetry and Drama' (1951), reproduced in *On Poetry and Poets* (London, 1957), pp. 79–81.


*Conrad Aiken*      A Trip to Canterbury      (1935)

. . . without any preliminary fuss or fanfare, without advertisements in the newspapers, or any advance announcements except through Church channels, a poetic play was staged in the Chapter House which may well mark a turning point in English drama.

Making every allowance for the extreme impressiveness of the surroundings – the hall of the Chapter House is, of course, magnificent – and for the extraordinary associational aid in the fact that a play about Thomas à Becket's martyrdom was being performed on the very spot where the martyrdom itself had been enacted – a combination of circumstances which must remain unique – nevertheless, one hadn't listened five minutes before one felt that one was witnessing a play which had the quality of greatness. If one had become uneasy about the effect of Eliot's churchward leanings on his poetry, one forgot that at once. Performed in a barn, and before an audience of sceptics, *Murder in the Cathedral* would still be a profound and beautiful thing. It transcends the particular beliefs on which it has been built – or, rather, it creates its own beliefs out of its own sheer

livingness – exactly as *Everyman* does, or *Oedipus Rex*, and, inciden-
tally, with striking technical resemblances to both. The use of the
chorus of ten women, and the choruses themselves, were superb.
One's feeling was that here at last was the English language literally
being *used*, itself becoming the stuff of drama, turning alive with its own
natural poetry. And Eliot's formalisation wasn't at all the sort of thing
one has grown accustomed to expect of poetic drama – no trace of
sham antique or artiness about it; nothing, in the 'dead' sense,
'poetic'. No, the thing was directly and terribly real, the poetry of the
choruses was as simple and immediate in its meaning as our own daily
lives, and the transition into satirical modern prose at the end, when
the four knights turned and addressed the audience, came without
shock. It is a triumph of poetic genius that out of such actionless
material – the mere conflict of a mind with itself – a play so deeply
moving, and so exciting, should have been written; and so rich,
moreover, in the various language of *humanity*. That is perhaps the
greatest surprise about it – in the play Eliot has become human, and
tender, with a tenderness and a humanity which have nowhere else in
our time found such beauty of form.

    The production by Martin Browne was perfect. The stage was of
the simplest, the actors approaching it from the centre aisle of the hall,
through the audience; the chorus, when not speaking, sitting at the
right and left in the niches between little columns, as if merely a part
of the design. Robert Speaight, as Becket, was superb. The other parts
were taken by amateurs, the Cathedral Players, who gave a
performance that professionals might envy. And the speaking of the
choruses was so beautiful that one actually resented at moments the
singing which served as a counterpoint for it, from the gallery at the
other end of the hall; for once, the spoken word was all one wanted.
Altogether, an event; and we shall be surprised if later this lovely
thing isn't given a run in the West End of London, or even put on by
the Theatre Guild in New York.

SOURCE: extract from review article of 1935; reproduced in *A
Reviewer's ABC* (1958), subsequently reissued as *Collected Criticism*
(New York and London, 1968), pp. 191–3.

*Herbert Howarth*       'Theatrical Ingenuity and
Tact'    (1965)

. . . Writing a religious drama for performance in a cathedral Eliot
could not use exactly the recipe which he had been elaborating with
the commercial stage in mind. But he would not admit a total
cleavage between a play for a cathedral and a play for the stage: that
would have been to abnegate his theories. With ingenuity and tact he
retained 'requisites' which either less adventurous or less steady
minds might have abandoned. Comedy? He admitted it: startlingly,
in the apology of the Knights; and yet even there with discretion, and
with a tragic note underlying the surface gusto. Ritual? That was
most easy: the story itself was a rite; the cathedral setting prepared the
audience to follow a ritual and to participate in it. But Eliot
apparently felt that he should not simply count on the cathedral to
involve the audience in the action. He developed a trick, very simple,
as good theatre tricks usually are, to engage them. His protagonist
directly addresses the spectators and tells them of their part. At the
end of the first act Thomas, who has been speaking as the
introspective man interpreting himself to himself, turns and speaks to
the audience, and tells them

> for every evil, every sacrilege,
> Crime, wrong, oppression, and the axe's edge,
> Indifference, exploitation, you, and you,
> And you, must all be punished. So must you.

Then the Interlude sermon is addressed to the audience, who
participate as the Christmas morning congregation. When the
Knights defend the assassination, they address the audience as
Canterbury, England, and their (non-impartial) jury. The audience
has something in common with the chorus. Like the Women of
Canterbury it becomes the common people, no matter in what place,
'who shut the door and sit by the fire' and whose burdens a martyr
transfers to himself.

*Murder in the Cathedral* is exemplary in that it has spoken to Britain
and won something like popularity without any surrender of elevation. It is austere. Its verses are demanding; they range from the long
chorics, as exploratory and encyclopoedic as Claudel's, to the terse,
muscled remolding of the alliterative measures of the Middle English
morality play. It examines the agon of one man, and presents his
struggle and its difficult choice without concession to the frailty of our
understanding.

Eliot's treatment of the crucial phase of the martyr's problem involves a theatrical difficulty which Hofmannsthal before him had encountered in the *Grosse Welttheater*, and had described with candour and with a characteristically incisive self-criticism in the *Dial*. The Beggar raises his axe to shatter society. Wisdom raises her hands in prayer, not for her own salvation nor for society but for the Beggar. And

what next takes place in him is outside the province and possibilities of the truly dramatic, and could not be said in a regular play, but only in a miracle.

. . . Becket's resistance to the first three of his Tempters is clear, his victory over them perfectly clear. But his resistance to the fourth Tempter involves a problem beyond the common experience, at any rate beyond the common awareness: in what state of mind will he receive the death on which he has resolved? In abstaining from the Tempter's offer, he wins a victory the nature of which must be, at the best, only very dimly intelligible to most of us in the audience. Eliot undertook a difficulty more subtle than Hofmannsthal. And perhaps he did not wholly solve it. To some extent we take Becket's decision on trust, leaning on the traditional medieval theatre of the tempting for the illusion and on the poetry of the whole play for our confidence. But the peculiar order of the events in the play is rather beautifully arranged to help us. Becket's inner agon is over by the end of the first act; he has combatted his tempters and made his mysterious choice. Now there follow the interlude, with its sermon, and the whole of the second act, to clarify his victory. It is not clarified by exposition; but it is *dramatised*: the scenes are written so that the actor may convey by his bearing, his tone, as much as by his words, what his decision entailed. Becket must *act* his right reason for dying; and Eliot's script makes it possible for him. . . .

*Murder in the Cathedral* is not the story of the Beggar, but of the hero, the exceptional man. But the common man has a part in it; the Women of Canterbury speak for the poor, the forgotten and overlooked. Eliot's motif is their justification: suffering, they perform their part in God's play of the world, as Hofmannsthal's Beggar does. Again, watching, witnessing, praying, they fulfill an essential role in the drama of creation. Yet the motif speaks for Becket, too; it defines the condition of mind in which, having refused the fourth Temptation, he suffers his martyrdom, and by suffering consummates his life. . . .

SOURCE: extracts from *Notes on Some Figures Behind T. S. Eliot* (London, 1965), pp. 319–20, 321–2.

*Helen Gardner*     'Sanctity versus Self-
Consciousness'    (1949)

. . . The martyrdom of Becket was an obvious choice for a Canterbury
play, made more attractive no doubt by the association of the saint's
name. The theme of the conflict of the spiritual and the secular
powers, the relation of Church and State, was topical, and is a subject
on which Mr Eliot has spoken much in prose. The story of Becket's life
would seem to hold great dramatic and tragic potentialities, for the
'deed of horror' takes place between persons who, though not closely
related, as Aristotle thought best, were at least closely bound by old
ties of friendship; and the deed has a peculiar horror by the addition of
sacrilege to the guilt of murder. But although the conflict of Church
and State is present in the play, it is subordinated to another theme,
and the drama of personal relationships Mr Eliot deliberately avoids.
The king does not appear and the knights are not persons, but at first
a gang, and then a set of attitudes. They murder for an idea, or for
various ideas, and are not shown as individuals, disturbed by
personal passions and personal motives. The central theme of the
play is martyrdom, and martyrdom in its strict, ancient sense. For the
word martyr means witness, and the Church did not at first confine
the word to those who sealed their witness with their blood; it was a
later distinction that separated the martyrs from the confessors. We
are not to think of a martyr as primarily one who suffers for a cause, or
who gives up his life for truth, but as a witness to the awful reality of
the supernatural. The actual deed by which Thomas is struck down is
in a sense unimportant. It is not important as a dramatic climax
towards which all that has happened leads. We are warned again and
again that we are not watching a sequence of events that has the
normal dramatic logic of motive, act, result, but an action which
depends on the will of God and not on the wills of men:

> For a little time the hungry hawk
> Will only soar and hover, circling lower,
> Waiting excuse, pretence, opportunity.
> End will be simple, sudden, God-given.

Nothing prepares us for the consummation. We are told rightly that

> the substance of our first act
> Will be shadows, and the strife with shadows.

Thomas can hardly be said to be tempted, for the play opens so near
its climax that any inner development is impossible. Except for the

last, the temptations are hardly more than recapitulations of what has now ceased to tempt, an exposition of what has happened rather than a present trial; and the last temptation is so subtle and interior that no audience can judge whether it is truly overcome or not. 'Solus Deus cogitationes cordium cognoscere potest.' What spiritual pride lurks in a martyr's heart, even in his last agony, is not to be measured by the most subtle and scrupulous self-analyst, far less by any bystander. Though Thomas may say

> Now is my way clear, now is the meaning plain:
> Temptation shall not come in this kind again,

a question has been raised that cannot be answered dramatically and that has simply to be set aside. We have to take it for granted that Thomas dies with a pure will, or else, more properly, ignore the whole problem of motives as beyond our competence and accept the fact of his death. If in the first act the strife is with shadows, in the second there is no strife at all. The martyr's sermon warns us that 'a martyrdom is never the design of man', and that a Christian martyrdom is neither an accident nor 'the effect of a man's will to become a Saint'. The hero has only to wait for his murderers to appear:

> All my life they have been coming, these feet. All my life
> I have waited. Death will come only when I am worthy,
> And if I am worthy, there is no danger.
> I have therefore only to make perfect my will.

When the knights rush in the momentary drama of their irruption breaks against the calm of Thomas, and the murder takes place as a kind of ritual slaughter of an unresisting victim, a necessary act, not in itself exciting or significant.

The attempt to present in Thomas the martyr in will and deed, with mind and heart purified to be made the instrument of the divine purpose, is a bold one. Success is hardly to be expected. There is more than a trace in the Archbishop of the 'classic prig' who disconcerts us so deeply in Milton's presentation of the tempted Christ in *Paradise Regained*. There is a taint of professionalism about his sanctity; the note of complacency is always creeping into his self-conscious presentation of himself. He holds, of course, the pastoral commission, and it is right that he should teach his flock, but his dramatic function comes to seem less to be a martyr or witness, than to improve the occasion, to give an Addisonian demonstration of 'how a Christian can die'. Thomas is indeed less a man than an embodied attitude, for

there is in this play an almost Gnostic contempt for personality and its
expression in acts. . . .

. . . The difficulty lies partly in the nature of dramatic presentation.
The protagonist of any play must be conscious and aware; that is part
of his function as protagonist. It is through him that the situation is
made clear to us, and we recognise implications hidden from other
persons in the drama. But if there is no true action, if the centre of the
play is a state of mind, the protagonist can only be *self*-aware and
*self*-conscious, and self-consciousness is incompatible with sanctity.
Mr Eliot has conceived his hero as a superior person. The nature of
his superiority can be expounded dramatically only by himself, for the
play assumes a gulf between the saint and the ordinary man.
Inevitably in the expounding the protagonist appears superior in the
pejorative sense.

But for all its lack of action and its unconvincing protagonist,
*Murder in the Cathedral* is intensely moving and at times exciting when
performed. The real drama of the play is to be found in fact where its
greatest poetry lies – in the choruses. The change which is the life of
drama is there: from the terror of the supernatural expressed at the
opening to the rapturous recognition of the 'glory displayed in all the
creatures of the earth' in the last. The fluctuations of the chorus are
the true measure of Thomas's spiritual conquest. They feel his failure
of faith after the last temptation. They know obscurely that if sanctity
is nothing in the end but a higher egoism, there is no value in any
human goodness. Only if the heroic has meaning can the ordinary
have dignity. . . .

SOURCE: extracts from *The Art of T. S. Eliot* (London, 1949; new edn
1968), pp. 133–5, 136.


*Stephen Spender*          'Martyrdom and Motive'
(1975)


. . . The true theme of Eliot's plays written after his conversion is the
discovery by heroes, and one heroine, of their religious vocation. It is
required of the hero that he perfect his will so as to make it conform
completely with the will of God. The play in which these aims are

revealed in a very pure state is *Murder in the Cathedral* (1935). The problem of Thomas Becket is not to attain the courage necessary for him to undergo martyrdom – from his first entrance on the stage he is set on being martyred – but to purify himself of all self-regarding motives for martyrdom. His conversations with the Tempters reveal this aim.

The dramatic purpose of the First and Third Tempters is not really to tempt, since they offer Thomas choices of pleasures and political partisanship which he has already clearly rejected. Their purpose is to set before the audience images of Thomas's past – the life of personal enjoyment, friendship with the king, and temporal power. These Tempters are ghosts from that past. The Second Tempter offers Thomas a choice which he has already rejected. However, this is a choice not just evocative of the past, it is one that needs to be defined and explained in order that the spectator may clearly understand Thomas's present position. It is the choice of doing material good in the temporal world, an action of which Thomas, as a spiritual leader in command of temporal power, might well undertake. The Second Tempter asks him to become Chancellor again in order that he may save the people from misgovernment. Thomas has no difficulty in rejecting the part of this temptation which concerns covering himself in worldly glory. But there is a further temptation which involves him in exacter definition of his aims. It is the temptation to use power in order to achieve good:

> Temporal power, to build a good world,
> To keep order, as the world knows order.

Thomas rejects this on the grounds that he has made a choice beyond that of doing good in the world through power. It is that of spiritual power and carrying out the will of God.

The Third Tempter, like the first two, offers temptation which can scarcely be expected to tempt. This is for Thomas to ally himself with the English barons against the King with whom his friendship has been broken. As a temptation this is meaningless. If he were concerned with temporal power, Thomas would be on the side of the King against the barons.

Finally there is the Fourth Tempter – the only one who really tempts Thomas because he echoes what are his own thoughts, the prospects of the 'enduring crown to be won' through martyrdom:

> What can compare with glory of Saints
> Dwelling forever in presence of God? . . .
> Seek the way of martyrdom, make yourself the lowest

On earth, to be high in heaven.
And see far off below you, where the gulf is fixed,
Your persecutors, in timeless torment,
Parched passions, beyond expiation.

Thomas recognises this voice which is the echo of his own and knowing this he cries:

Can sinful pride be driven out
Only by more sinful? Can I neither act nor suffer
Without perdition?

The hero or the martyr may be acting out of pride and the desire for glory. Although glory is indeed the crown of martyrdom, for the martyr to be martyred for this reason corrupts his action and puts him on the level of those concerned with their own power and glory. The will of the individual has to be absorbed within the objective will which is the love of God with such perfection that action becomes passive suffering, subjectively motiveless. There are, of course, theological arguments, going back to Aristotle, and resumed by Thomas Aquinas and Dante, which discuss this. But drama concretises abstractions as living situations, and the situation of Thomas Becket, with his tormenting doubt as to his motives, is real. . . .

The Fourth Tempter, having echoed and clarified for him Thomas's aspirations for the glory of martyrdom, now echoes his rejection of his own self-regard, his dedication to the aim of submerging every element of his own will within the will of God. The Fourth Tempter takes up indeed the very words that Thomas has himself spoken to the chorus:

You know and do not know, what it is to act or suffer.
You know and do not know, that action is suffering.
And suffering action. Neither does the agent suffer
Nor the patient act. But both are fixed
In an eternal action, an eternal patience
To which all must consent that it may be willed
And which all must suffer that they may will it,
That the pattern may subsist, that the wheel may turn and still
Be forever still.

This is a moment when Eliot merges his own poetry in what was for him the supreme moment of Dante – 'in his will is our peace'.

In his concluding speech of the first act Becket has moved forward spiritually into an area of lucid consciousness. The Fourth Tempter, echo of his own wishes (and perhaps his angel), has shown him his own heart's way to purge his soul of impure motivation:

> Now is my way clear, now is the meaning plain:
> Temptation shall not come in this kind again.
> The last temptation is the greatest treason:
> To do the right deed for the wrong reason.

The first three Tempters are now seen as visitations from the past, 'ghosts' (like Gomez and Mrs Carghill in *The Elder Statesman*). They are the occasion for a review of his past as friend of the King, and of confrontation with this fact that spiritual authority puts the soul in even deadlier danger than temporal power:

> For those who serve the greater cause may make the cause
>     serve them,
> Still doing right: and striving with political men
> May make that cause political, not by what they do
> But by what they are.

Thomas, addressing out of his past a 'modern' audience, knows that his history will seem to most of these onlookers futility, the lunatic self-slaughter of a fanatic. His aim is further elucidated in the sermon which he preaches in the cathedral on Christmas morning, 1170:

A Christian martyrdom is no accident. Saints are not made by accident . . . A martyr, a saint is always made by the design of God, for His love of men, to warn them and to lead them, to bring them back to His ways. A martyrdom is never the design of man; for the true martyr is he who has become the instrument of God, who has lost his will in the will of God . . . the martyr no longer desires anything for himself, not even the glory of martyrdom.

This way of thinking, culminating in his religion, had fundamentally been Eliot's since the discussion of the relation of the living poet to the whole past tradition in the essay on 'Tradition and the Individual Talent'. The poet is seen not as expressing his own personality but as surrendering and even extinguishing it within the objective life which is the tradition. The view of the relation of the subjective individual who has found his vocation to an impersonal objective life is sacrificial. Eliot has found beyond literature, beyond the tradition, that religious life which, in his view, creates living values.

The four knights, agents of the king, who come to murder Thomas and who explain at considerable length, in a style that owes something to Shaw's *St Joan*, their reasons for doing so, correspond to the four Tempters. In a sense they are indeed Tempters, not of Thomas but of the Chorus in seeking their approbation of the murder. They are also, just as much as Thomas, instruments whereby Thomas perfects his own will within that of God. Although agents of ultimate good, they are, nevertheless, wicked not only before God but in the temporal world. As Archbishop of Canterbury, Thomas Becket, their opponent, is a doughty champion of the war of the spiritual authority against the temporal powers, whether of the King or of the barons, in his time.

It is a very fine stroke whereby Eliot makes Thomas, a few seconds before his assassination, recover his sense of his real authority in the world, which derives from his offices and from Rome, and rebuke one of the knights who calls him traitor. He cries:

> You, Reginald, three times traitor you:
> Traitor to me as my temporal vassal,
> Traitor to me as your spiritual lord,
> Traitor to God in desecrating His Church.

The Women of Canterbury are not wicked, but vacillating, concerned with their own interest but capable of accepting the burden of participating in a drama which can offer them nothing but the worsening of their own material conditions. Their poetry is perhaps the greatest triumph of *Murder in the Cathedral*. It is unparalleled in Eliot's work.

The choruses of *The Rock* are preparatory exercises for it, but tend to provide examples either of spiritual exhortation (which does not fit well in the mouths of a chorus of common folk who are being exhorted) or of Eliot's mysticism. In *The Rock* Eliot is incapable of giving expression to the feelings of ordinary modern men and women, perhaps, because he cannot see them except as corrupted by the time. . . .

The Women of Canterbury are another matter. Eliot can see them as rooted in rituals of toil – rituals of the seasons – as sharing the dignity of their domestic and agricultural labour, as having their place within a hierarchy whose temporal head is the king, and whose spiritual head is the Archbishop, representative of the Pope in Rome. Eliot's picture of the people of Canterbury may not be historically exact but it is imaginatively moving. He is able to visualise their lives within the context of values and conflicts which the play is about. They obey the King. They go to Church. They work. They are afraid of the barons. They are therefore capable of commenting on the action which they first obscurely, and later luminously, understand. They are in a relation to Thomas which is that both of chorus and of a generalised protagonist capable of entering into dialogue with him.

In the magnificent series of choruses which follow on the declaration by the Knights of their intent to kill the Archbishop, Eliot, through these voices of the past, focuses his feelings of horror in a universal vision which includes the present as well as the past. . . .

SOURCE: extracts from *Eliot* ('Modern Masters' series, London, 1975), pp. 189–91, 192–5, 195–6.

## Michael Goldman
## 'Dramatic Effectiveness'   (1973)

. . . the pattern I have described [in his previous discussion of Eliot's later drama – Ed.] helps to account for *Murder in the Cathedral*'s dramatic effectiveness and points to meanings that have been overlooked in criticism and production. Let me begin with an objection that is frequently raised against the play: 'The determining flaw in *Murder in the Cathedral* is that the imitation of its action is complete at the end of Part One.'[1] I do not think this is true to our felt experience of the play, even in a good amateur production, nor to the dramatic intentions clearly indicated in the text.

It is true that by the end of Part One we have seen Thomas accept his martyrdom as part of a pattern to which he must consent for the right reasons, and that we see this acceptance re-enacted both in the sermon and in Part Two, with no modification of theme or deepening of Thomas's response. But the point of the play lies in the re-enactment, since everything is changed *for us* by each re-seeing. The aim of *Murder in the Cathedral* is to make its audience 'watch and wait', to 'bear witness' – to see the event in several perspectives, each enriching the other, so the pattern may subsist, so the action may be seen as pattern, and so that our own relation to the action, our part of the pattern, may be fully and intensely experienced – and this is not finally accomplished until the very end of the play.

Once more it is a question of knowing and not knowing. Even as the play begins, we know what its climax will be. But by the time we actually see Thomas murdered, after witnessing Part One and the sermon, we see that we knew and did not know. In the same way, the Knights and the Chorus, lacking the knowledge we have, both know and do not know what they are doing and suffering. And of course after the murder, the Knights' speeches show us yet one more aspect of the event that we knew and did not know.

It should be noted at this point that bearing witness, watching the events of the play, is from the first associated both with knowing and not knowing and with fear. In performance we are apt to be unaware of the powerful theatricality of the opening chorus. The theatrical problems of the Women of Canterbury are generally approached by way of voice production and enunciation, and we are grateful – and lucky – if the actresses recruited for the occasion manage to speak clearly and on the beat. Choral acting, as opposed to choral reciting, is usually beyond them. But Eliot understands, as no one except Lorca since the Greeks has understood, that choral writing is writing for the body, and the bodily excitement of the first Chorus derives from the way it joins the feeling of knowing and not knowing to the emotion of fear. The Chorus prefigures the action to come and combines it with a bewildered self-consciousness. We move, they say. We wait. Why do we move and wait as we do? Is it fear, is it the allure of safety, is it even the allure of fear? What kind of fear, what kind of safety? This is exactly the question the play will put about martyrdom, put to Thomas and to us. . . .

Thomas is an easier dramatic subject for Eliot than his later heroes, because he remains active all the time he is on stage, aggressive even while he waits and watches. He is supremely connected to this world and the next, secure in his being except for the crisis at the climax of Part One. As far as it bears on Thomas, the pattern of haunting is complete when he says, 'Now is my way clear'. The true nature of the shadows he must strive with has been revealed to him and he is no longer isolated. We have seen, however, that in the later dramas the pattern of haunting continues to the end of the play and works itself out in the lives of characters for whom such transcendence is not possible. I would like to urge that this pattern is also present in *Murder in the Cathedral*. The sustained pattern of haunting completes the play's design after Thomas's death, and by means of a carefully prepared shift of focus imparts to the whole drama a final richness of impression too easily neglected both in the study and on the stage. As the play finds its structure in our bearing witness to Thomas's martyrdom and, through the Chorus, associates our watching and waiting with a fear that is at times close to panic, so the haunting in the play, the fear in the way of the original title, is finally brought to bear not on Thomas but on the Chorus and on us.

The sequence of events that concludes the play, beginning with the moment the Knights attack Thomas in the cathedral, testifies to Eliot's remarkable control over the resources of his stage. Thomas cries out at length, and the murder continues throughout the entire

chorus which begins, 'Clear the air! clean the sky!' The stage
directions make quite certain of this. The drunken Knights, then, take
upwards of three minutes – a very long time on the stage – to hack
Thomas to death, while the Chorus chants in terror. Beyond the
insistent horror of the act itself there is a further effect of juxtaposition
achieved between the murder and the action of the Chorus. Properly
acted, the choral text unavoidably suggests that in its terror the
Chorus is somehow egging the murderers on, that the continuing
blows of the Knights are accomplishing what the violent, physical,
heavily accented cries for purgation call for: 'Clear the air! clean the
sky! wash the wind! take the stone from the stone, take the skin from
the arm, take the muscle from the bone, and wash them. Wash the
stone, wash the bone, wash the brain, wash the soul, wash them wash
them!' The Chorus brings to a flooding climax the ambivalent current
of fear that has haunted the Women of Canterbury from the opening
scene – attraction toward Thomas and a powerful aversion from him,
fear for and of the martyr. The murder is felt not only as a protracted
physical horror but as an action in which the Chorus has participated.

The speeches of the Knights that follow are of course sinister as well
as comic. The two effects are connected, as Eliot seems well aware, for
our laughter involves us, as their fear has involved the Chorus, in
aggression toward Thomas. We laugh with release from the con-
straints of fancy-dress. In the style they adopt, the Knights voice our
own impulse to deflate the bubble of archaism, poetry, and saint-
liness. We share their animus, and their arguments turn the point
against us. They have acted in our interests, as de Morville reminds
us. 'If there is any guilt whatever in the matter you must share it with
us.'

It is not the confident Third Priest with his dismissal of the Knights
as weak, sad men, who has the last word, but the Women of
Canterbury, who acknowledge themselves as types of the common
man, weak and sad indeed. At the end they dwell upon their fear,
which is no less strong for the transcendence they have witnessed. As
in all Eliot's plays, the glimpse of transcendence is in itself a source of
fear for those who have been left behind. They make the point the
Knights have made in argument and that the choral accompaniment
of the murder has powerfully enforced:

> That the sin of the world is upon our heads; that the
>     blood of the martyrs and the agony of the saints
> Is upon our heads.

I would suggest that everything that happens in the play from the

moment the Knights raise their swords has been designed to give
these lines a weight of conviction and a dramatic force that I hope I
may by now characterise with some precision – as haunting. . . .

SOURCE: extracts from 'Fear in the Way: The Design of Eliot's
Drama', in Arthur W. Litz (ed.), *Eliot in His Time* (Princeton, N.J.,
1973), pp. 174–6, 177–9.

NOTE

1. Denis Donoghue, *The Third Voice* (Princeton, N.J., 1959), p. 81.

## *Hugh Kenner*   'The Archbishop Murder Case'   (1960)

. . . Plainly, one function of the play is to distinguish analytic
cleverness from wisdom, and enterprising good sense from conformity
of one's will to the will of God. And Eliot's great dramatic problem is
that the distinctions he wishes to dramatise do not terminate in
distinct actions, but in the same action. In this dilemma he has
recourse to the unexploited contrast lurking in every detective story,
the contrast between actions as they were performed, a step at a time
into the unknown, will intersecting with will, hidden desire belying
overt conduct, and the same actions as the Sleuth glibly recounts
them in his context of omniscience. A detective story is a twice-told
tale; it is the second telling that we think we understand. The second
telling – the one in the last chapter – establishes this illusion by
reducing person to purpose and behaviour to design. Eliot's ingenious
stratagem was to give the first telling the substantiality of dramatic
exhibition, and produce the glib summing-up as a fatuous anticlimax.
That is why the Fourth Knight begins his reconstruction by installing
us in the world of Mrs Christie: 'What I have to say may be put in the
form of a question: *Who killed the Archbishop?*' That is also why several
lines from a Sherlock Holmes story are dovetailed into Becket's
dialogue with the Second Tempter, and why his exchange with the
Third Tempter opens with the figure of rhetoric the late Rev. Ronald
Knox christened the Sherlockismus:

THIRD TEMPTER: I am an unexpected visitor.
THOMAS:                                    I expected you.

(With which compare,

'How do you know that?'
'I followed you.'
'But I saw nothing.'
'That is what you may expect to see when I follow you.'
                    —Sir Arthur Conan Doyle, 'The Devil's Foot.')

That is also why Eliot proposed calling the play *The Archbishop Murder Case*, a way of playing at Possum in the very citadel of Shakespeare and Aeschylus.

Unhappily, three things combine to sidetrack this extremely promising device for throwing into dramatic relief the changed orientation of Becket's will. The first is the effectiveness of the second act, which so impresses us with Becket's human force, his energetic fortitude before death, that the interchange with the Fourth Tempter is obliterated from memory, and thus rendered inaccessible to the Fourth Knight's suicide verdict which ought to have recalled it and brought it viably into salience at the climax of the play. The second is opportunism; for Eliot did not deny his Third Knight a chance to score against the twentieth-century audience.

But, if you have now arrived at a just subordination of the pretensions of the Church to the welfare of the State, remember that it is we who took the first step.

This is the one part of the Knights' speeches the audience is likely to take seriously; in the film version, indeed, it is forced into prominence, as the Knight suddenly stands in darkness and speaks to the cinema audience:

. . . ask yourselves, who is more representative of the thing you are: the man you call a martyr, or the men you call his murderers?

– an excellent point, but one pertinent to a different play. And the third thing that muffles the dramatic scheme of *Murder in the Cathedral* is the language of the Chorus.

The language of the Chorus: their ululating logorrhea, doubling and tripling the image, assailing and bewildering the mind with that reduplication of epithets that caused Ezra Pound to turn off his radio in Rapallo with a despairing, 'Oh them cawkney woices'. ('I stuck it fer a while, wot wiff the weepin and wailin. Mzzr Shakzpeer *still* retains his posishun.') . . .

Eliot had first written choruses the year before, for a pageant-play entitled *The Rock*; and had quite possibly discovered that when enunciated simultaneously by seven men and ten women the most crisp and athletic verse he had it in him to write became unintelligible three rows from the footlights. Hence, one may conjecture, his new and counter-Eliotic tactic of accumulating epithets around a simple emotion, syntactic structure left in abeyance. The choruses of *Murder in the Cathedral* have this merit, that they are perfectly intelligible even when spoken by elocutionists. . . .

SOURCE: extracts from *The Invisible Poet* (London, 1960; reissued 1965), pp. 240–2, 243.

## *Francis Fergusson*  'Ritual Form of Ancient Tragedy'  (1954)

. . . In its conception, its thought, its considered invention of a whole idea of the theater, *Murder in the Cathedral* is unique in our time; . . .

The basic plot-structure appears to be derived from the ritual form of ancient tragedy. The first part corresponds to the agon. The chief characters are the Chorus of Women of Canterbury, three Priests, four Tempters, and Thomas. The issue – whether and how Thomas is to suffer martyrdom for the authority of the Church – is most explicitly set forth in the scenes between Thomas and the Tempters, while the Priests worry about the physical security of the Church, and the Women suffer their premonitions of violation, a more metaphysical horror. The First Tempter, a courtier, offers pleasure, 'kissing-time below the stairs'. The Second, a Royalist politician, offers secular power, 'rule for the good of the better cause'. The Third, a baron, offers the snobbish comfort of acceptance by the best people, the security of the homogeneous class or tribe. These three echo motivations from Thomas's past, which he has completely transcended, and can now dismiss as 'a cheat and a disappointment'. But the Fourth Tempter offers Thomas the same formula ('You know and do not know, what it is to act or suffer') which Thomas had himself offered the Women when he first appeared; and he shows Thomas that his acted-suffered progress toward martyrdom is motivated by pride and aims at 'general grasp of spiritual power'. For the first time, Thomas nearly despairs: 'Is there no way, in my soul's sickness / Does not lead to damnation in pride?' he asks. There follows a chorus in four parts, triumphant Tempters, Priests and Women, envisaging and suffering Thomas's danger in their various ways; after which Thomas sees his way clear, the 'right reason' for suffering martyrdom. This is the climax and peripety of Thomas's drama and the dramatic center of the play; . . . It concludes the first part.

There follows an Interlude: Thomas's Christmas sermon addressed directly to the audience. He sets forth the timeless theory of the paradox of martyrdom: mourning and rejoicing, living and dying in one: the bloody seed of the Church. From the point of view of the dramatic form, it corresponds to the epiphany following the agon and the choral pathos of Part I. It is also another demonstration, in another mode of discourse and another theatrical convention (the sermon), of the basic idea of the play.

Part II is, from the point of view of Thomas's drama, merely the overt result, the more extended pathos and epiphany, of his agon with the Tempters: he merely suffers (and the audience sees in more literal terms) what he had foreseen at the end of Part I. This part of the play is in broad, spectacular effects of various kinds. First there is the procession of the Priests with banners commemorating three saints' days: those of St Stephen, St John the Apostle, and the Holy Innocents. The four Knights (who replace the Tempters of Part I and, as a group, correspond to them) come to demand that Thomas yield to the King, and then they kill and sanctify him at once. The killing is enacted in several steps, including a chorus in English (one of the best in the play) while the Dies Irae is sung off-stage in Latin. After the killing the Knights advance to the front of the stage and rationalise the murder in the best British common sense political style. The immediate effect of the Knights is farcical – but, if one is following the successive illustrations of the idea of the play, their rationalisation immediately fits as another instance of wrong reason. If it is farce, it is like the farce of the Porter in *Macbeth*: it embodies another aspect of the subject of the play. Part II as a whole, corresponding to a Shakespearean last act and to the catastrophe with chorus and visual effects at the end of a Greek tragedy, is rhythmic, visual, exciting and musical – contrasting with Part I which is addressed essentially to the understanding. . . .

Source: extract from *The Idea of a Theater* (New York, 1954), pp. 223–5; first published in 1949, with subsequent new editions.

*Gareth Lloyd Evans*     The Dramatist in Search of
a Language   (1977)

. . . Eliot achieved a major dramatic success with this play and it is the
more to be acclaimed because the evidence is that he was by this
copious and exhaustive manipulation of language patterns, experi-
menting to find the way into the one unified form of expression. But
metrics and beats are what affect (or should affect) audiences without
attention being drawn to them. It is the words, their colour and pace
and place that are nearer to the audience's conscious listening. And it
is in this relatively unregarded area of sensibility that we will find the
reason why *Murder in the Cathedral* is such a fine play while,
paradoxically, it is also such a self-consciously written play.

We can best see it by dividing our examination into three parts.
First, to reveal Eliot's technical variety, second to show how his
language creates character, third to realise the interrelationship of
language and theme. We are essentially looking at the function of
words as they occur, not at the elusive effects of metrics as they exist.

In the first chorus of the play, for example, there is an impressive
variety of technical skill, all designed to increase the dramatic activity
of the line. Emphasis is achieved by repetition of 'Here let us', and this
is given urgency by repeated single words – the hammer-blows, for
instance, of 'what'. Contrast is achieved by the change from the dull
urgencies of the language of the first eight lines to the pictorial and
atmospheric language of what follows – indicating a shift from
apprehensiveness to cherished memories of certainty about the
inevitable rhythm of the seasons – 'golden October', 'sombre
November', and the simplicity of natural actions, '. . . the labourer
kicks off a muddy boot and stretches his hand to the fire'.

Curiosity is induced by the economical use of questions. Eliot, a
devotee of the skills of the music-hall artist in holding suspense and
inciting the audience into wondering what happens next, is a master
of what, in television and radio drama serials and comedy, is called
'the cliff-hanger'.

> He is at one with the Pope, and with the King of France,
> Who indeed would have liked to detain him in his kingdom:
>
> FIRST PRIEST: But again, is it war or peace?

One example out of context may not convince, but even to read a page
or two of the play is to be assured that Eliot is well aware of the
dramatic tightening he is achieving by questions:

> Who shall have it?
> He who will come.
> What shall be the month?
> The last from the first.
> What shall we give for it?
> Pretence of priestly power.
> Why should we give it?
> For the power and the glory.

The plainness of the verbal content of the questions of the second example above is yet another very characteristic technical device. Some of the most effective dramatic moments of the play come not as a result of *what* is said or of *what* happens but because of a quite sensational bareness or terseness, sometimes even banality of statement which is altogether unexpected:

> We have seen births, deaths and marriages,
> We have had various scandals,
> We have been afflicted with taxes,
> We have had laughter and gossip,
> Several girls have disappeared
> Unaccountably, and some not able to.
> We have all had our private terrors,
> Our particular shadows, our secret fears.
> But now a great fear is upon us, a fear not of one but of many,
> A fear like birth and death, when we see birth and death alone
> In a void apart. We
> Are afraid in a fear which we cannot know, which we cannot
>      face, which none understands,
> And our hearts are torn from us, our brains unskinned like the
>      layers of an onion, our selves are lost lost
> In a final fear which none understands.

Sometimes these have the force of understatement, but with, inevitably, Eliot's typical assumption of irony:

> I see nothing quite conclusive in the art of temporal government.

These accessions of the apparently ordinary gain a lot of force from being placed, more often than not, either in the midst of, or immediately after sections of highly wrought language – the sudden bareness is like seeing a single rock in a field.

In this play Eliot does not commit the error of overworking this particular device. Indeed he seems to have been much more concerned with avoiding slackness here than in his later plays. At times we have a feeling that he senses a need to pull together the

strands of his language. So we have many examples of a gathering up
of matters which might become disparate. Eliot, indeed, never lost a
predisposition to collect together qualities or factors which add up to
a whole in a tight Bristol-fashion unity.

Eliot's Chorus in *Murder in the Cathedral* is far more dramatically
successful than that of *The Family Reunion* which seems to form and
undo itself on a kind of self-willed ad hoc basis. One of the reasons for
the success is the extent to which Eliot relies upon it to fulfil a
traditional function – a function which Shakespeare (although, of
course, his choruses were not multi-peopled) gladly employed. It is
really quite a simple matter but it is extraordinary how rarely its
importance in Eliot has been allowed. This Chorus sets the scenes for
us, and is able, verbally, to take us on a visual journey to those areas
which it is necessary that we should see in our imaginative eye. It
fulfils the function of piecing out the imperfections of the theatre by
working on our visual imaginations. Through the Chorus, we see
Canterbury *outside* the cathedral, we experience the seasons, we watch
peasant, king and priest at work and at talk, and we see even great
ceremonies – all this germane to what we need to know to experience
the play fully.

The second feature of Eliot's language in this play concerns
character. Although Thomas uses several different kinds of speech in
the play Eliot immediately distinguishes him from the moment he
enters into the action. There is a much more gravely formal
architectural quality in Thomas's first speech than anything that has
gone before:

THOMAS: Peace. And let them be, in their exaltation
  They speak better than they know, and beyond your understanding.
  They know and do not know, what it is to act or suffer.
  They know and do not know, that action is suffering
  And suffering is action. Neither does the agent suffer
  Nor the patient act. But both are fixed
  In an eternal action, an eternal patience
  To which all must consent that it may be willed
  And which all must suffer that they may will it,
  That the pattern may subsist, for the pattern is the action
  And the suffering, that the wheel may turn and still
  Be forever still.

And this is a policy Eliot employs for all characters of any consequence.
One of the most fascinating and revealing exercises is to examine how
Eliot carefully designates each of the Three Tempters. Every sentence
of the First Tempter's opening speech is either a specific or an implied

question. In the latter respect we should take notice of this implication in the lines:

> Fluting in the meadows, viols in the hall,
> Laughter and apple-blossom floating on the water,
> Singing at nightfall, whispering in chambers,
> Fires devouring the winter season,
> Eating up the darkness, with wit and wine and wisdom!

– and, if we mentally insert a question mark after each phrase – one which is almost there anyway – we are immediately aware of the nature of this temptation. The actor who will succeed in this speech is the one who recalls that temptation is something which, in a sense, questions the ability to push it aside.

Indeed one might say that this Tempter is 'histrionically' created – that is, the methods used in the language to designate him are larger-than-life, extrovert, drawing attention to themselves. The use of alliteration is hypnotic in effect, and the use of coiled rhyme gives the sense of cosy self-satisfaction – like a cat curled about its satisfied sleep:

FIRST TEMPTER: You see, my Lord, I do not wait upon ceremony:
  Here I have come, forgetting all acrimony,
  Hoping that your present gravity
  Will find excuse for my humble levity
  Remembering all the good time past.
  Your Lordship won't despise an old friend out of favour?
  Old Tom, gay Tom, Becket of London,
  Your Lordship won't forget that evening on the river
  When the King, and you and I were all friends together?

But the Tempter is a man whose ability to employ the rhetoric of beguilement is not matched by any ability to hide his shallowness, his insincerity. With remarkable skill, Eliot, having produced him as a dangerous talker, allows him to demolish himself through his own mouth. After the billing blandishments, the empty clichés fall thick and fast, like the tired winks and nods of a faded Pandarus: 'A nod is as good as a wink'; 'I am your man'; 'The easy man lives to eat the best dinners'; 'Leave well alone'. He defeats himself.

The Second Tempter is immediately established as a man of decision, who keeps a good diary:

> Your lordship has forgotten me, perhaps. I will remind you.
> We met at Clarendon, at Northampton,
> And last at Montmirail, in Maine . . .

The language is clipped, it does not have the limpidity of Tempter
one. Only in one respect does it resemble it – in its sudden access of
alliteration.

> King commands. Chancellor richly rules.
> This is a sentence not taught in the schools.
> To set down the great, protect the poor,
> Beneath the throne of God can man do more?

But the effect is noticeably different from the alliterative language of
the First Tempter, where the soft vowel noises between alliterating
consonants produced a mesmeric effect:

> Spring has come in winter. Snow in the branches
> Shall float as sweet as blossoms. Ice along the ditches
> Mirror the sunlight. Love in the orchard
> Send the sap shooting. Mirror matches melancholy.

One of the most affecting episodes in the play is Becket's sermon. It
grips the emotions in several ways. First, it is a remarkable sermon,
dealing with a particular issue in an authoritative and graceful
manner. Second, it is a splendidly constructed and modulated piece of
prose – it has style without drawing attention to itself, in the manner
of all the best and most memorable sermons. Third, coming, as it
does, after the intricate verse-structure of the first part, it works by
contrast. This does not mean that it is simple in structure but that, by
comparison, it compels the reader's or listener's mind to concentrate
without, at the same time, expecting it to contend with great shifts of
pace or mood or style.

From the point of view of its dramatic and theatrical status it is an
important and clear example of the third element of Eliot's technique
– the close relationship between his language and his theme. It is, on
examination, obviously a prose written by a poet, not in the sense that
it is done with a flourish or is packed with the more apparent poetic
devices of imagery and rhythm; but certain technical resources and
the manner in which they are used bespeak the workings of a poetic
imagination. To this extent it is an example of Eliot's conception of a
dramatic style which had no definite break between a poetic and
prose mode, but accepted gradation between the one and the other.

Three elements – two of which are themes, the other a concept
which is personalised – dominate the sermon. 'Peace' and 'martyrdom' are the content, so to speak, over which 'God' the Father
presides in the sermon. 'Peace' is repeated at intervals throughout the
sermon as the formal theme for the Christmas celebration. But, at a
certain point, the theme of martyrdom is announced and the word

'martyr' becomes a noticeable part of the motif. What happens is that the more subjective theme of martyrdom is always ready to oust the formal one, but never succeeds. Martyrdom, it says, should never be sought, should never be allowed to dominate the consciousness – the way in which the word is kept at bay in the speech is itself a demonstration of this persistent note in the play. But both concepts – peace and martyrdom – are under the control of 'He', 'His', 'Our Lord', 'God'. The words are interspersed throughout the sermon and become the third point in this verbal triangle of forces.

It is superbly achieved, and gives an incantatory quality and a tension to a piece of writing which is also an exercise of a kind of logic. The major part of the speech which begins 'consider also one thing of which you have probably never thought' goes from step to step in the proposing of an argument, but the triangle of faces gives the argument both a religious and an emotional impetus.

And, in the last paragraph, 'peace', 'martyr' and the variants of 'God' are suddenly joined by a very personal 'I' (the 'I' of Thomas himself). The effect is a remarkable example of dramatic contrast. The rich and formal architectonics of language have given place to an utter simplicity – Thomas's aspiration for humility in the face of impending death and martyrdom are a poignant dying fall to the robust affirmatives of the major part of the sermon.

A crucial and persistent critical argument about this play concerns the appearance of the Knights, in what Eliot called 'the public meeting' scene, what they say and how they say it. There are extremes of attitude ranging from a belief that their intervention thoroughly allows the play to impinge on the modern consciousness (because both their language and attitudes are 'modern' in content, form and tone) to an assertion that they jar on the ear and fracture the play's unity.

There can be no doubt that the appearance of the Knights is a shock, not only because of their language – which is of a quite different order from that of the rest of the play – but because they directly address the audience. This latter point is often ignored in any assessment of whether they upset the play's elegant design. The shock they give us frequently gives place to a regret that what has been a grand and noble dramatic creation has been both thematically and dramatically compromised for the sake of a coup de théâtre.

It is not easy to dismiss this opinion, but it does not take us very far in understanding what is implied in the appearance of the Knights. What underlies the implications has a good deal to do with language. The shock is verbal and we might say that, in a sense, the language is

almost too dramatic. It is well suited for stage delivery, being full of
contrasts and modes and moods ranging from the comic to the
pompous, and it has a great range of pace. But it is a fundamentally
different kind of dramatic language from that used in the rest of the
play, including the sermon. It is essentially the language of the
temporal, visible, material world – it is the speech of man in his
environment and in no way echoes any other world, any other
environment. Because of this it can concern itself only with the
realities of the visible world, but its presence cannot be justified by
claiming that this is exactly what Eliot intended – that we are meant
to see how the Knights' raucous speech interrupts the complex rituals
of Becket's world as comprehensively as the Nurse's demotic noise
crashes into the lyrical designs of Romeo and Juliet's love at their first
meeting.

*Murder in the Cathedral* becomes a different play from what we had
been led to expect from its first two-thirds, by the intervention of the
Knights. Moreover it is a difference which seems less a result of design
than of accident. Whereas the first two-thirds is a sensitively achieved
exploration of a man's soul, the coming of the Knights drastically
changes the theme to an ironic melodrama about aims and motives.
What should alert us to the possibility of this shift being accidental is
the fact that what the Knights have to say about aims and motives has
already been covered by the Tempters. The attitudes of the Knights,
the permutations of why and wherefore and if, have been more subtly
conveyed already. No dramatic reason therefore exists for their
interference in this scene – they are essentially a theatrical happening.

The play recovers as ritual language re-establishes its claim on
Eliot's theme and communication and, in the final analysis, the
Knights' scene has no lasting damaging effect. They are, nevertheless, interesting because they make us inquire into the reasons for
their appearance. Martin Browne, who seems to have had a good deal
of responsibility for the allocation of speeches to the various Knights,
is of no direct help. But it appears that Eliot was not short on
suggestions from outside sources. Ashley Dukes had something to say
about characterising each Knight by an introductory phrase, for
example. Perhaps Robert Speaight, who played Becket originally,
and those who actually played the Knights also contributed their
opinions.

The tone of the scene, the theatricality of its presentation, the fact
that it does not really contribute much to the theme, all suggest the
possibility that Eliot (or someone) felt that some kind of relief from the
high tension of the preceding events was necessary. Perhaps the

existence of this scene is proof positive that Eliot's frequent doubting of his own dramatic instinct and capability found expression in practice as well as theory.

What *Murder in the Cathedral* amply shows is that Eliot's doubts about his own ability were unfounded. He went on to write plays of progressively less dramatic credibility because he seems, on his own testimony, to have doubted whether the language of *Murder in the Cathedral* was viable for any other kind of drama. What he seems not to have realised is that far from any other play requiring a quite different language-pattern, what he had created for *Murder in the Cathedral* might very well be capable of infinite variety. He moved, however, further and further away from a mode which allowed of both a high degree of poetic resource as well as a judiciously calculated amount of low-tensioned prose, into a prose medium which eventually lost all sense of contrast, variation of pace, colour, as it desperately tried not to seem 'artificed', dependent, in any way, on those resources of poetry. . . .

Source: extract from ch. 8 in *The Language of Modern Drama* (London, 1977), pp. 153–61.

*Raymond Williams*   'Dramatic Pattern'
(1968)

. . . The achievement of *Murder in the Cathedral* is dramatic pattern, a pattern which 'is the action'. Only at times is this completeness threatened, perhaps most notably in the Sermon and in the speeches of the Knights. In the Sermon, when one comes to phrases like these–

A martyrdom is always the design of God, for His love of men, to warn them and to lead them, to bring them back to His ways. It is never the design of man . . .

– one feels that the 'meaning' which they bear is a crude addition to the fully dramatic communication which is the total action. It is natural self-explanation by Becket, and natural exposition; but it lacks the intensity of the play as a whole. Similarly, the speeches of the Knights to the audience can be theoretically justified, as a dramatic

device to indicate the speciousness of their reasoning; and the tone is
an interesting variation in the movement of the play. But there is a
distinctly Shavian element of 'knowing comedy' which seems to me
essentially sentimental.

When we look at the whole action of *Murder in the Cathedral*, we find
that Eliot, though using the familiarity of the Canterbury theme, is
not writing the history of Becket, but is dramatising a contemporary
consciousness of separation and martyrdom; Becket is in that sense a
Sweeney. The Tempters, matching the Knights, who come to
dissuade Becket, offer not only the usual rewards of material power,
but also the false glory – the intellectual pride – of wanting to be a
martyr. It is this that is finally rejected, in what is described as a total
submission to the will of God. This is the action, in formal terms, but
in its substance *Murder in the Cathedral* is based on yet another rhythm:
not so much of martyrdom as of sacrifice. The dominant imagery is of
the land and the seasons: of the relation between the lives of men and
the lives of beasts; of what can be seen as redemption but also as
increased fertility through the spilling of blood. Redemption is an
awareness that the natural and human order, without this kind of
sacrifice, is merely bestial. It is the act of blood, and the receiving of
blood, which creates consciousness and separates man from the
beasts. The whole drive of the play is to gain acceptance, through the
chorus, of this feeling. We have already seen the movement from

no action<br>
But only to wait and to witness

to

the blood of the martyrs and the agony of the saints<br>
Is upon our heads.

The participation is formally in a Christian recognition, through the
acceptable and familiar phrases of orthodoxy. But the substantial
design is the need for sacrificial blood, for the renewal of common life.
This need is not discovered within a common experience, but is
brought to the people by an exceptionally conscious man: Becket.
This is, in another form, the variation of levels of consciousness we
have seen described in *Sweeney Agonistes*: it is the structure of feeling on
which all Eliot's work is based – the many unconscious, the few
conscious. The act of martyrdom, but more crucially the act of drama,
as Eliot conceives it, links the two groups, in an achieved common
action.

The power of *Murder in the Cathedral* is that it succeeds in
communicating a personal structure of feeling as if it were traditional

and even conventional. The strangeness of Eliot's vision – the rejection of ordinary life, the insistence on separation and sacrifice – is made to seem familiar and acceptable:

> We thank Thee for Thy mercies of blood, for Thy redemption by blood.
> For the blood of Thy martyrs and saints
> Shall enrich the earth, shall create the holy places.

When Eliot moved on to his explicitly contemporary plays, the problem was not only one of dramatic convention, without the basis of the liturgy. It was also of conveying a strange consciousness – here masked by orthodoxy – in its own surprising and even shocking terms. . . .

SOURCE: extract from *Drama from Ibsen to Brecht* (London, 1968), pp. 182–3.

# PART THREE

# Plays for the Theatre

1. *The Family Reunion*      (1939)
2. *The Cocktail Party*      (1949)
3. *The Confidential Clerk*      (1953)
4. *The Elder Statesman*      (1958)

# 1. *THE FAMILY REUNION* (1939)

## *T. S. Eliot* Comment (1951)

... What we have to do is to bring poetry into the world in which the audience lives and to which it returns when it leaves the theatre; not to transport the audience into some imaginary world totally unlike its own, an unreal world in which poetry is tolerated. What I should hope might be achieved, by a generation of dramatists having the benefit of our experience, is that the audience should find, at the moment of awareness that it is hearing poetry, that it is saying to itself: '*I* could talk in poetry too!' Then we should not be transported into an artificial world; on the contrary, our own sordid, dreary daily world would be suddenly illuminated and transfigured.

I was determined, therefore, in my next play to take a theme of contemporary life, with characters of our own time living in our own world. *The Family Reunion* was the result. Here my first concern was the problem of the versification, to find a rhythm close to contemporary speech, in which the stresses could be made to come wherever we should naturally put them, in uttering the particular phrase on the particular occasion. What I worked out is substantially what I have continued to employ: a line of varying length and varying number of syllables, with a caesura and three stresses. The caesura and the stresses may come at different places, almost anywhere in the line; the stresses may be close together or well separated by light syllables; the only rule being that there must be one stress on one side of the caesura and two on the other. In retrospect, I soon saw that I had given my attention to versification, at the expense of plot and character. I had, indeed, made some progress in dispensing with the chorus; but the device of using four of the minor personages, representing the Family, sometimes as individual character parts and sometimes collectively as chorus, does not seem to me very satisfactory. For one thing, the immediate transition from individual, characterized part to membership of a chorus is asking too much of the actors: it is a very difficult transition to accomplish. For another thing, it seemed to me another trick, one which, even if successful, could not have been applicable in another play. Furthermore, I had in two passages used the device of a lyrical duet further isolated from the rest of the dialogue by being written in shorter lines with only two stresses. These passages are in a sense 'beyond character', the speakers have to be presented as falling into a kind of trance-like state in order to speak them. But they are so remote from the necessity of the action that they are hardly more than passages of poetry which might be spoken by anybody; they are too much like operatic arias. The member of the audience, if he enjoys this sort of thing, is putting up with a suspension of the action in order to enjoy a poetic fantasia: these passages are really less related to the action than are the choruses in *Murder in the Cathedral*. . . .

It was not only because of the introduction of passages which called too much attention to themselves as poetry, and could not be dramatically justified, that I found *The Family Reunion* defective: there were two weaknesses which came to strike me as more serious still. The first was, that I had employed far too much of the strictly limited time allowed to a dramatist, in presenting a situation, and not left myself enough time, or provided myself with enough material, for developing it in action. I had written what was, on the whole, a good first act; except that for a first act it was much too long. When the curtain rises again, the audience is expecting, as it has a right to expect, that something is going to happen. Instead, it finds itself treated to a further exploration of the background: in other words, to what ought to have been given much earlier if at all. The beginning of the second act presents much the most difficult problem to producer and cast: for the audience's attention is beginning to wander. And then, after what must seem to the audience an interminable time of preparation, the conclusion comes so abruptly that we are, after all, unready for it. This was an elementary fault in mechanics.

But the deepest flaw of all, was in a failure of adjustment between the Greek story and the modern situation. I should either have stuck closer to Aeschylus or else taken a great deal more liberty with his myth. One evidence of this is the appearance of those ill-fated figures, the Furies. They must, in future, be omitted from the cast, and be understood to be visible only to certain of my characters, and not to the audience. We tried every possible manner of presenting them. We put them on the stage, and they looked like uninvited guests who had strayed in from a fancy dress ball. We concealed them behind gauze, and they suggested a still out of a Walt Disney film. We made them dimmer, and they looked like shrubbery just outside the window. I have seen other expedients tried: I have seen them signalling from across the garden, or swarming on to the stage like a football team, and they are never right. They never succeed in being either Greek

goddesses or modern spooks. But their failure is merely a symptom of
the failure to adjust the ancient with the modern.

A more serious evidence is that we are left in a divided frame of
mind, not knowing whether to consider the play the tragedy of the
mother or the salvation of the son. The two situations are not
reconciled. I find a confirmation of this in the fact that my sympathies
now have come to be all with the mother, who seems to me, except
perhaps for the chauffeur, the only complete human being in the play;
and my hero now strikes me as an insufferable prig. . . .

SOURCE: extracts from 'Poetry and Drama' (1951); reproduced in
*On Poetry and Poets* (London, 1957), pp. 82–3, 83–4.

*Hugh Kenner*          'The Play's Poetical Context'
(1960)

. . . Approaching *The Family Reunion*, not as Eliot's first play for the
commercial stage, but rather as his next poem after 'Burnt Norton',
we discover a woman who has attempted for eight years to enforce, at
a country house named Wishwood, a protracted artificial timeless
moment ('Nothing has been changed. I have seen to that'); a man
who is more dogmatically convinced than the musing voice at the
'Burnt Norton' opening that

> all past is present, all degradation
> is unredeemable,

but who has nonetheless returned to his first world to seek out the
presences that move without pressure over its dead leaves; and a
chorus of strained, time-ridden faces, distracted from distraction. The
man who has come back recalls a life transacted in a more lurid
facsimile of the 'Burnt Norton' underground

> The sudden solitude in a crowded desert
> In a thick smoke, many creatures moving
> Without direction, for no direction
> Leads anywhere but round and round in that vapour—
> Without purpose, without principle of conduct
> In flickering intervals of light and darkness. . . .

In this subterranean void he has willed a deed of violence, which he has incurred the obligation of expiating; for he has discovered that he cannot simply leave the past behind, just as his mother needs to discover that she cannot simply keep it with her.

Through time, however, time is conquered. He gains the means of liberation from his nightmare past by acquiring, in Wishwood, insight into a still earlier past which he had never comprehended. His father, a presence out of his first world, becomes intelligible to him, 'dignified, invisible', and his own crime, which he had been concerned to expiate in isolation, turns out to be simply the present cross-section of a family crime projected through generations. As he has willed to kill his wife, so his father, it turns out, had once willed to kill his.

> The trilling wire in the blood
> Sings below inveterate scars
> And reconciles forgotten wars;

and Harry, the purpose of his visit to the great house with its garden now accomplished, takes his departure.

It is easy to see the application to Harry's plight of the enigmatic epigraphs from Heraclitus which Eliot affixed to 'Burnt Norton': 'Though the law of things is universal in scope, most men act as though they had insight of their own'; and 'The way up and the way down are one and the same.'

> Whether in Argos or England,

The *Family Reunion* Chorus proclaims,

> There are certain inflexible laws
> Unalterable, in the nature of music.

Harry has supposed himself the centre of a totally sick world which has arranged itself around his unique malaise. When he tells his impercipient uncles and aunts that they have gone through life in sleep, never woken to the nightmare, and that life would be unendurable if they were wide awake, it is because he supposes himself a privileged person, habituated to 'the noxious smell and the sorrow before morning'. But though it is true that

> . . . the enchainment of past and future
> Woven in the weakness of the changing body,
> Protects mankind from heaven and damnation
> Which flesh cannot endure,

nevertheless the 'inflexible laws, unalterable, in the nature of music', are not the iron chains Harry supposes them to be; like the laws of music, they define the conditions of freedom.

> Only by the form, the pattern,
> Can words or music reach
> The stillness, as a Chinese jar still
> Moves perpetually in its stillness.

By approaching it from 'Burnt Norton', we see the intelligible play Eliot was attempting to write. Looking at it as a first night audience, we are more likely to behold an impenetrable screen of symbols that do not declare themselves and events that do not occur. The ending is particularly troublesome. Harry goes,

> the consciousness of [his] unhappy family,
> Its bird sent flying through the purgatorial flame,

and where he is going and what he proposes to do, what will be the nature of his liberated existence, these are of obvious dramatic importance. But 'Burnt Norton' does not carry things that far, and the fundamental thinking for the play is what is contained in 'Burnt Norton'. The problem is in fact a pseudo-problem, forced upon the play by the exigencies of dramatic construction; for, as we learn from subsequent poems, the state promised in the garden at 'Burnt Norton' is, like the reorientation of Becket's will, not reducible to terms of exhibited action, but rather an invisible inflection of whatever action one performs. If this consideration spoils *The Family Reunion*, it lends itself intimately to further meditative poems; and in 1940, the year after the performance of the play, Eliot published 'East Coker'. While working on it, he conceived the sequence of four poems to which 'Burnt Norton' was ultimately transferred, and by 1942 had completed *Four Quartets.* . . .

SOURCE: extract from *The Invisible Poet* (London, 1960; reissued 1965), pp. 258–61.


*John Peter*     'An Artistic Failure'     (1949)


. . . Though agreement as to what is good and bad in the play is not, I suppose, likely to be general, no one will presumably wish to deny that it offers grounds both for admiration and for something less. I wish first, very briefly, to consider what seems to me its merits; and then . . . to make what I take to be the main criticism that must be lodged against it.

The first positive quality to notice, since it is the simplest, is probably the overall neatness of the construction. As in *Murder in the Cathedral*, there are none but the baldest stage directions – doubtless a reaction from the garrulity of Barrie and Shaw – and this matches the general economy in the writing. 'Insets' to give depth and perspective to what is going on are often of the briefest,[1] and a convention allowing the characters to fall into 'trances' in which they speak their secret thoughts also works admirably in the interests of concentration. At the same time certain recurrent phrases help to give symmetry and stability to the play, holding it together against the centrifugal thrust of the expanding theme. Amy's reference to clocks that may 'stop in the dark', for example, is repeated both at the opening and the end of the play. The reunion is 'a very particular occasion', until at last, with Amy's death, it does indeed become so. Harry's decision ('I must follow the bright angels') is taken up in the refrain of the last chant by Mary and Agatha: 'Follow, follow.' And so on. Wishwood is repeatedly called 'a cold place', except for the occasion when Agatha (and Harry, in a different place) remembers 'A summer day of unusual heat for this cold country'. The previous insistence helps, of course, to give the reminiscences the intensity they need. Throughout Part II Harry is given a series of questions about his father; and these, while being, as we might say, an admirable dramatic device for presenting the subjective process of introspection, also help to build up expectation for Agatha's disclosures, which crown his inquiries at the climax of this part of the play. Most palpable of all, perhaps, is the protracted *George and Margaret* device with the younger brothers, Arthur and John. Continually expected, they never arrive; yet the mere reiteration of their names, with the business occasioned by it, helps sensibly to hold the dialogue and the incidents of the plot together.[2]

These – neatness and integration – may seem somewhat formal qualities. Even if we find them so, however, there are others which may be more easily accepted. Consider, for instance, the element of verisimilitude in the play, that is, the touches of authenticity which Eliot has given to the details of his plot. We may find an example of this in Harry's description of the respite he enjoyed after the murder –

I lay two days in contented drowsiness;
Then I recovered

– though the precision here is, I think, a little weakened by its being repeated in a later speech by Downing:

> CHARLES: You've looked after his Lordship for over ten years . . .
> DOWNING: Eleven years, Sir, next Lady Day.

One is also impressed by the circumstantiality with which the background of Harry's childhood is made to unfold. The hollow tree, a symbol of freedom and autonomy, the sense of everything being 'referred back to mother', John falling off the pony ('and always on his head'), 'the low conversation of triumphant aunts' – these memories of an unhappy childhood come naturally and convincingly forward. They are all, moreover, apposite, and help to give correct definition to the picture of Harry's present suffering.

Equally fine, in that it shows a dramatist keenly sensitive to the need for at any rate an apparent credibility, is the touch which makes the paragraph about Arthur's accident 'not very conspicuous'. Had it been more prominent we might have wondered why Charles had not noticed it before. Again, and more significantly, there is special sensitiveness, both to theme and characters, manifest in that passage in which the 'murder' is so mildly introduced:

> It was only reversing the senseless direction
> For a momentary rest on the burning wheel
> That cloudless night in the mid-Atlantic
> When I pushed her over.

Harry is allowed to speak casually of the act because the suggestion must be that it is not itself intrinsically important; while, conversely, Violet and the others (the representatives of incomprehension) are made to fasten upon the act alone, not on its causes or consequences. It is the same sensitiveness in the playwright that assigns to Harry just the right tone of coolness and unastonishment when he hears that his father once planned to murder his mother.

> In what way did he wish to murder her?

One can, so to speak, hear the next question – 'By drowning?' – without its being intruded into the text.

As a study in the implications of personal and family relationships the play is, indeed, necessarily concerned with character, and this close and analytical observation of the chief protagonists is everywhere apparent. Amy is another case. We are made to see how she has substituted a tie with Wishwood for the lost tie with her husband, and how, through Wishwood, she struggles to retain the love of her sons:

> I keep Wishwood alive
> To keep the family alive, to keep them together,
> To keep me alive, and I live to keep them.

Yet this, too, like the proposed marriage with Mary, never comes off. 'Nothing has been changed,' she says, 'I have seen to that.' And Harry, for whom this arrest has been imposed – perhaps because he is himself a neurotic – at once recognises it as a symptom of neurosis: 'the loop in time', that is, the wish to linger in the past instead of living forward, into the future. Speaking to Mary he deprecates his mother's attitude:

> It's very unnatural,
> This arresting of the normal change of things:
> But it's very like her. What I might have expected.

Amy is, in sum, the parasite-mother, preying for her life upon the lives of her children, especially Harry. This is why she collapses when she realises that Harry's decisions have passed beyond her control. Wishwood, the family, the whole complex, clock-like organisation has 'stopped in the dark'.[3]

I have said that the main characters are carefully observed. It would be true, on the whole, also to say that his observation is sympathetic – or at least neutral. The characters of the Chorus (Ivy, Violet, Charles, Gerald), on the other hand, are prosecuted with a consistent irony that sometimes comes dangerously close to malice. Charles, deploring the younger generation's proclivities for smoking and drinking, is made simultaneously to help himself to sherry and a cigarette. It is true that Gerald is more subtly ridiculed when he replies:

> You're being very hard on the younger generation.
> I don't come across them very much now, myself;
> But I must say I've met some very decent specimens
> And some first-class shots – better than you were,
> Charles, as I remember.

One might say that this comes near to being what Middleton Murry, speaking of Jane Austen, has called 'a perfect right and left'.[4] But subtlety is the exception here. Violet is given the merciless line, 'I do not seem to be very popular tonight'; and Ivy, with her diagnosis as to the death of Harry's wife ('She may have done it in a fit of temper'), is also brought down to a level of caricature.

On a careful reading I think it does indeed become apparent that the treatment of the Chorus offers the first intimation of a possible defect in the play. Cognate with it, a sort of obverse of the same limitation, is the note of priggishness often to be found in the speeches of Harry and Agatha. It is irritating time and again to encounter in these the same stilted tone of omniscience, the same assumption of superiority over the other characters:

> Thus with most careful devotion
> Thus with precise attention
> To detail, interfering preparation
> Of that which is already prepared
> Men tighten the knot of confusion
> Into perfect misunderstanding. [Agatha]

> . . .I think it is probably going to be useless,
> Or if anything, make matters rather more difficult.
> But talk about it, if you like. [Harry]

> It seems a necessary move
> In an unnecessary action
> Not for the good that it will do
> But that nothing may be undone
> On the margin of the impossible. [Agatha]

There are, of course, inevitabilities here. One of the play's preoccupations is with a concept of 'consciousness' – awareness, more or less, of the complexity, perilousness, even the horror of life – and Harry and Agatha have to be shown more fully 'conscious' than the lesser characters. At the same time it is unfortunate that the playwright has given them a near-oracular intonation to make this point clear. One does not want Othello, so to speak, to insinuate his own nobility and courage. Even if the device is to be thought of as a convention it still contrasts jarringly with the conversational accents of the Chorus. Frequently, too, it grows monotonous. I have heard a rustle of relief and agreement run through an audience at Violet's

> This is just what I expected. But if Agatha
> Is going to moralise about it, I shall scream.

I doubt whether it assists the sympathetic understanding of Harry or Agatha to raise this kind of prejudice against their speech.

There are, then, let us say, uncertainties in the expression which limit its effectiveness. Side by side with the sensitive understanding with which, say, Mary is presented we have these touches of pompousness in Harry and Agatha; and side by side with the excellent dramatic irony that enriches the scene between Harry and Winchell – the adroit play with the ambiguous term, 'her Ladyship' –

we have the rather clumsy ironies with which the characters of the
Chorus are attacked. An even greater uncertainty (not, I think,
unconnected with these former) is to be found if we consider the
intensity of Harry's reaction to his 'crime':

> It's not being alone
> That is the horror – to be alone with the horror.
> What matters is the filthiness. I can clean my skin,
> Purify my life, void my mind,
> But always the filthiness, that lies a little deeper . . .
> I was like that in a way, so long as I could think
> Even of my own life as an isolated ruin,
> A casual bit of waste in an orderly universe.
> But it begins to seem just part of some huge disaster,
> Some monstrous mistake and aberration
> Of all men, of the world, which I cannot put in order.
>
> In and out, in an endless drift
> Of shrieking forms in a circular desert
> Weaving with contagion of putrescent embraces
> On dissolving bone.

The accent is quite unmistakable, an accent of naked revulsion. One
may query, however, how much it is supported by the play as a whole.
For such an accent of despair to be properly subjugated to the facts of
the plot there would have, I think, to be something patently
unpleasant about the act of murder itself. Otherwise the effect of the
play is to attribute Harry's consciousness of 'filthiness' merely to his
general hereditary neurosis: which is no more than to say that it is
Harry's distress that causes his distress – to make him a lunatic,
obsessed. Eliot has written of the attitudes of Pascal and Swift in a
paragraph which furnishes a useful commentary here:

. . . A similar despair [to Pascal's], when it is arrived at by a diseased
character or an impure soul, may issue in the most disastrous consequences
though with the most superb manifestations; and thus we get *Gulliver's
Travels*; but in Pascal we find no such distortion; his despair is in itself more
terrible than Swift's, because our heart tells us that it corresponds exactly to
the facts and cannot be dismissed as mental disease; but it was also a despair
which was a necessary prelude to, and element in, the joy of faith.

This, surely, applied to *The Family Reunion*, helps to bring out a very
important point. If, that is to say, Harry's 'despair' is disproportion-
ate, then he is (like Swift) subject to 'mental disease'; and, this being
so, his acceptance of religious responsibility must be very much closer
to regression than to development, a mere evasion of the pitted

which is not properly supported by the facts of the plot. It is perhaps
advisable to quote his own words:

The only way of expressing emotion in the form of art is by finding an
'objective correlative'; in other words, a set of objects, a situation, a chain of
events which shall be the formula of that *particular* emotion; such that when
the external facts, which must terminate in sensory experience, are given, the
emotion is immediately invoked. If you examine any of Shakespeare's more
successful tragedies, you will find this exact equivalence . . . The artistic
'inevitability' lies in this complete adequacy of the external to the emotion:
and this is precisely what is deficient in *Hamlet*. Hamlet (the man) is
dominated by an emotion which is inexpressible, because it is in *excess* of the
facts as they appear.

Here we come, seemingly, to the very heart of the matter. If the
objective correlative is 'precisely what is deficient in *Hamlet*', it is,
equally precisely, what is deficient in *The Family Reunion*. Two forces
are pulling in opposite directions. The requirement of the total theme,
on one side, demands that the 'murder' should be as nebulous as
possible; and, on the other, the ferment of the personal experience
required the murder to be a very real and substantial 'objective
correlative'. It cannot, however, be both; and in effect Harry becomes
(what Eliot would have us believe Hamlet becomes) no more than a
mouthpiece for obsession, disturbing and impairing the play in which
he figures. If, in fact, *Hamlet* is to be accounted 'most certainly an
artistic failure', then *The Family Reunion* must, I am afraid, be set as
low. It is, after all, in that most central of his essays, *Tradition and the
Individual Talent*, that Eliot has written the truest criticism of this play:
I mean that well-known passage where he says that 'the more perfect
the artist, the more completely separate in him will be the man who
suffers and the mind which creates'. All the small defects of the play –
the rancour towards the Chorus, the occasional hysteria or smugness
in Harry's speeches, the general secretiveness – seem to group
themselves into one radical deficiency: the lack of what Eliot has
taught us to call 'impersonality'. Beyond a doubt there is a failure
here, a failure on the part of the poet, a failure that the prescient critic
has already diagnosed. One cannot but feel, regretfully, that it is the
critic who is right.

SOURCE: extract from an essay on the play in *Scrutiny*, XVI, 3 (1949);
reproduced in F. R. Leavis (ed.), *A Selection from 'Scrutiny'*, vol. 1
(Cambridge, 1968), pp. 62–9.

struggle in his own consciousness. To make Harry a lunatic, in fa
to destroy the significance of the play. Some fact in the plot, some
*d'appui*, must be found to support his attitude of horror and dis
and that fact, when found must provide an *adequate* support.
correspondence of emotion to fact must be preserved.

But the only sufficient support for the despair is, surely,
murder. To attribute Harry's despair to his neurosis is, as I have
seriously to risk branding him as an irresponsible psychopath; an
more concrete terms, it is also to locate a prime mover in the pl
guilt – outside the compass of 'the facts' as they are presented by
plot. Had the murder been an act in its nature particularly br
there would obviously have been a very full and valid 'cause' for
fervour of Harry's emotion. But, as we have seen, while being
than compelling in itself (if anything, a push), the act is consiste
glossed over – *has* to be glossed over in order to bring out the
significance of the theme. We are left with the picture of a chara
who, while speaking of 'filthiness' and 'putrescent embraces',
explain these feelings no more satisfactorily than by referring then

> The accident of a dreaming moment,
> Of a dreaming age, when I was someone else . . .

How, one may ask, is this sharp disparity to be explained, and how
does it indicate a defect in the conception of the play?

Inevitably, I would suggest, we are thrown back, for the explai
tion upon an earlier observation that I made: namely, that the play
roughly, a transference of emotion from a personal experience to
fictitious setting. From time to time this transference is, throu
Harry, almost admitted:

> I am not speaking
> Of my own experience, but trying to give you
> Comparisons in a more familiar medium.

Two experiences are present in the play, and even the phantor
presence of the personal experience (it is perhaps not fanciful to
equate this with the personal experience represented by *The Was
Land*) is enough to blur the story of Harry, its fictitious equivalent.

Explanation is, however, only half the problem. It yet remains t
find some standard by which to gauge the seriousness of thi
insecurity – to see how far it constitutes a failure in the play. And her
we can conveniently go back to the essay on *Hamlet* in *The Sacred Wood*
There, it will be remembered, Eliot makes the point that *Hamlet* mus
be adjudged an artistic failure because there is in it an emotional tone

NOTES

1. One may instance the Doctor's mention of his first patient, the cancer-sufferer, and the admirable passage in which Downing recalls the night of the drowning.

2. There are, of course, more substantial reasons for these references to the younger brothers. They are the two sons who have surrendered to their mother's will, thereby earning for themselves the reputation of 'reliability' among the family. To make them miss the reunion which Harry, the runaway, attends, is to comment upon that reliability and so, in an extended fashion, upon the success of their mother's methods. Moreover, there is a parallel between the three sons of each generation, and in this sense John and Arthur are clearly to be identified with, respectively, their uncles Gerald and Charles. Whatever is said about the nephews is accordingly applicable, in part, to the uncles; and thus the device becomes another instrument of economy.

3. Only in relation to Amy's death can the play be called a tragedy, and to make that the pivot of the play is manifestly absurd. One might perhaps contrast Ibsen's *Ghosts*, where the tragedy is that of Mrs Alving, not of her son.

4. J. Middleton Murry, *The Problem of Style*, p. 69.


## *Raymond Williams*   'The Drawing-Room of Naturalism'   (1968)

. . . The scene of *The Family Reunion* is the family drawing-room of naturalism. The persons of the play include several 'everyday, insignificant characters', such as Ibsen had introduced. These elements are framework rather than structure, however. The play draws a measure of initial acceptance from the familiarity of its surface; from its resemblance, indeed, to the conventional country-house detective play. But there is a further relation to naturalist method, and particularly to Ibsen. The close-knit family drama; the *incidental* revelations of certain aspects of character; the development through retrospect so that the present is continually deepened to include the past: these are manners inherited, directly or indirectly, from Ibsen; and perhaps also from the novel. The drama has moved out of the church, and the former continuity and contact is not available. New links have to be forged.

The critical issue is raised sharply by these now notorious lines:

What's the use of asking for an evening paper?
You know as well as I do, at this distance from London,
Nobody's likely to have this evening's paper.

On their own, certainly, these lines are flat. It is easy to object that for
so commonplace a remark, verse is not necessary, or is even
ridiculous. And it would be possible to make an anthology of passages
from the play, of similar apparent vapidity. No proper critical
conclusion could be drawn from them, however, for it is the total
verse-form that is important.

Consider an example from the first scene:

IVY:                           The younger generation
Are undoubtedly decadent.
CHARLES:                       The younger generation
Are not what we were. Haven't the stamina,
Haven't the sense of responsibility.

This minutely stylised deadness is very characteristic of Eliot's earlier
work, and indeed of *Sweeney Agonistes* itself. The imitation and
repetition of commonplace speech, and then its contrast with
intensity, is one of Eliot's permanent methods. The organisation of
different kinds of statement can be seen very well in an exchange of
this kind:

GERALD: That reminds me, Amy,
When are the boys all due to arrive?
AMY: I do not want the clock to stop in the dark.
If you want to know why I never leave Wishwood
That is the reason. I keep Wishwood alive
To keep the family alive, to keep them together.
To keep me alive, and I live to keep them.
You none of you understand how old you are
And death will come to you as a mild surprise
A momentary shudder in a vacant room.
Only Agatha seems to discover some meaning in death
Which I cannot find.
—I am only certain of Arthur and John,
Arthur in London, John in Leicestershire:
They should both be here in good time for dinner.

The sudden deepening of level with the first line of Amy's speech is the
test of Eliot's essential organisation. The verse-form of the whole play
must be such that it can, when necessary, be intensified into the
statement of a complex experience, while retaining its affinity with the
verse of ordinary conversation through which the audience is led into

the play. It is a form designed to express the interpenetration of different levels of reality; not merely as a dramatic device, but because this interpenetration is the condition of experience of the play as a whole. The passage I have quoted seems to me successful in its aim, and it succeeds very largely because the transition of level is not consciously pointed by the author. When attention is drawn to the transition, there is dislocation, because the uncertainty of the convention is revealed. Here, for example:

AGATHA: When the loop in time comes – and it does not come for everybody –
The hidden is revealed, and the spectres show themselves.
GERALD: I don't in the least know what you're talking about. You seem to be
wanting to give us all the hump.

This play for laughter as a smooth transition, back to 'normality' from too great an intensity, is of the same order as a significant passage in a play of Granville-Barker's: *Waste*:

T.: I'm offering you the foundation of a New Order of men and women who'll
serve God by teaching His children. Now shall we finish the conversation in
prose?
C.: What is the prose for God?

or the end of a speech in Denis Johnston's *Moon in the Yellow River:*

. . . I suppose the Devil can do nothing for us unless God gives him a chance.
Or maybe it's because they're both the same person. Those glittering
sorrows, eh? Asleep? Well, here endeth the first lesson.

The level of experience, and so the character of the language, has gone beyond the tone of established probability. But then instead of contrast – the dramatic contrast of kinds of experience – the mixing of levels is accepted as uneasy, and is manipulated, negotiated, by a self-conscious – a falsely self-conscious – uneasiness. There are several such manipulations of tone in *The Family Reunion*, typified perhaps in Aunt Violet's conscious play with the audience:

> I do not understand
> A single thing that's happened.

The failure is in fact a dramatic timidity, an uncertainty of the audience's acceptance of the convention, so that a need is felt to offer reassuring explanations in naturalist terms. It is a serious corruption of a possible form. When Harry and Agatha, after virtual soliloquies, ask: 'What have I been saying?' the effect is perhaps right; but the interpenetration of levels is most successful when Eliot is confident of his convention, and offers no explanation. When a writer is launched into a form of this kind, the middle of the play is no place to express technical hesitations.

This kind of failure is what might be expected of Eliot's attempt to come to terms with the methods of the naturalist theatre. Within the total form which he has attempted, the attraction of certain of the superficial elements seems to have been too great. The policeman, for example, is a weary caprice, hoping that the audience will be reassured by having the familiar figure around. Similarly, the chauffeur's exposition of the death of Harry's wife involves an overfamiliar piece of business:

> But you know, it is just my opinion, sir,
> That his lordship is rather psychic, as they say.

It is the familiar comic exercise, the *Punch* tradition; a character in the shadow of Mr Forster's Leonard Bast and Mrs Woolf's sudden insensitive charwomen. The fault is partly social, a real corruption of the common language. More immediately, it is part of the general anxious reassurance of the audience; and the question is not whether the audience is in fact reassured, but whether such reassurance helps the communication of the play. Comic episodes may serve communication, by setting the central experience in relief (it is in this sense that the serious use of comic relief is best understood); they may also, like Mr Eliot's policeman, simply distract. The experience of *The Family Reunion* is revelation, but the coincidence of the word does not demand that this should involve character-revelation of the familiar naturalist kind. The 'inside stories' of the newspapers are revelations, and for spiritual autobiography of the special interview variety one does not need the talent of an Eliot.

> I shall have to stay till after the funeral.
> Will my ticket to London still be valid?

This is one of Eliot's theatrical aunts; and while it is an amusing appeasement of certain appetites of the contemporary theatre, it is the kind of thing which blurs the significant communication of the play.

The problem which faces the critic is of deciding whether these things are mere blemishes, a minor residue of confusion as to means; or whether they are local indications of some more fundamental disharmony in the play. Harry's experience is the search for redemption, which cannot come while he flies from the pursuing Eumenides, but only when he recognises them and their significance. This he is able to do, with Agatha's help, in a moment of illumination when his own and his family past becomes realised in the present. In this revelation his guilt is transformed; the Furies will not continue to pursue him, but he, instead, will 'follow the bright angels'. The series of events which Eliot has created to embody this experience is in a way adequate; but there is also a sense of the form being fitted, as a secondary process, to an already considered experience. This is why we ask how Harry's wife really died: not because guilt requires some overt crime, but because we get the impression of a sustained bluff, and even a certain arrogance: what has happened is too difficult for *us* to understand: 'I gotta use words when I talk to you.' Some part of this difficulty is inherent in the nature of the experience, but it is too persistent to be dismissed with a gesture towards the 'incommunicable'. For we have, as it happens, an immediate basis for comparison, in the *Four Quartets*. The central experience of the poems is similarly 'incommunicable', but in fact, in each of the poems, and particularly in *The Dry Salvages*, there is a convincing achievement of resolved experience beside which *The Family Reunion* pales. . . .

Source: extract from *Drama from Ibsen to Brecht* (London, 1968), pp. 184–8.


*Ronald Gaskell*     'Dramatic Anguish'     (1972)


. . . At the heart of *The Family Reunion* is the anguish whose source and nature Harry seeks to understand. The urgent rhythms, forcing home the imagery of defilement, mount to a climax in the violence of his recognition (in the scene with Mary) of the presence of the Eumenides. But this anguish, dramatic because struggling into consciousness, is not fully accounted for until later. Its immediate cause is, indeed, located at once in Harry's sense of responsibility for the death of his wife. But the parallel with Sweeney is misleading. For we are told explicitly that Harry's suffering dates not from his wife's death but from his marriage (or even before it?):

> One thinks to escape
> By violence, but one is still alone
> In an over-crowded desert, jostled by ghosts.
> It was only reversing the senseless direction
> For a momentary rest on the burning wheel

> That cloudless night in the mid-Atlantic
> When I pushed her over.

Whether Harry did in fact push her is shrugged off as irrelevant; and in the theatre, even more than when we read the play, this casualness ('What of it?') sticks in one's throat. Is it really, as Agatha suggests, of no moment whether Harry killed his wife or merely wanted to? For the Christian, Eliot's commentators tell us, a sin willed is morally indistinguishable from the same sin actually committed. This may be so. For the victim, however, the distinction between murder and intended murder is not negligible. Eliot's failure to imagine the wife as a person in her own right – a person whose life and death could matter – denies her any existence except as the occasion of Harry's suffering.

Dramatically, then, the drowned wife remains a cipher. Harry's wish to kill her, on the other hand, is established with sufficient strength to bring to bear on him the earlier, analogous, sin he has to expiate: the loveless marriage of his parents. The central action of *The Family Reunion* is the dragging into light of this sin, this 'origin of wretchedness' which has lain behind Harry's childhood and destroyed his marriage. The future, as Agatha remarks, can only be built upon the real past; and the point on which the play converges is Harry's discovery of the real past and of what it requires of him.

The relation of the family to this is important. Individually, their placid unconsciousness sharpens the edge of Harry's suffering. In chorus, their anxiety mines below our normal conception of reality (time), preparing for the rejection of this conception in the scenes between Harry and Mary, and Harry and Agatha.

Since the entire weight of the moral action falls on this rejection of time, it is worth while tracing the preparation for these scenes in detail.

The play opens with a deliberate recognition of time passing:

> Not yet! I will ring for you. It is still quite light.
> I have nothing to do but watch the days draw out
> Now that I sit in the house from October to June,
> And the swallow comes too soon and the spring will be over
> And the cuckoo will be gone before I am out again.

The day is specified as Amy's birthday and the family, together for the first time for eight years, await Harry's return and the arrival of his brothers. Nothing has been changed at Wishwood, for Amy's hope is that Harry will agree to deny his marriage by returning to the home he left. Agatha is sceptical:

When the loop in time comes – and it does not come for everybody –
The hidden is revealed, and the spectres show themselves.

The first threat to the family security – the first remark to provoke the habitual response 'I don't in the least know what you're talking about' – is this hint that time may be less reliable than we suppose. For the family, time is irreversible: an impenetrable medium of change, or arrested change, which enables them to disown the past. This attitude Harry rejects at once:

> Time and time and time, and change, no change!
> You all of you try to talk as if nothing had happened.

A moment later he goes to the heart of the matter:

> All that I could hope to make you understand
> Is only events: not what has happened.
> And people to whom nothing has ever happened
> Cannot understand the unimportance of events.

The distinction is between two concepts of time. In the world of events the family are at home; to the world of moral action they are totally blind. Harry is explicit:

> You have gone through life in sleep,
> Never woken to the nightmare. I tell you, life would be unendurable
> If you were wide awake. You do not know
> The noxious smell untraceable in the drains,
> Inaccessible to the plumbers, that has its hour of the night; you do not know
> The unspoken voice of sorrow in the ancient bedroom
> At three o'clock in the morning. I am not speaking
> Of my own experience, but trying to give you
> Comparisons in a more familiar medium. I am the old house
> With the noxious smell and the sorrow before morning,
> In which all past is present, all degradation
> Is unredeemable. As for what happens –
> Of the past you can only see what is past,
> Not what is always present. That is what matters.

The imagery is strained, the particularity of the phrase 'Inaccessible to the plumbers' a little grotesque in the light shed by the line that moves the passage out of time:

> The unspoken voice of sorrow in the ancient bedroom.

But the force of the rhythms has made possible an advance beyond the vocabulary of physical experience. If all time is in fact eternally present, all time is 'unredeemable'; for redemption from time can

come only with the free act of a will not determined by the past. Harry
has still to find such freedom.

In the scene with Mary he is given a glimpse of it. As in the first
scene of the play, the dialogue in Scene II (between Mary and Agatha)
opens with the expectation of spring, the season of sacrifice. Harry
notices for the first time that nothing at Wishwood has been changed:

> It's very unnatural,
> This arresting of the normal change of things.

People, indeed, change; but what has happened remains. Harry has
returned to Wishwood in the hope that the unreality of the last eight
years would fall into place. But there is no escape in a simple return to
the past, for the past, which has shaped the present, is itself unclean.
In a sense, therefore, everything that has emerged from it is unreal. It
is Mary who first recognises this, though only as a possibility:

> Even if, as you say, Wishwood is a cheat,
> Your family a delusion – then it's *all* a delusion,
> Everything you feel – I don't mean what you think,
> But what you feel.

And with this, the image of

> the distant waterfall in the forest,
> Inaccessible, half-heard

points to the agony of death and birth, the way of freedom Harry is to
follow.

The years of marriage have been unreal; this he recognises. But he
has not yet learned that his entire life in time has been unreal, because
rooted in his parents' sin. There is more to understand: hence the
appearance of the Eumenides to balk the premature hope of escape.

The pressure of past on present has lifted for a moment. In the next
scene, Warburton's casual reference to murder wakens the sense of it
again in Harry's voice:

> Your ordinary murderer
> Regards himself as an innocent victim.
> To himself he is still what he used to be
> Or what he would be. He cannot realize
> That everything is irrevocable,
> The past unredeemable.

This horror of time as an inescapable, determined and determining
element is reinforced by the Chorus, its uneasiness now for the first
time defined:

I am afraid of all that has happened, and of all that is to come;
Of the things to come that sit at the door, as if they had been there always.
And the past is about to happen, and the future was long since settled.

Agatha's prayer, which ends the first part of the play, focuses the sin
(though the word is not yet admitted) which has lain and lies still,
pressing for expiation, in the house:

> May the crossed bones
> In the filled-up well
> Be at last straightened.

The image is significant. The bones may have been covered by the
leaves of successive autumns; but they remain crossed. An action is
not altered by the time that has borne it into the past.

In the scene between Harry and Warburton which opens Part
Two, the presentness of the past is merely glanced at. It gathers in the
Chorus that takes up again the image of the house:

> In an old house there is always listening, and more is heard than is spoken.
> And what is spoken remains in the room, waiting for the future to hear it.
> And whatever happens began in the past, and presses hard on the future.

The image is developed in detail and advances to explicit affirmation
of an order beyond time:

> There is no avoiding these things
> And we know nothing of exorcism
> And whether in Argos or England
> There are certain inflexible laws
> Unalterable, in the nature of music.

But this is the family speaking. It is not till the scene between Harry
and Agatha that the sin that has lain at Wishwood can be brought to
consciousness.

The scene parallels the duologue between Harry and Mary in the
first part. Again, as he moves into the duet, Harry senses the unreality
that his life has been:

> Perhaps my life has only been a dream
> Dreamt through me by the minds of others.

As the sin is brought fully into light, the years of illusion, of unreality,
are shed (with a violence not altogether convincing). Harry's
rejection of these years, of the whole of his life in time, brings the scene
to its climax:

> I was not there, you were not there, only our phantasms
> And what did not happen is as true as what did happen

O my dear, and you walked through the little door
And I ran to meet you in the rose-garden.

The words are to be taken literally: what did not happen is as true as
what did. The unreal past is annihilated. The future is to be built
upon the real past – the love of Agatha and Harry's father, the love of
Agatha for Harry who should have been her child. But this is only the
beginning; for the freedom Harry has reached is freedom to choose,
and the choice is made:

A care over lives of humble people,
The lesson of ignorance, of incurable diseases.
Such things are possible. It is love and terror
Of what waits and wants me, and will not let me fall.

The strengthening of the religious vocabulary (expiation, election,
redemption, pilgrimage, intercession) in this and the following scene
has been made possible by the gradual deepening of Harry's
understanding of his suffering; and this has come not simply with
disclosures of the past but through the illumination of past and
present by the insights captured in the scenes with Mary and Agatha.

These insights are into a reality beyond time. And it is this that
aligns *The Family Reunion* with *Four Quartets* rather than with *Sweeney
Agonistes*. In *Sweeney Agonistes* there is an agonising sense of the
meaningless repetitiveness of life in time, and as in *The Family Reunion*
this sense is focused in the consciousness of a man whom sin has
wakened. In the later play, however, the permanence of the act of sin
in the flux of time is emphasised. Sin in *The Family Reunion* is not an act
only but an inheritance; and the struggle to become conscious of this
inheritance requires a development of the theme at greater length.

The choice of naturalism as the mode of development is curious.
For Eliot's problem is to distinguish sin from guilt: to establish,
without overt reference to the Christian tradition, a moral order to
which man is responsible. And the recognition of this order, though a
considerable dramatic achievement, is obscured by the naturalistic
texture of the play. . . .

Source: extract from *Drama and Reality in the European Theatre since
Ibsen* (London, 1972), pp. 130–5.

## 2.  THE COCKTAIL PARTY        (1949)

### T. S. Eliot      Comment      (1951)

... You will understand, after my making these criticisms of *The Family Reunion*, some of the errors that I endeavoured to avoid in designing *The Cocktail Party*. To begin with, no chorus, and no ghosts. I was still inclined to go to a Greek dramatist for my theme, but I was determined to do so merely as a point of departure, and to conceal the origins so well that nobody would identify them until I pointed them out myself. In this at least I have been successful; for no one of my acquaintance (and no dramatic critics) recognised the source of my story in the *Alcestis* of Euripides. In fact, I have had to go into detailed explanation to convince them – I mean, of course, those who were familiar with the plot of that play – of the genuineness of the inspiration. But those who were at first disturbed by the eccentric behaviour of my unknown guest, and his apparently intemperate habits and tendency to burst into song, have found some consolation in having their attention called to the behaviour of Heracles in Euripides' play.

In the second place, I laid down for myself the ascetic rule to avoid poetry which could not stand the test of strict dramatic utility: with such success, indeed, that it is perhaps an open question whether there is any poetry in the play at all. And finally, I tried to keep in mind that in a play, from time to time, something should happen; that the audience should be kept in the constant expectation that something is going to happen; and that, when it does happen, it should be different, but not too different, from what the audience had been led to expect. . . .

SOURCE: extract from 'Poetry and Drama' (1951); reproduced in *On Poetry and Poets* (London, 1957), p. 85.

# Raymond Williams 'A Theatrical Compromise' (1968)

. . . Ten years separated *The Family Reunion* and *The Cocktail Party*, and the new play was awaited with more than ordinary interest. Eliot's influence at this time was considerable, and his choice of method was certain to have important effects. He might have returned to the deliberately formal pattern of *Murder in the Cathedral*, which had been his most complete success; or he might continue with the experiment of using current theatrical forms and trying to raise them to the status of poetic drama by the use of a flexible overall verse convention, as he had done in *The Family Reunion*. His choice, as we now know, was the latter. *The Cocktail Party* almost entirely abandoned even those elements of ritual which had been retained in *The Family Reunion*: the use of an occasional chorus, of interspersed lyrics, and of 'runic' recital. The chorus of *The Family Reunion* had not been very satisfactory: the verse was adequate, but the formal convention depended upon a sudden change of function by the aunts and uncles, who had been set in a deliberate comic characterisation and were required suddenly to become agents of a formal commentary; this was not easy to accept. The lyrics had been used to express certain of the moments of illumination; a good example is given to Mary, beginning:

> I believe the moment of birth
> Is when we have knowledge of death.

The 'runes' had been used as a formal ending to each part, spoken by Agatha:

> Round and round the circle
> Completing the charm
> So the knot be unknotted
> The crossed be uncrossed
> The crooked be made straight
> And the curse be ended.

Unlike the lyrics, the placing of these passages had made transition into conversational speech unnecessary, and for this reason they were more successful. This is the only formal device of the kind retained in *The Cocktail Party*; it is used in the libation near the end of Act Two:

ALEX: The words for those who go upon a journey.
REILLY: Protector of travellers
  Bless the road.

ALEX: Watch over her in the desert
    Watch over her in the mountain
    Watch over her in the labyrinth
    Watch over her in the quicksand.
JULIA: Protect her from the Voices
    Protect her from the Visions
    Protect her in the tumult
    Protect her in the silence.

With this exception, *The Cocktail Party* uses no formal devices which are not already familiar from the average prose play. Its main formal device is the overall verse convention.

The verse of *The Cocktail Party* is similar in function to that of *The Family Reunion*, with its capacity for sudden change of level from light conversation to conscious statement:

EDWARD: Celia? Going to California?
LAVINIA:               Yes, with Peter.
    Really, Edward, if you were human
    You would burst out laughing. But you won't.
EDWARD: O God, O God, if I could return to yesterday
    Before I thought that I had made a decision.
    What devil left the door on the latch
    For these doubts to enter? And then you came back, you
    The angel of destruction – just as I felt sure.
    In a moment, at your touch, there is nothing but ruin.

The function is similar to that in *The Family Reunion*, but the quality of the verse is very different. In the first place, the verse of conversation, particularly at the beginning of the play when the measure needs to be established, is very closely stylised, in the manner of *Sweeney Agonistes*:

PETER: I like that story.
CELIA:       I love that story.
ALEX: *I'm* never tired of hearing that story.
JULIA: Well, you all seem to know it.
CELIA:       Do we all know it?

or, again:

JULIA: The only man I ever met who could hear the cry of bats.
PETER: Hear the cry of bats?
JULIA:       He could hear the cry of bats.
CELIA: But how do you know he could hear the cry of bats?
JULIA: Because he said so. And I believed him.

The device is obvious in print, but in speech it is virtually an unconscious form, since the repetitions on which the rhythm depends are normal elements of conversation.

The second and more important difference in the verse of *The Cocktail Party* is that it is always, at every level, *statement*, of a deliberate lucidity, and with the minimum of imagery and evocation. In *The Family Reunion* the speech of Harry and Agatha is full of the characteristic imagery of Eliot's general poetry: the corridor, the footfall, the door opening into the garden. The words 'have often a network of tentacular roots, reaching down to the deepest terrors and desires.' In *The Cocktail Party* the language is never, or hardly ever, of that kind. It is verse of the surface, although not superficial. It is conscious, lucid statement, with a generality which is quite unlike the normal verse of *The Family Reunion*. Here, for example, is a speech which will illustrate the change:

EDWARD: No – not happy; or, if there is any happiness,
  Only the happiness of knowing
  That misery does not feed on the ruin of loveliness,
  That the tedium is not the residue of ecstasy.
  I see that my life was determined long ago
  And that the struggle to escape from it
  Is only a make-believe, a pretence
  That what is, is not, or could be changed.
  The self that can say 'I want this – or want that'
  – The self that wills – he is a feeble creature.
  He has to come to terms in the end
  With the obstinate, the tougher self; who does not speak
  Who never talks, who cannot argue;
  And who in some men may be the *guardian* –
  But in men like me, the dull, the implacable,
  The indomitable spirit of mediocrity.
  The willing self can contrive the disaster
  Of this unwilling partnership, but can only flourish
  In submission to the rule of the stronger partner.

The third and fourth lines of this speech are in the recognisable manner of *The Family Reunion* and of much of Eliot's poetry, but the dominant tone in the passage is something quite different; it is deliberate, contained statement. It is a remarkable achievement, for it is both eminently speakable and also the instrument of complete precision in the expression of feeling. This distinct manner is the main strength of the play; it can be very widely exemplified from the best scenes, those between Edward and Reilly; Edward and Celia; Edward, Lavinia and Reilly; Reilly and Celia. However the play as a whole may be judged, this development of a flexible, lucid verse manner, based very closely on speech and yet capable of great precision, is an important achievement.

The speech of Edward which I have quoted provides one key to the theme of the play: the concept of the *guardian*. The play is concerned with the salvation, not of an individual, but of a group, and the elements of this salvation are the guardians Reilly, Alex, and Julia. The word is certainly *salvation*, although for a considerable part of the play one could substitute *cure*. This double sense is an important element of the play, and it is this above all which has caused difficulty. The double sense is most clearly expressed in the character of Reilly, who is at once psychiatrist and confessor. Reilly's treatment of Edward and Lavinia is in the familiar psychiatric tone, even if it is never quite orthodox:

> I learn a good deal by merely observing you,
> And letting you talk as long as you please,
> And taking note of what you do not say.

The cure of the delusions and dishonesties of Edward and Lavinia is a cure *within* society:

> . . . my patients
> Are only pieces of a total situation
> Which I have to explore. The single patient
> Who is ill by himself, is rather the exception.

What Reilly does is to bring Edward and Lavinia to knowledge of themselves and their situation, and to forward the process of reconciliation:

> The best of a bad job is all any of us can make of it.

This is Eliot's familiar description of the unreality of commonplace experience, and the limited possibilities of any growth in its terms. These are the 'unconscious majority', brought to local recognition. And beyond them, as before, is the 'conscious minority': the exceptional person:

> The best of a bad job is all any of us can make of it,
> Except of course the saints.

Delusion, irreconcilability, have been seen with the others as part of the habitual mask; health lies in acceptance of the reality. But delusion must be carefully defined: Reilly says to Celia:

> A delusion is something we must return from.
> There are other states of mind, which we take to be delusion
> But which we have to accept and go on from.

This is Celia's case:

CELIA: It's not the feeling of anything I've ever *done*
  Which I might get away from, or of anything in me
  I could get rid of – but of emptiness, of failure
  Towards someone, or something, out of myself;
  And I feel I must . . . *atone* – is that the word?

This is not delusion, but

It is, as Reilly comments, 'most unusual'.

Celia chooses, not the first way of 'cure', of reconciliation; but the second way, of atonement:

REILLY: The first I could describe in familiar terms
  Because you have seen it, as we all have seen it
  Illustrated, more or less, in lives of those about us.
  The second is unknown, and so requires faith –
  The kind of faith that issues from despair.
  The destination cannot be described
  You will know very little until you get there;
  You will journey blind. But the way leads towards possession
  Of what you have sought for in the wrong place.
CELIA: . . . Which way is better?
REILLY:        Neither way is better.
  Both ways are necessary. It is also necessary
  To make a choice between them.
CELIA: Then I choose the second.

The way of atonement need not necessarily lead outside society. Some who have chosen it –

               . . . lead very active lives
            Very often, in the world.

But Celia's way leads to isolation and to a terrible death.

Here the shock that had been masked in *Murder in the Cathedral* – the intense insistence on separation and sacrifice – is made open and explicit. The details of the death were softened, after the first production, but there is still a direct preoccupation with an exposed physical suffering, and this is ratified:

            she paid the highest price
      In suffering. That is part of the design.

What Eliot does, in *The Cocktail Party*, is to bring to the level of recognisable action the structure of feeling by which he had always been determined, but which had been mainly expressed, elsewhere, as a rhythm or as an image. This is the real irony of his acceptance of

the methods of the naturalist theatre. The comic-strip figure of
Sweeney could be made to say

> I knew a man once did a girl in
> Any man has to, needs to, wants to
> Once in a lifetime, do a girl in

without involving, with any closeness, a human death. In *The Cocktail
Party*, in what is offered as a probable life, the pattern is the same, but
the effect is different. And yet it is not the death that is most shocking;
it is the consequent version of life. The play shows, convincingly, an
empty round: the superficial society of the title. It is a world of
temporary relationships, transience and bright emptiness: the
'unconscious majority', for all their sophistication. But then there is a
further irony. For this kind of life, which is Eliot's image of a common
condition, is particularised in a place and among people who belong,
essentially, to the theatrical mode which he has chosen as his
dramatic means. Anxiously reassuring his audience about the surface
of his play – here the bright talk of a London flat; there the known
habits of an English country house – he involves himself in a profound
deception: what he is offering as a surface becomes the substance, and
the intended counter-statement, of the separation and sacrifice of
Celia, has, in its turn, to be negotiated in just such a world. 'The soul
cannot be possessed of the divine union, until it has divested itself of
the love of created beings': this is still the pattern, but the substance of
the play is in fact an attachment, to a chosen social mode. Whatever
the ultimate action means, the visible action accepts the world from
which Celia is separated. The scene in which her death is reported, as
the guests reassemble and go on with the cocktail party, is no longer,
dramatically, the interpenetration of states of consciousness; it is the
absorption, the negotiation, of that savage death, and the reduction of
its meaning to a story at a cocktail party. In moving so far into the
conventional theatre, giving its modes and tones an effective priority,
Eliot succeeded in displacing the lonely intense experience, which
had always been his essential concern, to a reported event: a story to
point at. It is not only the guests, coming together and going on with
the familiar round, but also the dramatist, who is making the best of a
bad job. The play could have followed 'the bright angels', pursued the
'agony in the desert'; but it chooses not to; it delights too much in its
chosen particulars, its reassuring social tone. What was once a
dramatic tension has become a theatrical compromise.

SOURCE: extract from *Drama from Ibsen to Brecht* (London, 1968),
pp. 188–94.

## *John Peter*      Sin and Soda     (1950)

Though the play seems very much closer to *Sejanus* than to *Every Man in his Humour* one cannot feel that it was strange of Jonson to call *Volpone* a comedy. Some such description was usual on the title-pages of his times and of the two chief he chose the least misleading. But when Mr Eliot calls his new play a comedy he seems to me to be closer to the position of a Shakespeare calling *Macbeth* a comedy on the strength of the Porter Scene. Only the incidentals in the play are, in fact, comic and, though on the stage they should be much more effective, on paper they barely deserve the adjective. I suppose that the more perspicacious readers will think of Dante and accept the description in the very limited sense in which it seems intended; the rest are likely, however, to yield to the general chorus of the dramatic critics, to accept the play as 'witty' and 'delightful', and to get little further into it than the title might seem to tempt them to get. If they find it unsatisfactory it will be on the grounds that parts of it are dull and not because – what is surely the real criterion for judgement – it is unsuccessful on the terms that it prescribes for itself.

A good deal of the play, and particularly that part of it that relates to Celia Coplestone, is a development of the ideas handled in *The Family Reunion*, and the reader will be well advised to discard any presuppositions which the use of the term 'Comedy' may raise and to treat the play with the same sobriety that he would bring to its predecessor. Like *The Family Reunion* it is an attempt to discuss religious topics in theatrical terms and, again like that play, it essays this discussion by using situations from modern life. Both plays, that is, attempt something much more difficult than is attempted in *Murder in the Cathedral*, where the remote historical setting allows even the sceptical among the audience to concur in the argument without, as it were, feeling themselves too personally or immediately implicated in it. The difficulty in both the later plays is to effect the necessary emotional synthesis between the world of ideas, of belief, in which the topics discussed may be said to exist, and the mundane world of taxis and boiled eggs which is the *milieu* of the characters. This is not to suggest that there is an inveterate hostility between these two worlds, but rather to indicate how comparatively easily a dramatist seeking to fuse them may be betrayed into, on the one hand, bathos and, on the other, seemingly gratuitous lurches towards sublimity. I think that it is significant that the single (fairly long) quotation in *The Cocktail Party* should be a neo-Platonic passage from *Prometheus Unbound*:

> For know there are two worlds of life and death:
> One that which thou beholdest; but the other
> Is underneath the grave. . .

That we should be given such lines seems to indicate that the
playwright is aware of the dichotomy in his material and apprised of
the difficulties inherent in his task. We begin, then, by looking at the
play to see whether it has improved upon its predecessor in the
handling of these difficulties.

Two improvements can be at once perceived. In the first place,
because Sir Henry Harcourt-Reilly is made a professional consultant
his analytical probings, comments and advice are given a more than
individual authority, and seem far less queerly oracular than do the
rather similar speeches of Agatha in the earlier play. This is so, I
think, even when he ceases to speak as a doctor and reveals himself as
a 'Guardian', intent upon the health of the soul rather than that of the
body. His authority tends to pass over with him from the one role to
the other, and if we are responding naturally we shall tend not to
question it. In the second place the development of Celia Coplestone
(we might call her Harry Monchensey in the guise of a young woman)
is really only half the play, the other half being concerned with the
marital difficulties between Edward and Lavinia Chamberlayne. If
not the most important part of the play this other half is at least the
most prominent and this has the effect, not only of making the martyr
seem more exceptional, more of a departure from the average (as she
surely should seem), but also of giving a more balanced picture of
religious experience than that given in *The Family Reunion*. The
Chamberlaynes are shown as following a religious development of
their own which, while quite different from it, is yet supplementary to
that of Celia. As Reilly says:

> Neither way is better.
> Both ways are necessary. It is also necessary
> To make a choice between them.

The impression is thus quite different from that given by *The Family
Reunion*. There we are left with the sense that virtue is somehow the
prerogative of a limited class of 'sufferers', an esoteric quality to which
more normal persons cannot hope to attain; here, on the other hand,
martyrdom is only one of several varieties of religious experience, and
that one of the less common. To an audience composed (let us hope)
of non-'sufferers' the latter view is much more likely to recommend
itself.

Another difference between the two plays is that there are evidently intended to be no fundamentally bad or trivial characters in *The Cocktail Party*. This may seem so slight a point as hardly to be worth noticing but in fact I think it is crucial. In life, I suppose, we are only aware of virtue negatively, and through knowing the virtuous party for some time. Sobriety is consistent but unaggressive abstaining from drunkenness, charity from malice or unkindness, humility from arrogance or condescension, and so on. As soon as these qualities become too positive or overt, as soon as we have a man who ostentatiously refuses a drink or sententiously refuses to criticise his neighbour, we have, not virtue, but hypocrisy or priggishness. It is by their works that we know the virtuous and not by their professions, and it usually takes time before our knowledge ripens into any sort of assurance. Now where a dramatist means to present a virtuous character he has obviously to work in firmer and more immediate stuff than this and it is understandable that he usually employs his own sort of negative approach by playing the character off against a number of others who are palpably less virtuous. At times, indeed, as in some of the Elizabethan and Jacobean plays, he is content to work almost entirely in negative terms – that is, through a cast of villains – and to allow his moral positives to present themselves merely as implications or inferences. Dramatically speaking, either of these approaches has obvious advantages over the direct approach, where the good characters have to be positively established *as* good, because they do not involve the characters in description or suggestion of one another's goodness, and so give rise to something more convincing than a dull assortment of eulogies. 'Damn braces, bless relaxes', said Blake: the relevance of this to drama should be self-evident.

In this play Eliot is trying to present virtue directly, without the traditional advantage of a contrast with its opposite, and it seems to me that he is often perilously close to relaxation of the kind I take Blake to have meant. At the end of the play Edward is clearly on the way to regeneration, his relations with Lavinia clearly more unselfish, yet how is this presented? Partly, to be sure, it is a matter of contrast with their previous relationship. But the dramatist does not leave it there. He goes on to give Edward a string of compliments and 'thoughtful' remarks that are as monotonous as they are unconvincing – 'I hope you've not been worrying'; 'It's you who should be tired'; 'I like the dress you're wearing'; 'You have a very practical mind'; 'You lie down now, Lavinia'. Even if this is meant to suggest that Lavinia is pregnant it is surely an unhappy way of drawing attention to domestic harmony. Happiness in marriage would inhere in far less definite particulars – a glance, a touch, a tone of voice. Edward is, in fact, in a position analogous to the ostentatious professor of virtue: he has himself to *show* how virtuous he is, and we accordingly at once suspect that he is only mimicking the real thing. This is not charity but solicitude. Yet how else, granted the chosen approach, could the point be made? Celia is another focus for this sort of weakness, though she is at least removed off-stage when her decision is complete. It is true that Alex's laconic narration of her martydom is effective, true also that the reactions of the other characters are at first simple and convincing enough. But very soon they begin to magnify her image into portentousness so that it cracks and allows her validity as a symbol to drain away:

> I've only been interested in myself:
> And that isn't good enough for Celia.
>
> Do try to come to see us.
> You know, I think it would do us all good –
> You and me and Edward . . . to talk about Celia.
>
> I cannot help the feeling
> That, in some way, my responsibility
> Is greater than that of a band of half-crazed savages.

It seems to me that the unprejudiced reader will find this insistence almost as tiresome as the muscular Christianity of the foreman in *The Rock*, and will react away from rather than towards the values sought to be embodied in the martyr. His recollections of her pleasantly sensitive normality at the opening of the play will hinder him from seeing her in these large and cloudy terms, and he may even feel that she would have merited more sympathetic attention had she remained the woman she at first sight appears. Skilful acting could doubtless conceal some of these weaknesses but the play is not to be called successful because that is so.

It is not only to Celia, however, that this sort of jar, between an initial and a later character, is confined. Julia and Alex, who with Reilly make up the group of 'Guardians', have an even more striking metamorphosis from their initial selves. This is so palpable that it must be intentional, a sort of deliberate convention, and we are no doubt intended to take Edward's remark about 'the guardian' as a clue showing how to accept the convention:

> The self that wills – he is a feeble creature;
> He has to come to terms in the end
> With the obstinate, the tougher self; who does not speak,
> Who never talks, who cannot argue;
> And who in some men may be the *guardian*. . .

In the light of this the Julia and Alex of Acts Two and Three are presumably the inner selves of their analogues in Act One, and not real people at all. Yet the contrast between the selves in each case is almost wantonly exaggerated, and most readers or members of an audience must surely find it impossible to accept. Alex is at first vain ('I'm rather a famous cook') and suspicious ('Ah, so the aunt Really exists') and it would appear that he is also not above drinking half a bottle of Edward's champagne. As for Julia, she is vapid ('Lady Klootz'), avaricious ('Are there any prospects?'), featherbrained . . . and inquisitive, and vain enough to take umbrage when Reilly sings his song. To transform this figure into a 'Guardian' of such potency that she can condescend ('You must accept your limitations') even to her fellow Guardian, the perspicacious Reilly, seems to me preposterous. Are we to infer that no matter how stupidly vicious people may be on the surface they can be spotless within? The human Julia's flippant mention of St Anthony is scarcely sufficient to bridge the yawning void between herself and her *alter ego*, and in fact it is difficult to see how, given two such different quantities, it could be bridged.

Obviously, it will be retorted, Eliot has not tried to bridge it: why impugn him for not doing what it was no part of his intention to do? This is easily said but I do not think that in this instance it is a valid defence. The fact is, as I have pointed out, that there is already something of a tension between the two worlds handled in the play, and to make the contrast between the Julia of the real world and the Julia of the spiritual world so gross is only to increase that tension to a point at which the play begins to tear apart. Where the play should be forcing us to see the interdependence of the two worlds, forcing us to admit that the spiritual underlies and informs the actual, we get instead the impression that they are so distinct, so little related, that to move from one to the other is like putting on an impenetrable disguise. What, after all, besides the name, have these Julias in common? Could we identify the one after being acquainted only with the other? That the deliberate convention of 'inner selves' should at first sight give an impression of simple ineptitude is thus not its chief defect. What is serious is that in another way it is itself inept, and draws attention to a material dichotomy which it was part of the business of the dramatist to dissolve or remove. I have not seen the play and I am aware that it might be argued that this contrast, between the earlier and the later Julia, is less serious on the stage. With a book one can turn back to the early pages and make comparisons; but on the stage there is a temporal progression which leave us dependent on memory and for this reason we may tend to accept the changed figure more readily. The play's popularity may be evidence that the convention works better in the theatre than in the study, and I should be happy to believe that it does. On the other hand there may be other reasons for its popularity, reasons more properly the province of the sociologist than of the critic. Even in the study do we, after all, *need* to turn back to the early pages for the contrast to be felt, and felt disturbingly?

These might be called structural criticisms. I should like to conclude by observing that the flaccidity of the verse does little to compensate for them. Some of Celia's speeches to Reilly in Act Two are so inexplicit that one is tempted to call them Eliotese. They seem to rely on certain concepts such as 'love' and 'shame' and 'aloneness' (I use this barbarism because the state is clearly neither loneliness nor solitude), yet they do nothing to make these concepts real. This is at all events what seems to me to be taking place in such a speech as Celia's on p. 123. Again, at other times the verse is so obviously *not* verse that to have printed it as such gives one much the same pause as does the 'Comedy' of the title-page:

> Well, Peter, I'm awfully glad, for your sake,
> Though of course we . . . I shall miss you;
> You know how I depended on you for concerts,
> And picture exhibitions – more than you realized.
> It *was* fun, wasn't it! But now you'll have a chance,
> I hope, to realize your ambitions.
> I shall miss you.

'Anyone who tries to write poetic drama, even today', Eliot has written, 'should know that half of his energy must be exhausted in the effort to escape from the constricting toils of Shakespeare.' This was well said, and it is to his credit that in *The Family Reunion* and, more particularly, *Murder In The Cathedral* Eliot has written dramatic verse that is both verse and underivative. The impression left by *The Cocktail Party*, however, is rather that the 'constricting toils' have been, if that is possible, too thoroughly cast off. It is not that the dramatist here eschews Shakespeareanisms – no sane reader would throw that in his teeth – but that the verse is of so poor a quality as to make them unthinkable. Even a quotation from Shakespeare rather than Shelley would throw up its context in all too harsh a light. One seems to see the shade of William Archer smile ironically.

SOURCE: review essay, 'Sin and Soda', in *Scrutiny*, XVII (1950); reproduced in F. R. Leavis (ed.), *A Selection from 'Scrutiny'*, vol. 1 (Cambridge, 1968), pp. 69–75.

## *Stephen Spender*      'The Search for Religious Vocation'   (1975)

... *The Cocktail Party* is another study of the search for religious vocation. Celia Coplestone is the mistress of Edward Chamberlayne who, at the opening of the play, has been left by his wife, Lavinia. With Lavinia away, Celia believes that all problems between her and Edward are solved and that they will live openly together. However, Edward does not see it in this way: his wife's disappearance makes him realise that he wants her back. Celia has to face the unpleasant truth that from Edward's point of view his relationship with her depends on his being respectably married, with a wife in evidence whom he does not love. Her disillusionment at the lack of passion which is the hollow reality of Edward's character has a positive aspect. It makes her realise that this love which she thought she believed in was not what she really sought. This transforms her into one of Eliot's characters whose problem is to fulfil a religious vocation. In realising this she is greatly assisted by an *éminence grise* of the psycho-analytical world, the mysterious Sir Henry Harcourt-Reilly. Harcourt-Reilly has been identified by Eliot exegesists with various mythical figures from Greek tragedy and anthropological mythology. Eliot may well have had associations of this sort in mind. As player of a role in other people's lives the character to whom he most obviously approximates is the Duke in Shakespeare's *Measure for Measure*.

In the early scenes of *The Cocktail Party* Harcourt-Reilly does not reveal his name. Unknown to them, by wire-pulling from Harley Street, he affects a reconciliation between Edward and Lavinia who are reunited on the basis of *faute de mieux* on both sides, and, ultimately, the death by martyrdom of Celia Coplestone: a result which he reviews with self-congratulatory self-complacency. Despite his attempts to render himself convivially human by gin-drinking and singing the very bawdy song of which *The Cocktail Party* presents a bowdlerised version, Reilly is best described by a phrase from current American juvenile slang. He is a high-class 'creep'.

Reilly is assisted in his administrations by two of the guests at Edward's cocktail party, on which the first scene of the play opens. These are Julia, an elderly indefatigable cocktail party frequenter (modelled scrupulously on certain London specimens), and a bright young man called Alex. These are called Guardians, and at the end of the second act, together with Reilly, they perform a ritualistic libation to celebrate the fact that Celia has set forth on her spiritual journey. (One person who proves resistant to salvation is Peter Quilpe, a young guest at the original cocktail party who is head-over-heels in love with Celia.)

The religious activities of Julia and Alex, though perfectly consistent with the mixture of frivolity and seriousness which often enters into English upper-class life, seem not intensely imagined. A well-meaning young man like Alex who, when one has been deserted by one's wife, interrupts one's solitude in order to make one an omelette according to some recipe he has learned in Tibet, is not by any law of his nature also a Guardian (or Christian Missionary among the upper classes), without something further being explained about his motives. According to the eccentricities of high society he well might be, but, according to those of creative art, his case deserves more complex treatment than that with which Eliot provides it.

In his role of priest Reilly interviews Celia and prescribes for her a sanatorium which is evidently some kind of curative ecclesiastical establishment. Reilly explains that she need take nothing with her to this institution (not even a toothbrush?), and that there will be no expenses: which makes it one up on professionally conducted psycho-analytical therapeutic sanatoria. Yet upon this shaky structure of suspect spiritual institutionalism Celia's spirit does spread wings. She obeys Reilly's injunction to 'work out her salvation diligently'. She feels the love which is beyond that of human creatures, the call to sainthood, which is also a return to some past vision. As she explains to Reilly:

> You see, I think I really had a vision of something
> Though I don't know what it is. I don't want to forget it.
> I want to live with it. I could do without everything,
> Put up with anything, if I might cherish it.
> In fact, I think it would really be dishonest
> For me, now, to try to make a life with *any*body!
> I couldn't give anyone the kind of love –
> I wish I could – which belongs to that life.
> Oh, I'm afraid this sounds like raving!
> Or just cantankerousness . . . still,
> If there's no other way . . . then I feel just hopeless.

This is not the ecstatic communication of those who share with one another the knowledge of the Buried Life – Harry and Agatha – or who seek a burning solitude – Harry departing on his journey across deserts. But it is authentic – extraordinarily touching – the voice of a lost girl like that in Blake's poem.

*The Cocktail Party* ends with a second party, balancing that with which the play opens, and with the same uninvited guests present. Peter Quilpe comes in to inquire of news of Celia because he is in a position to recommend her for a role in a film to a director. Alex tells him that Celia is dead, having gone to Africa as a missionary and been 'crucified . . . near an ant-hill' by some 'heathens' who were making an insurrection. Peter speaks with feeling about his love for Celia. Reilly explains that when she came to his office for her interview with him:

> I saw the image, standing behind her chair,
> Of a Celia Coplestone whose face showed the astonishment
> Of the first five minutes after a violent death . . .
>                                        So it was obvious
> That here was a woman under sentence of death.

He explains that he did not know what form her death would take but that he directed her 'in the way of preparation':

> That way, which she accepted, led to this death.
> And if that is not a happy death, what death is happy?

Part of the happiness, he goes on to explain, is that Celia suffered far more than any one of them would ever be able to suffer, being more conscious.

>                         She paid the highest price
> In suffering. That is part of the design.

No one, not even Peter Quilpe, who was in love with Celia and who is not a Guardian, challenges the assumptions behind Reilly's statement. The most striking of these is that her death was not defensible as a risk undergone for the sake of doing real good to ignorant people (she was, it seems, one of the three Sisters of some religious order working in that area), but triumphant because it was the means whereby she perfected her will, bringing it into conformity with the will of God and thus achieving her martyrdom. Julia interrupts to point out that Celia has made her choice, that Peter Quilpe now also has to make his choice – which is to go and make the film he is working on – that the Chamberlaynes in becoming reconciled have also made their choice, and that they must all now make their choice which is to entertain guests who are arriving for the cocktail party. Lavinia says: 'But all the same . . . I don't want to see these people'. To which Reilly characteristically replies: 'It is your appointed burden. And as for the party,/I am sure it will be a success.' Soon after this the doorbell rings and the curtain falls before the party begins.

There is doubtless something of the parable of the talents in Eliot's idea of choices which are made, the duty of each person being to follow his calling. Edward's and Lavinia's choice is to become reconciled and carry on with their lack-lustre marriage. A problem for Eliot as a playwright is that for him the choice of eternity is so obviously preferable to that of life on this earth that it is difficult for him not to make actual living seem second-rate.

SOURCE: extract from *Eliot* ('Modern Masters' series, London, 1975), pp. 203–7.

## Michael Goldman   'Eliot's Most Successful Play' (1973)

. . . In *The Cocktail Party* the isolated cell of the poems has become a modern flat where a man cannot get a moment's privacy, but it confirms a prison still. One achievement of *The Cocktail Party* is its transposition of so much that is haunting in modern life – the horror and boredom and glory that attack and pursue the central sensibility of *The Waste Land* – into the modes of light comedy, but though any production of the play must maintain a proper lightness, it must also be careful not to slight the real pressures that even the most farcical turns of the action apply to the major characters, especially Edward. The first act is a series of humiliations for him, all the more humiliating because they are initiated by the typical raillery and contretemps of drawing-room comedy. And it is exactly this contrast between the convention and his response that allows the play to reveal with lucidity and precision the real sources of humiliation in his life.

Though the later plays are in some respects more profoundly conceived and contain concluding passages of a theatrical beauty quite unique to them, *The Cocktail Party* is still Eliot's most successful play, because in it the vivacity of the author's line-by-line response to his theatrical opportunities is at its height. We feel this most strongly in two ways – first in the interaction of the characters, and second in the use of all the elements in the mise en scène to advance the action

and to intensify and render more subtle our experience of it, in
particular to heighten our sense that the characters are haunted. In
*Poetry and Drama* Eliot complains that too many of *The Cocktail Party*'s
characters stand outside the action, but of all his plays it is *The Cocktail
Party* whose characters most thoroughly act upon each other in their
dialogue. Not surprisingly, *The Cocktail Party* has of all the drawing-
room plays the most definite spine, which can be expressed in the
phrase *to begin*. From the beginning of the play, when Alex is called
upon to begin his story again (the story being drowned, as Julia's soon
will be, in the very effort to begin it), until the end, when the bell rings
and Lavinia says, 'Oh I'm glad. It's begun', the characters are
constantly trying to begin and to begin again. And their efforts to
begin – if only to leave the room or start a conversation – elaborate the
process of haunting and heighten our sense of the fragmentation and
isolation of the self that Edward, Lavinia, and Celia experience.

The mise en scène contributes throughout to the sense of an illusory
connectedness badgering and isolating the central characters. Take,
for example, the strange variety of food that is prepared, consumed, or
recommended in the opening scenes. The inadequate tidbits, Alex's
culinary fantasies and inedible offerings, the remedies of Norwegian
cheese, curry powder, prunes and alcohol, even the unwanted
champagne, all forced upon Edward as he suffers in his constantly
interrupted yet unbreakable solitude – these like the genteel disarray
of the set, the post-cocktail-party depression (and it has been a badly
managed, underfed and underpopulated cocktail party) – like the set,
and with a wit and variety that makes the audience alert and
sympathetic to nuance, the food plays upon the isolation and debility
of the untransfigured individual in the ordinary world. It is a horror
and boredom expressed no less exactly than that of the poor women of
Canterbury.

All this reinforces the attack Edward undergoes in the course of the
first act, the series of humiliations whose insubstantial and amusing
surface constantly reminds us how illusory is the ostensibly dense
social continuum in which Edward has his being. He cannot be alone
for a minute; everyone wants to feed him. He has no privacy; in the
nicest way he is interrogated and exposed – but in truth he has
nothing but his privacy, and it is a privacy that leaves him with
nothing. Left to himself he 'moves about restlessly', while the doorbell
and the phone keep ringing. Throughout the act, Eliot emphasises a
nagging connection with the outside world by a series of exits and
entrances that require Edward to half-leave the stage – to be invisible
for an instant, open the door and return with his caller. Edward's

world, like drawing-room comedy itself, is a network of insistent
social connections which, like his marriage, fail to free him from
aloneness and emptiness. In the first scene, he wafts his guests and
interrupters out, then phones Celia only to receive no answer. The
lights go down and come up again. We are immediately aware that no
considerable interval has passed; the time elapsed has been pointedly
insignificant. Edward sits among the debris as before – potato crisps,
glasses, bottles, a forgotten umbrella – playing solitaire.[1]

These examples have all been taken from the first act. Each of the
devices referred to – the emphasis on communications, the treatment
of food and drink, the behavior of characters when alone – is used in
later acts to underline that awareness of transformation which I have
argued is essential to Eliot's dramatic technique – awareness that the
true nature of the haunting in the play is being revealed. This
dramatic imagery is employed with a distinctive wit, a kind of
half-explicit mocking of its own recurrence and tendentiousness that
sustains the play's tone. Sir Henry's office with its plot-expediting
intercom and its carefully scheduled arrangement of exits and
entrances contrasts nicely with the nagging persistence of bells and
callers in Act One. Similarly, the toasts that are drunk in the course of
the play form a sequence that guides our attention from the ordinary
to the transcendent. And in the last act we have a cocktail party to
contrast with that of the first. The work of the caterers and the new
reputation of the Chamberlaynes' parties for good food and drink
makes itself felt as a welcome improvement in this ordinary drawing-
room world. Even the exits and entrances have been improved – by
the presence of a caterer's man who announces the guests. In this
world, decent social arrangements still mean much, for they are still
the means by which the guardians make their presence known.

As for the behavior of the characters in private, let me take just one
example – the moment when Reilly lies down on his couch. In part,
this is a joke – a piece of raillery typical of the play but aimed directly
at the audience. The couch is one of the indicators by which we have
recognised the psychiatrist's office. It has remained empty throughout Reilly's interviews with Edward and Lavinia. Both conventional
psychiatry and our conventional dramatic expectations are being
mocked. This orchestrates the real shift in expectation, both for us
and the characters. The problems of this marriage are not to be
located in the usual psychological sources, but in an abiding spiritual
deficiency. At the same time the scene marks another transition in the
action and in our understanding of the characters. Reilly's moment of
exhaustion precedes the entrance of Julia ('Henry, get up') and the

interview with Celia; it prepares for our discovery that Reilly does not occupy the highest place in the play's spiritual hierarchy and our dawning sense of what that hierarchy may mean. Again let me stress that the spiritual world is felt as haunting, that it exerts an unsettling and mysterious psychic pressure on the characters. If Reilly's questions and Julia's snooping haunt Edward in the first act, Celia's martyrdom haunts the marital contentment of the last. . . .

SOURCE: extract from 'Fear in the Way: The Design of Eliot's Drama', in Arthur W. Litz (ed.), *Eliot in His Time* (Princeton, N.J., 1973), pp. 166–70.

NOTE

1. Later, in the midst of their painful interview, when Celia leaves the room for a moment, 'EDWARD goes over to the table and inspects his game of Patience. He moves a card.'

*Herbert Howarth*          'The Supreme Result'
(1965)

. . . In *The Family Reunion* he first realised his method. Without that play *The Cocktail Party* could not have been written. But though it is high praise of the *Reunion* to say that it made the later plays possible, there remains a further word due to it: that, if Eliot had died in 1940 and *The Cocktail Party* had not followed, *The Family Reunion* would have stood as a considerable play in its own right.

But *The Cocktail Party* is the supreme result of Eliot's long battle with and for the drama. Instead of alternating between tragedy and comedy, he interfuses them. He manages speech and poetry, so that the poetry sounds like speech yet dances. He masters the doubleness of comic poetry. He leads into the rites without suspending the action. He elicits a doubleness of plot: working from Euripides's *Alcestis* so freely that one spectator may ignore it and enjoy the play, another, sensitive to the hinter-phenomenal, may discern it, as if it were the psyche, the unconscious world, beneath the conscious action of the stage.

In 1938 he had published in the *Criterion* McEachran's article on the pattern of rebirth in the drama from *Alcestis* to *Hamlet*. It is not surprising if, long a student of anthropology, Eliot was drawn to *Alcestis* as a pattern for a modern play, and if, as a Christian and a polemicist of his faith, he wanted to apply McEachran's principle: that the Christian dramatist reproduces the ancient ritual of the sacrifice of the hero-victim at 'a higher level'. He has [subsequently] told how his plan for *The Cocktail Party* grew as he thought about the Greek story and asked himself, 'What happened afterwards?' After Admetus received Alcestis back from the dead, how did husband and wife put up with each other? Playing with the question, he invented a series of felicitous transpositions of archetypal material into terms at once acceptable in the commercial theatre and yet not overfamiliar there. In *The Beating of a Drum* he had noticed the peculiar importance of the doctor in English medieval drama, and he knew Jessie Weston's remarks on the role of the doctor in the *Rig-Veda*. He recognised that the modern doctor of souls, the psycho-analyst, the clinician-priest, is also the modern Hercules: he goes down to the tomb and recovers the souls of the living dead. So he pivoted his play on Harcourt-Reilly. He was also concerned, as always, with that proper theme of the Christian dramatist: the saint. In *The Rock* he had written:

> And the Son of Man was not crucified once for all,
> The blood of martyrs not shed once for all,
> The lives of the Saints not given once for all:
> But the Son of Man is crucified always
> And there shall be Martyrs and Saints.

*Murder in the Cathedral* had been the play of England's most famous saint. He now conceived the play of one of the saints who shall be. By a combination at first sight the most unpromising, the combination of the story of the emergence of a new saint with the story of a marriage, Eliot found a way to raise the pattern of rebirth to the 'higher level'. *The Cocktail Party* tells of a soul brought back from the dead; and tells it twice. Two souls are recovered from the dark in two different senses. Hercules restores a selfish wife to a selfish husband, so that they can learn to endure each other and to endure the reflection of themselves in each other. Even this is, in its degree, a higher level. But at a higher level still, Hercules brings back Celia's soul from the dead; from destitution, desiccation, evacuancy and inoperancy, he restores her to life. And there is a third recovery. In restoring her to a life which is the saint's death, he restores the world from sickness to life. Again, in letting Celia go as she chooses, to perform the Roycean act of atonement, Eliot restores life and meaning to the religious act of atonement – restores the meaning of the act in the minds of his audience and readers.

The myth of fertility, which underlay *The Waste Land*, underlies *The Cocktail Party*. And though Eliot is not normally given to Joyce's neatly naturalised equivalences, he admits one into *The Cocktail Party*. '. . . You do need to rest now', says Edward to Lavinia as they prepare their party in the Union days of the last act. Evidently the marriage is to be fruitful. The fertilisation lacking in love at *The Waste Land* era now belongs to it. To Celia the glory, whose choice of death has fertilised the earth. But Eliot adds that a simple glory also belongs to those who choose the household life and decently endure and propagate. In fact the saint would have no vocation if there were no common men to save; they save the saint, if she saves them.

*The Cocktail Party* was the conquest of the West End and Broadway to which the Harvard of 1910 had marshalled its talent. In one sense the play was received at the expense of its meaning. Very few of the audience recognised the meaning, few accepted it if they were aware of it, some were shocked; for as Eliot had warned his Rochester audience in 1937, the original Biblical events are, 'if we regard them with fresh eyes, profoundly shocking' – and the Imitation of a saviour must be shocking. Yet the play made its points, and the beliefs out of which it grew are circulating wherever it has gone, for they are integrated with the art and the entertainment, and to enjoy it is to absorb them. Very few people come away without enjoying it. But where do the art, entertainment, and success reside?

Partly in the skill and knowingness (but this does not weaken the seriousness) with which the 1949 interest of England and America in psycho-analysis and the transactions of the consulting room is exploited. More, in the comedy. In *The Cocktail Party* he perfected his comic art. His comedy is alive as a succession of diverting incidents, especially in the sequence in which Julia and Alex appear and reappear to interrupt and safeguard Edward and Celia. It is alive in the conversational and debating thrusts of the dialogue. It is alive in the metrics of the dialogue. . . .

The poetry of *The Cocktail Party* is the poetry of speech which Eliot had imagined a quarter of a century earlier: the new mode for English poetic drama: with metrics delicately pulsing, with phrases which effloresce though they are authentic spoken phrases. It is an astonishing linguistic phenomenon: the dialect of Mayfair reproduced, and yet bettered, by a poet whose native dialect is a combination of St Louis and Boston. It is tinged with the influence of

great predecessors: of Hofmannsthal exploiting his own Viennese
dialect; of Pound's excursions among the dialects in search of energy;
of Ford's and Pound's insistence on the use of genuine speech; and of
Browning's sense of the poetry of the spoken language. Yet it is
peculiar to Eliot, who reached it by his gift for separating, in the work
of friends and forerunners, what he could use from what he could not,
and his perseverance in rumination and exercise.

The poetry was the *transparent* poetry for which he had been
working. Towards the end of the play Eliot draws attention to his
success. Harcourt-Reilly asks, 'Do you mind if I quote poetry?'
Edward and Lavinia are polite enough, or cowed enough, to
encourage him, and he quotes the Zoroaster lines from *Prometheus
Unbound*. It is a crucial moment of the play, and Shelley in his seer
mood is right for it, but the humourist and the technical critic as well
as the seer in Eliot have their part in the choice and want us to note
that traditional poetry sounds unmistakably different from the new
poetry, the transparent medium, that he has invented after a lifetime
of discipline.

SOURCE: extract from *Notes on Some Figures Behind T. S. Eliot*
(London, 1965), pp. 326–9, 331–2.

## *Hugh Kenner*    (1960; 1975)

### I: 'Something Happens At Last'    (1960)

. . . Because the first of the drawing-room plays [*The Family Reunion*] is
crammed with intractable matter, and the succeeding one contains
less and less of the familiar Eliotic traffic with the viscera of language,
they are sometimes regarded as a spent poet's hobby. On the
contrary, they register the effort of one very cunning writer to devise a
stage verse which shall *set the characters free*, and enable him to
construct his plots around a theme of liberation. What is usually
called poetry on the stage is rhetoric, and what rhetoric signifies we
are in a position to know; T. S. Eliot spent one career dissociating it
into moral components. Rhetoric clangs on the prison bars of
self-dramatisation. In *The Cocktail Party* rhetoric is gone, and *The
Cocktail Party* is the first Eliot work (excepting *Ash Wednesday*) in which

anything happens. The situation expounded in Act I gets resolved into a new situation in Act II. That Act III is (as the author has himself said) an epilogue rather than a finale doesn't diminish the fact that Prufrock's hell has undergone transformation for the first time since it was posited in 1911. 'That is not what I meant at all', says the Lady to Prufrock in his recurrent hallucination, 'settling a pillow or throwing off a shawl, and turning toward the window'. Lavinia Chamberlayne says to Edward,

> . . . you kept on *saying* that you were in love with me –
> I believe you were trying to persuade yourself you were.
> I seemed always on the verge of some wonderful experience
> And then it never happened. I wonder now
> How you could have thought you were in love with me.

Edward can only answer,

> Everybody told me that I was;
> And they told me how well suited we were.

Throughout *The Waste Land*, in *Sweeney Agonistes* and in *The Family Reunion*, Prufrock, disguised as Sweeney and as Harry, drowned this woman over and over. The only thing that could happen was a deed of violence, which isn't an Aristotelian action but only an occurrence. In *The Cocktail Party* something happens at last. The 'dead' woman is restored; and then, as the doom Becket accepts looks from the outside like the one he was tempted to court, so Edward and Lavinia return from Harcourt-Reilly's office to a life which is superficially their former life, yet which no longer courts

> the final desolation
> Of solitude in the phantasmal world
> Of imagination, shuffling memories and desires.

Now this is possible because the verse is of a new kind. In Eliot's last plays the language has developed a quite inimitable explicitness, as though people were capable of saying what they wanted to.

> It will do you no harm to find yourself ridiculous.
> Resign yourself to be the fool you are.
> That's the best advice that *I* can give you.

Or,

> Your conscience was clear.
> I've very seldom heard people mention their consciences
> Except to observe that their consciences were clear.

This verse is neither a dense medium lying in wait for effects of full intensity and damping out anything slighter, nor is it apt to be set twittering by random trivialities. It is seldom quotable, nearly devoid of fine lines; dry, not dessicated; not prosaic because more explicit than prose. The characters make themselves understood to each other and to us with preternatural efficiency and wit, and as they enlighten one another they grow more and more separated before our eyes. This is why audiences are usually disquieted. For no defect of communication can be attributed to the language, and yet the total communication on which modern liberalism has staked its faith does not occur. The characters discover and affirm their own inalienable privacy, indistinguishable from identity. They do not advance toward a shared illumination; they do not all, once freed from the illusions with which the play concerns itself, do similar things or elect similar lives. And yet no one echoes Sweeney's complaint that he has to use words. It took Eliot twenty-five years to develop a language against which that imputation would not lie. It is the thing his verse does that prose cannot do; mere English prose cannot be so explicit.

Colloquial prose does not define emotional meanings. Prose sketches in what it can and then says, 'You know what I mean'. Hence prose, a system of reference to meanings already shared, draws interlocutors together, when the dramatist is representing them as understanding one another; and when they are represented as not understanding each other, that is because the language is defective. But a speech in verse can be as clear as a scientific law, its intelligibility residing in the structure of what is said, not in another's guess at its purport. So it is possible for the verse dramatist, if he understands this use of verse, to build up gradually a structure of meaning which clarifies to everyone on stage everything that can be formulated. What is then left unstated is simply each speaker's wordless experience of himself, the essential life in the possession of which he experiences both the freedom and the isolation of the finite centres. No one, in the late Eliot plays, makes a Laurentian fuss about this. It is simply so.

Clarity of discourse, then, is the function of the verse. It is secured by using only those components of poetry which can enhance the defining powers of colloquial speech: rhythm and syntax, brought to the assistance of images no more salient, though more tidily developed, than those that occur in enlightened speech. And clarity, once secured, determines the moral climate of the plays. Establishing as it does the separateness of the characters – each actor's part, speech by speech, a marvel of explicitness – it lends definition to Eliot's

familiar theme, the difficulty of understanding that another person
exists not simply as a figure in your inner drama, but in his own way,
and the necessity of arriving at that understanding in order that both
you and he may be free. . . .

SOURCE: extract from *The Invisible Poet* (London, 1960; reissued
1965), pp. 284–7.

## II: 'Private Agonies'    (1975)

. . . Vivien Eliot, long deranged, had died in 1947. During 1948 T. S.
Eliot began and brought to nearly final form his unsettling drawing-
room comedy, with its psychiatrist-Herakles, a bold lift from the
*Alcestis* of Euripedes, offering to bring back a lost wife from a place we
cannot imagine. Eliot's Sir Henry Harcourt-Reilly is as suavely
elusive a figure as his creator. If we are never told he is Herakles, we
are never told that he is a psychiatrist either, much as we are tempted
to think so. He drinks a great deal (gin and water), breaks into song,
dispenses oracular wisdom, traffics in supernatural rites. Though his
drawing-room manners are impeccable, he is meant to disorient the
securities of a drawing-room play; as Alec Guinness played him,
equivocally smiling, he fascinated Edinburgh and Broadway audiences, who had no idea either that the playwright was exposing
private agonies or that they were looking at a Greek play transposed;
or that its theology was (somehow) Christian, or – in all cases anyhow
– that it was written in verse (one Edinburgh reviewer mentioned
'deathless prose' repeatedly). . . .

SOURCE: extract from *The Pound Era* (London, 1975), p. 524.

*Roger Kojecký*      'The Role of the Guardians'
(1971)

. . . The guardians' identity as a group, their relationship with one
another, is never fully made clear. At the party with which the play
opens, Julia seems not to know Reilly, and afterwards, when he has

left, asks Edward Chamberlayne who the unidentified guest was. But at Reilly's consulting-room, only some weeks later, Julia and Alex appear to be accomplices of Reilly's, and Julia protests her long-standing confidence that Celia would choose a high vocation. 'I knew from the beginning', she says, thereby giving grounds for the inference that she had all along been party to the whole plan affecting Edward, Lavinia and Celia. Alex, evidently a man of practical resource, the sort of person who is asked by the Foreign Office to take part in tours of inspection in remote corners of the Commonwealth, is the guardian whose forte is outside relations. It is not only that he seems to know important people in the right places, but that he is in touch with guardians the world over. In the libation scene at the end of the second act, where Reilly, Julia and Alex invoke supernatural protection for their charges, Alex insists that he hopes well for Peter Quilpe: 'You know, I have connections – even in California.' There is an obvious, though indirect, reference to the world-wide Christian Church. Moreover the guardians, whose name links them to the most responsible class in Plato's *Republic*, bear a strong resemblance to the section of society Eliot called the Community of Christians in his *Idea of a Christian Society* [1939]. There he described the role of an élite possessing Christian awareness and outlook:

The Community of Christians is not an organisation, but a body of indefinite outline; composed of both clergy and laity, of the more conscious, more spiritually and intellectually developed of both. It will be their identity of belief and aspiration, their background of a common system of education and a common culture, which will enable them to influence and be influenced by each other, and collectively to form the conscious mind and conscience of the nation.

This certainly accords with Reilly's efforts to point out to the Chamberlaynes and Celia the issues by which they were confronted.

The vagueness of the guardians' interrelation, and the ignorance of their operations which they foster in those whom they help, have sometimes caused critical unease. Some critics appear to have been put in mind of an order like the Jesuits, and to regard the play as dramatising the building up of a 'Christian conspiracy'. Celia indeed joined a 'very austere' nursing order, and it could be said that Edward and Lavinia took out some form of associate membership. Moreover, about ten years before he wrote this play Eliot had been involved in joint-Church discussions at Lambeth Palace about the formation of a new religious order, and a name put forward for it in another context had been, curiously enough, the 'Christian Conspiracy'. (Presumably the name 'Conspiracy' was intended to express the idea of common inspiration.) But the suggestion of anything sinister would have been the last thing Eliot sought. Quite probably he enjoyed the sort of arrangements which the guardians engineered, and he makes the most of them dramatically; but at the same time the freedom of Reilly's patients is insisted upon. Edward chose reconciliation with his wife at a time when he believed Reilly to be persuading him of the advantages of separation. Celia's most important question to Reilly was whether there is a better than the good life, for she wanted it whatever the cost.

The guardians are there to offer illumination and to render help. In Edward and Lavinia's case, Reilly could throw light on the psychological and moral contours of their circumstances. In Celia's, he could indicate the spiritual direction opened by her sense of sin and her vision of the joy of selfless love. He himself had only limited competence, and admitted, 'When I say to one like her "Work out your salvation with diligence", I do not understand What I myself am saying.' He could help, not only through Julia and Alex, but also by means of the sanatoria, appropriate to different types of patient, to which he gave access. These sanatoria, which connote both medical institutions and spiritual houses (both of which Eliot found useful to him in the course of his life) coincide with the hierarchical conception underlying the play. There are three ways: the hell of 'final desolation . . . shuffling memories and desires', the good life of common routine and tolerance, and the way of sainthood in which 'the human is transhumanised'. Above Reilly are higher powers. He invokes their protection for his patients; he himself looks to 'the Saint in the desert'.

SOURCE: extract from *T. S. Eliot's Social Criticism* (New York, 1971), pp. 110–12.

# 3.  THE CONFIDENTIAL CLERK      (1953)

## E. Martin Browne    'A Producer's Retrospect'
## (1981)

[Browne is recalling, in later years, some of his preoccupations in mounting the play's first performance.] . . . I could not help being troubled by the improbability of the plot, even if the characters brought to it their own genuineness. I also questioned its period: 'Is it set in 1904?' The title suggested the master-servant relationship of that period which was now almost extinct, but which indeed existed between Sir Claude and his 'confidential clerk' Eggerson, from whom young Colby seemed at first ready to carry it on. Could the characters in this play be regarded as living the 'contemporary life' which Tom wanted to depict? The question was particularly pertinent because the post-second-world-war theatre was opening itself to relationships of such a different kind. *Look Back in Anger* was only three years ahead, and many signals of that breakthrough were appearing. Was the poetic drama of today sacrificing its poetry for a contemporaneity which it was failing to attain?

Perhaps though, I thought, that was the wrong question. After all, the play, after a slow start, was entertaining and the complications could add to the fun. With such a plot, it must be seen, not as realism, but as high comedy analogous to that of Oscar Wilde, and the relationships must be presented with his kind of sparkle. The danger was that the author's deep concern for his people kept breaking in. Could the two styles be successfully combined? The verse must help here: it would not be noticeable, the speech hardly ever rose to the intensity of poetry, but it supplied rhythm that unified height with depth, farce with feeling.

This it achieved in its first production [in 1953, at the Edinburgh Festival], and *The Confidential Clerk* enjoyed a considerable success; but it has very seldom been played since. I cannot help wondering whether, if he had not been living the inward-turning life demanded by a possessive invalid, Tom would have acclimatised himself to the post-war social revolution and let it appear in his work. The scene between Colby and Lucasta in Act Two suggests that he would have, for it is full of the loneliness, the restlessness, the longing for love. One is profoundly moved by those two young people: then the incongruities of farce intervene, Lucasta resumes her mask, and Colby, the central figure, retreats into shadow. Perhaps it is this play, rather than *Murder in the Cathedral*, that Tom should have called 'a dead end'. . . .

SOURCE: extract from *Two in One* (Cambridge, 1981), p. 203.

*Northrop Frye*       'Atmosphere of Demure Farce'
(1963)

. . . *The Confidential Clerk* turns on the ancient device of the recognition scene, where hero or heroine discover their long-lost parents. There are seven characters, four in an older generation, Sir Claude Mulhammer, his wife Lady Elizabeth, his 'confidential clerk' Eggerson, the pivot of the dramatic action, and Mrs Guzzard, who has a role like that of Buttercup in *Pinafore*. These four sit around a table and identify their offspring among the other three: Colby Simpkins, the hero and Eggerson's successor as confidential clerk, Lucasta Angel, the heroine, and B. Kaghan, who marries her. Mrs. Guzzard, the dealer in this curious poker game, assigns Simpkins to herself, though both Sir Claude and Lady Elizabeth are convinced that he is a son of theirs by a previous liaison, and he finally goes off in a foster-son relationship to Eggerson. Thus everybody of the older generation in the play claims him as a son, though his real father, the late Mr Guzzard, does not appear. Lady Elizabeth's son is Kaghan and Lucasta is Sir Claude's daughter.

The atmosphere of demure farce is sustained throughout, and, as the hero remarks rather dazedly, everybody seems to have a heart of gold. The plot-complications are closer to Menandrine New Comedy than to *Ion* (to which however New Comedy owed a good deal), and still closer to Wilde's *Importance of Being Earnest*, though it lacks the exuberance of Wilde ('marry into a waiting-room, and contract an alliance with a parcel?'). The word 'farce' reminds us of the high respect for farce that Eliot shows in his dramatic essays, where he speaks of it as the creation of a distorted but self-consistent world, found in Rabelais, Dickens, and even Marlowe. *Sweeney Agonistes*, with its pounding jazz rhythms and its weird expressionistic staging, is farce in this sense. *The Confidential Clerk* is a different kind of farce, a comedy in which the structure has been deliberately over-complicated, and so turned up one notch from the conventional well-made play into a parody of such a play.

The imagery of this comedy is confined to the inner worlds, here symbolised by the suburban garden and the 'City', and the upper world is entered by marriage. Sir Claude has for his 'secret garden' a frustrated desire to be a potter. Simpkins falls into the same pattern as long as he believes himself to be Sir Claude's son, though his ambition is to be an organist. Unlike Marvell, Simpkins is not satisfied to be in his garden alone:

> If I were religious, God would walk in my garden
> And that would make the world outside it real
> And acceptable, I think.

This remark indicates a possibility of further growth in him. He resents the fact that he will never be a first-rate organist, but when he learns that his real father was a frustrated organist too, humility comes to his aid and he becomes an organist on his own level. Like Harry, he transfers allegiance from one self to another, hence Lucasta can say:

> . . . You're either an egotist
> Or something so different from the rest of us
> That we can't judge you.

SOURCE: extract from *T. S. Eliot* (Edinburgh and London, 1963); new edn – *T. S. Eliot: An Introduction* – (Chicago, 1981), pp. 95–6.

*Carol H. Smith*  'Christian Implications and Greek Myth' (1963)

. . . The Christian implications of the events and characters of *The Confidential Clerk* become clearer when their prototypes in Eliot's Greek source, Euripides's *Ion*, are examined. The *Ion* is also a story of a misplaced child and the conflicting parental claims upon him. In the prologue to the Greek play it is revealed that Apollo had once ravished Creusa, princess of Athens, and the child Ion was born of the union. Creusa abandoned the child to the elements, expecting him to die of exposure but Apollo, unwilling to see his own son destroyed, sent Hermes to rescue Ion and take him to the shrine at Delphi to be reared by the priestess and to become a servant of Apollo at the temple. Creusa, meanwhile, had married Xuthus, never revealing the birth of her child by the god. The action of the play takes place years later when Creusa and Xuthus, their marriage childless, journey to the oracle to ask for aid. Apollo, wishing Ion to claim his birthright of the kingdom of Athens, reveals to the king through the oracle that the first person he meets after leaving the temple will be his natural son. Apollo plans to reveal Ion's identity secretly to his mother later. Xuthus meets Ion outside the temple and, embracing him as his son, plans to take him home and establish him as his heir. Ion, however, is not eager to leave his sacred life for the wealth and power of life at court. He points out to Xuthus that Creusa may be displeased by being forced to accept her husband's child, but the king tells him that he must learn to be happy with his lot. Xuthus plans to keep Ion's identity secret until he can gain the approval of Creusa, but before this can be accomplished, the chorus interferes and tells the queen of Xuthus's new son. In her jealousy and anger at Apollo for favoring her husband, she plans the murder of Ion, but when her plan miscarries she is forced to seek refuge at the altar of the god. She is met there by Ion seeking vengeance, but before he can take action the altar priestess intervenes and, showing the cradle, wrappings and birth trinkets, reveals to mother and son their true relationship. In disbelief, Ion asks Apollo directly for the truth and the god sends Pallas Athene to confirm Ion's parentage and his inheritance.

In Eliot's version of this story Colby is, of course, Ion and Lady Elizabeth and Sir Claude the childless Creusa and Xuthus. Colby, born of the union of humanity and divinity, has an obligation to both worlds, but whereas in Euripides's play Ion must accept his human heritage and leave the altar of Apollo, Eliot focuses the interest of his plot on the divine parentage of his hero which takes precedence over every human relationship. Both plays, however, emphasise the point that human desires are not always fulfilled as men would wish but instead as the gods determine. Just as Apollo does not wish his son to go without his birthright, so the Christian God finds a birthright for Colby superior to that of wealth or power, and at the play's end Eggerson becomes Colby's substitute father.

Lady Elizabeth and Sir Claude, like Creusa and Xuthus, have a childless marriage, but both have lost children earlier whom they desire to discover. In *The Confidential Clerk* Lucasta and B. Kaghan, the 'true' children of the Mulhammers, replace Colby, who as the child of Apollo follows *his* true father. Thus Colby inherits his 'musical' nature naturally, or, more accurately, supernaturally, as the child of the god of music. As Ion was reared by the temple priestess of Apollo, Colby has been raised by Mrs Guzzard, and her role as granter of divinely approved wishes comes from Eliot's merging of Apollo's priestess and Pallas Athene into one character.

Although Eliot has avoided supernatural disruptions of the play's surface, important elements of the ritual scheme still remain in *The Confidential Clerk*. Renewal by divine agency is still the fundamental dramatic theme, although the author has now expanded his conception of the meaning of renewal beyond the ascetic confines expressed in his first plays. The secular renewal portrayed in *The Confidential Clerk* is achieved by the rejection of the false substitutes tried by the older generation – Sir Claude's attempt to atone to his dead father in the wrong way and Lady Elizabeth's inadequate efforts to find religious inspiration – and the replacement of these false aspirations by the understanding of one's own nature and of one's own family. The domestic circle is fuller in *The Confidential Clerk* than in *The Cocktail Party* because the dramatist has added the relationship of parents and children to his earlier treatment of Christian marriage as a means of following the Affirmative Path to salvation. Thus the marriage relationships of both the older and the younger couple will be complemented by their mutual roles as parents and children; Colby's renewal will be of a different kind – the consecration of a life of service to the musical principle of the spirit. . . .

SOURCE: extract from *T. S. Eliot's Dramatic Theory and Practice* (Princeton, N.J., 1963), pp. 204–8.

# 4.  *THE ELDER STATESMAN*  (1958)


*Raymond Williams*      'Spectres of a Dying
Theatre'  (1968)


... *The Elder Statesman*, in 1958, was a dramatic epilogue. It brings
together the two themes of the epigraphs to *Sweeney Agonistes*: the
relation between human and divine love; and the consciousness of the
Furies. The first of these themes is beyond Eliot's power, though for
different reasons from the failures in *The Cocktail Party* and *The
Confidential Clerk*. The love of Monica and Charles is defined, it is true,
by their being Monica Claverton-Ferry and Charles Hemington; a
dry, tight-lipped idiom, in a world of social formalities, which makes
the talk of love like the faint rattle of spoons; dry sticks, saying the
words to each other, as the old man dies in the garden. But the
consciousness of guilt, in the elder statesman himself, waiting for
death, brings a return of some of the earlier power. The Furies, it is
true, are theatrically negotiated; the endless trouble of having them
materialise in the window recess, in *The Family Reunion*, has been
avoided by making them Federico Gomez and Mrs Carghill: a cross
between the grotesques of the early poems and familiar theatrical
types. It is not in that action that any significance is achieved, but in
what has been forced back – after all the years of dramatic
experiment, after the still conscientious construction of a theatrical
framework – to monologue:

> But waiting, simply waiting
> With no desire to act, yet a loathing of inaction.
> A fear of the vacuum, and no desire to fill it.

As nearly forty years before, in *Gerontion*:

> Here I am, an old man in a dry month,
> Being read to by a boy, waiting for rain.

When this feeling is touched, Eliot's recognisable verse returns:

> Say rather, the exequies
> Of the failed successes, the successful failures,
> Who occupy positions that other men covet.

and

> What is this self inside us, this silent observer,
> Severe and speechless critic, who can terrorise us
> And urge us on to futile activity,
> And in the end, judge us still more severely
> For the errors into which his own reproaches drove us?

The ostensible action, which provokes and resolves this emotion, never begins to be convincing. It is a given emotion, to which the memories and the hauntings of Gomez and Mrs Carghill are no more than a rough correlative sketch. Its issue again is private:

> They are merely ghosts:
> Spectres from my past. They've always been with me
> Though it was not till lately that I found the living persons
> Whose ghosts tormented me, to be only human beings,
> Malicious, petty, and I see myself emerging
> From my spectral existence into something like reality.

It is Eliot's familiar conclusion: the release, through consciousness, from an unreal ordinary life, 'only human beings'; the acceptance, in death, of another reality. It can be spoken with a shadow of his old conviction, but it can not be enacted; Claverton must die, off stage, under the beech-tree, in a traditional literary reminiscence; while on the stage the spectres of a dying theatre go through the motions of being human. And what we then see is a tragedy of another kind, in which this powerful voice – intense, articulate, memorable – finds and then loses, in experiment and accommodation, a new and serious dramatic form.

SOURCE: extract from *Drama from Ibsen to Brecht* (London, 1968), pp. 197–8.

## *Michael Goldman*       'Acceptance of Loss and Limitation'   (1973)

... In *The Elder Statesman*, Lord Claverton tells us that Gomez and Mrs Carghill are ghosts – ghosts of his past, of past crimes. In all the senses announced at the beginning of the play, their power to haunt Claverton turns out to be illusory; the crimes are not real crimes; their threats are insubstantial. But in another sense the ghosts and what they represent are inexpungeable; to face them they must be accepted, for their power to haunt lies in their reflection of the facts of Claverton's own character, which he must accept if he is to cease to be 'hollow'. For once, the burden is eased for those left on stage. Monica and Charles are brought closer to each other and to Claverton because his confrontation and acceptance of the ghosts has issued in a transforming love. But the discovery, a version of which has been hinted at in the final tableau of *The Confidential Clerk*, depends on clear-eyed acceptance of a haunting loss and limitation.

The great point about the encounter at the end of *The Elder Statesman*, and the great dramatic surprise, is that Claverton does not make his ghosts disappear or render them innocuous by facing them. They continue to be what they always were, and their power for evil is all the more felt for being more fully faced. The price Claverton pays is his son, Michael, but the meaning of the price, as he tells us, is love. If *The Elder Statesman* goes beyond *The Confidential Clerk* by presenting human love as a path to Divine Love, it is significant that the parent-child relation it requires as a dramatic pivot is much grimmer than that between Sir Claude and his daughter. Lucasta is quite clearly a bright angel, as her name suggests. Michael Claverton is not, and he follows Gomez and Carghill.

The pattern I have been describing is suggestive in a number of ways as to the meaning and method of Eliot's drama. What I wish to stress now is its relation to the convention he finally chose to work in – the convention of boulevard entertainment whose fourth-wall realism and bourgeois milieu sustain the workings of a well-made plot. The exact genre may vary with the mood required, but it is always well-made, whether it be the plot of detection, love-intrigue, farce or melodrama – always the mechanism of secrets to be discovered, obstacles to be overcome, communications to be rechannelled and restored. It will already be clear that the transition from false ghost to true ghost corresponds to the development in every one of Eliot's plays by which the expectations of the convention are subverted. *The Family Reunion* is not an Agatha Christie-like story of crime and punishment but of sin and expiation. The love-tangles of Edward and Celia, Lavinia and Peter, do not lead to complications in the second and third act. Mrs Guzzard's revelations do not solve the problems carefully established in the first two acts of *The Confidential Clerk*, but show that the problem as it has been stated is irrelevant, and so on. More important, the change in our understanding of the ghosts develops its special meaning and intensity only by virtue of taking place in this type of setting and growing out of this type of dramatic convention. . . .

SOURCE: extract from 'Fear in the Way: The Design of Eliot's Drama', in Arthur W. Litz (ed.), *Eliot in His Time* (Princeton, N.J., 1973), pp. 161–3.

*Carol H. Smith*    'Love and Self-Knowledge:
Badgley Court'   (1963)

. . . In *The Elder Statesman* Eliot further explores the idea of the role or dramatic mask given us by others, or assumed to protect ourselves from others, which must fall off before love can be freely offered or received. Lord Claverton must strip himself of his false roles as distinguished statesman, retired executive of 'public companies', and irreproachable father and husband, and accept the truth about his real nature and his shabby past. Only by confession to his daughter Monica can he fully experience self-acceptance in the peace of her forgiveness and love. The stripping off of false masks before death makes up the chief dramatic action of the play.

Both the tone and the structure of *The Elder Statesman* are carefully arranged to stress the importance of love in the process of self-knowledge. Although the most important part of the play's content deals with the events leading to Lord Claverton's death, the author opens the play with a love scene between Monica and her suitor, Charles. The developing relationship between the young lovers is used throughout the play to exert an emotional control over the other events and to reflect the effect of these events upon their love. The first view of the lovers shows them in a graceful drawing-room scene engaged in a playful courtship argument. Having accompanied Monica home after luncheon and a shopping expedition, Charles vainly tries to be alone with her in order to propose, while she teasingly keeps him at a distance. Their conversation serves to introduce the play's more serious dilemma of love: the relationship between Monica and her father, which is chiefly responsible for keeping Charles and Monica apart.

Lord Claverton, after a highly successful political career followed by a term in 'public companies', is about to begin an enforced retirement on doctor's orders at Badgley Court, an expensive convalescent home. Charles is jealous of Lord Claverton's dependence on Monica and remonstrates against her father's insistence that she accompany him. The lightness of the opening love scene suddenly changes at the moment when Monica first recognises and admits her love for Charles:

> How did this come, Charles? It crept so softly
> On silent feet, and stood behind my back
> Quietly, a long time, a long long time
> Before I felt its presence.

While Monica expresses love newly discovered, Charles describes the negative side of the same emotion – the torment of unexpressed and unaccepted love and the lover's desperate need for reassurance. Their conversation states the theme which is developed throughout the stages of Lord Claverton's spiritual re-education. They recognise the transforming power of love which he is finally brought to recognise when, after a life spent in selfish exploitation of others because of his inability to face the responsibilities of loving and being loved, he is visited by the ghosts of his guilty past. It is only at the end of the play that Lord Claverton discovers that his ghosts can be exorcised by his hard-won recognition of what loving costs and its curative effects on the soul.

The love duet between Charles and Monica gives ample evidence that Eliot has learned to integrate his poetic dramatic goals. His first dramatic use of the love duet was in the 'beyond character' scene between Harry and his cousin in *The Family Reunion*; the fact that the playwright purged such poetic 'intrusions' from his later plays is an indication that he judged such devices to interfere with the dramatic expression of his theme. In *The Elder Statesman* he has reintroduced the poetic interlude, but it now serves to forward the main love theme of the play. The lovers' discovery of a private world in the midst of the public world is conveyed by Charles's question:

> I'm not the same person as a moment ago.
> What do the words mean now – *I* and *you*?

and Monica's astonished reply:

> In our private world – now we have our private world –
> The meanings are different. Look! We're back in the room
> That we entered only a few minutes ago.

In these lines and in Lord Claverton's final spiritual cure, the poet expresses the necessity of a private world of personal love before either selfhood or salvation can be achieved. Neither the pretence of a public personality nor the isolation of a private life filled with unconfessed secrets can give a sense of identity. Lord Claverton has sacrificed his private world of personal relationships for his public roles and has lost hold of both worlds. The love of Monica and Charles is meant to exemplify the positive and beneficial power of love, while Lord Claverton's unawakened state before his act of contrition exemplifies the destructive and malignant power of love perverted and betrayed. . . .

Eliot's choice of Sophocles's *Oedipus at Colonus*[1] as his Greek source for *The Elder Statesman* suggests that he wished the play to express the final resolution of his theme of spiritual quest. At the time of the first production of *The Family Reunion*, Eliot had written to his director, E. Martin Browne, that 'Harry's career needs to be completed by an *Orestes* or an *Oedipus at Colonos*'.[2] *The Elder Statesman* is the fulfillment of that promise. It is indicative, however, of Eliot's changed conception of the qualifications necessary for salvation that between *The Family Reunion* (1939) and *The Elder Statesman* (1958) Harry had been replaced as the archetype for the penitent by a hero less spiritually gifted, less ascetically oriented, and more corrupted by personal sin. Eliot's choice of the old king Oedipus as his prototype for Lord Claverton stresses expiation by prolonged suffering and devotion to the will of the gods.

In Sophocles's *Oedipus at Colonus* the exiled king has grown old expiating his youthful crimes of patricide and incest; having arrived at a state of reconciliation and acceptance, he nears the sacred grove of the Eumenides, where it is ordained that he is to die. Because of his blindness, he is led by his faithful daughter, Antigone, and later joined by his other daughter, Ismene, who assists him in conducting his prayers to the gods. Oedipus begs Theseus, king of Athens, for asylum and protection, and Theseus grants his request since his death place has been ordained by Apollo and since his burial at Colonus will bring a blessing on the city.

However, the oracle has also prophesied that if Thebes is to prosper, Oedipus must be buried there, and his peaceful and sacred death is threatened by the appearance of Creon, who desires to take him back to Thebes by force if necessary. Creon's motives are those of personal ambition, for by insuring his city's salvation he hopes to regain the crown which has been wrested from him by Polynices and Eteocles, Oedipus's two sons. Finally, with the help of Theseus,

Oedipus is able to resist all efforts to take him away from the sacred grove of the Eumenides.

Oedipus is then visited by his son Polynices, who, having been exiled by his brother, is planning to attack Thebes by force. Polynices comes to ask his father's blessing on his endeavor, but Oedipus, instead, curses both his sons for thinking only of the throne instead of recalling him when they received word of the oracle. Thunder is heard and, after a loving farewell to his daughters, Oedipus obeys the divine summons which urges him toward his fated place of death.

In Eliot's version of Sophocles's play, Lord Claverton re-enacts the final purgation of the aged Oedipus, laden with sins but purified and blessed by the gods before death. Lord Claverton, like Oedipus, has been blind to his guilt and has lived in a state of spiritual darkness. The sins of his past parallel those of Oedipus. He has run over an old man, lived with his wife without recognising her identity, and reared a son who, like Polynices, is an outcast from the world of spirit. Michael's desire for worldly power and wealth can be equated with Polynices's planned attack on Thebes, which represents a city of destruction, pestilence and conflict. The irony of Lord Claverton's public role as elder statesman in the face of his private guilt is made painfully clear when his correspondence to the aged Oedipus is seen, for Oedipus is an elder statesman in the most grotesque sense.

As Oedipus is supported in his purgation ordeal by his faithful daughter Antigone, so Lord Claverton is both supported and finally cured by the love of Monica. And as Antigone vowed to carry out the burial rites for her brother Polynices if his assault on Thebes failed, Monica assumes the obligation of being her brother Michael's link with his lost self, thus insuring his ultimate means of salvation.

Finally, as Oedipus is drawn to the sacred grove of the Eumenides, Lord Claverton is drawn to the great beech at Badgley Court where he will find salvation. The emphasis in both plays is on obedience to the will of God and faithful observance of the bonds of love as a means of redemption.

By using *Oedipus at Colonus* as his source, Eliot is able to emphasise a more positive side of the ritual symbolism than that used in his other plays. In his earlier portrayal of the ritual battle, the struggle between the old and the new involved the violent rejection and annihilation of the corrupt old god and the complete endorsement of the new and the young. In *The Elder Statesman*, however, while the representative of corruption dies, it is not as the result of a struggle with the new principle in the person of the young hero. Rather, the struggle is now enacted within the hero himself, who represents both the sin-laden old god and the reborn new god. . . .

SOURCE: extracts from *T. S. Eliot's Dramatic Theory and Practice* (Princeton, N.J., 1963), pp. 216–19, 228–31.

NOTES

[Reorganised and renumbered from the original – Ed.]

1. [Ed.] Cf. Eliot's comment in his interview with Donald Hall, *The Paris Review*, 21 (Spring–Summer 1959), p. 61, where – while affirming *Oedipus at Colonus* to be 'the play in the background' – he disliked its being called the 'model': 'I wouldn't like to refer to my Greek originals as models. I have always regarded them more as points of departure.' Conceding that *The Family Reunion* was, to its disadvantage, 'rather too close to the *Eumenides*', he observed that, subsequently, he took 'the Greek myth as a sort of springboard, . . . . After all, what one gets essential and permanent, I think, in the old plays, is a situation.'

2. Eliot's letter is quoted in F. O. Matthiessen, *The Achievement of T. S. Eliot* (New York, 1935; 2nd edn, revised & enlarged, 1947), pp. 167–8.

# SELECT BIBLIOGRAPHY

Some few books, additional to those excerpted for this Casebook, are indispensable in the study of Eliot as a dramatist.

The most obvious is E. Martin Browne's *The Making of T. S. Eliot's Plays* (Cambridge, 1969): a detailed account of the staging of all the plays from *The Rock* to *The Elder Statesman*; and further insights can be gleaned from E. Martin Browne (with Henzie Browne), *Two in One* (Cambridge, 1981), from which an extract is reproduced in our selection.

D. E. Jones, *The Plays of T. S. Eliot* (London, 1960) remains the most straightforward single-volume account of Eliot's aims and achievements in drama.

Denis Donoghue's account of modern British and American verse drama – *The Third Voice* (Princeton, N.J., 1959) – is invaluable; and no study of Eliot is complete without reference to Grover Smith's *T. S. Eliot's Poetry and Plays: A Study in Sources and Meaning* (Chicago, 2nd edition 1974), which examines the sources of the plays and shows how these contribute to an analysis of them.

Although unauthorised by the poet's literary executors, Peter Ackroyd's biography, *T. S. Eliot* (London, 1984) will serve us well enough until an authorised biography appears. Caroline Behr's *T. S. Eliot: A Chronology of his Life and Works* (London, 1983), as its title suggests, gives a year-by-year account of the important events in Eliot's life.

# NOTES ON CONTRIBUTORS

CONRAD AIKEN (1889–1973): American poet and critic. It was he who introduced Eliot's poetry to Ezra Pound, and his autobiographical novel *Ushant* (1952) contains reminiscences of the poet, who is called 'the Tsetse'.

BERNARD BERGONZI: Professor of English Literature, University of Warwick; his publications include *Heroes' Twilight* (1965) and the Casebook on T. S. Eliot's *Four Quartets*.

MURIEL C. BRADBROOK: Professor Emerita of English in the University of Cambridge and formerly Mistress of Girtom College; her publications include *Elizabethan Stage Conditions* (1932) and studies on Shakespeare and on Renaissance and Modern Drama.

E. MARTIN BROWNE (1900–80): British director and actor; a key figure in the revival of verse drama and in religious drama, he directed all of Eliot's plays.

GARETH LLOYD EVANS (1923–84): formerly Reader in Dramatic Literature in the Department of Extra-Mural Studies at Birmingham University. His publications include *The Language of Modern Drama* (1977).

FRANCIS FERGUSSON: drama critic, poet and Visiting Professor of Literature at Princeton University (1969–75); he previously taught drama and the humanities at Bennington College until becoming director of the Princeton Seminars in Literary Criticism: his publications include studies on Greek literature, on Dante and on Shakespeare. His *Poems* were published in 1962.

NORTHROP FRYE: Canadian literary critic, for many years Professor of Literature, University of Toronto; a strong influence in modern criticism, his publications include *Anatomy of Criticism* (1957), *The Critical Path* (1976), *Spiritus Mundi* (1976) and *Creation and Recreation* (1980).

HELEN GARDNER: Merton professor of English at Oxford (1966–75); her books on poetry and literary criticism include *The Business of Criticism* (1959), *The Composition of 'Four Quartets'* (1978) and *In Defence of the Imagination* (1982).

RONALD GASKELL: Senior Lecturer in English (now retired) in the University of Bristol.

MICHAEL GOLDMAN: American poet and Professor of English at Princeton University. His publications include *Shakespeare and the Energies of Drama* (1972) and *The Actor's Freedom: Toward a Theory of Drama* (1975) which won the George Jean Nathan Prize for Dramatic Criticism in 1976.

RONALD HAYMAN: British theatre critic and historian; his publications on the modern drama include *The First Thrust* (1975), *How to Read a Play* (1977) and *The British Theatre since 1955* (1979).

HERBERT HOWARTH: lived in London in the mid 1950s but then went to America and held various posts in English at the Universities of Pittsburgh, Montana, Manitoba (Canada) and Pennsylvania. He died in 1971. Publications include *The Tiger's Heart* (1969) – a collection of essays on Shakespeare.

ANDREW KENNEDY: Hungarian-born scholar-critic, a graduate of Bristol University and currently lecturing in the Department of English, University of Bergen; his publications include *Six Dramatists in Search of a Language* (1975).

HUGH KENNER: Canadian-born critic, Mellon Professor in Humanities at Johns Hopkins University; his books include *A Homemade World: The American Modernist Writers* (1975) and studies of Eliot, Pound, Joyce and Beckett.

ROGER KOJECKÝ: a great admirer of T. S. Eliot; his Ph.D. was published in 1971 as *T. S. Eliot's Social Criticism*.

JOHN PETER: British scholar-critic, closely associated with the *Scrutiny* circle; his academic appointments include teaching in the Department of English, University of Manitoba.

CAROL H. SMITH: Professor of English, Rutgers University.

STEPHEN SPENDER: English poet and critic; he assisted Cyril Connolly in editing *Horizon*, and co-edited *Encounter* (1953–65); his works of literary criticism include *The Destructive Element* (1935), *The Creative Element* (1953), *The Struggle of the Modern* (1963) and *The Thirties and After* (1978).

RAYMOND WILLIAMS: formerly Professor of Drama at Cambridge (retired 1984) and one of the best-known of English Marxist critics; among his publications are *Drama from Ibsen to Eliot* (1952 – largely rewritten as *Drama from Ibsen to Brecht*, 1968), *Drama in Performance* (1954) and *Modern Tragedy* (1966).

KATHARINE J. WORTH: Professor of Drama Studies at Royal Holloway College, University of London, and a member of the Society for Theatre Research; her publications include *Revolutions in Modern English Drama* (1972).

# ACKNOWLEDGEMENTS

The editor wishes to thank Derick Mirfin whose idea this book was; the editor and publishers wish to thank the following who have given permission for the use of copyright material: E. Martin Browne, extract from 'Two in One' (1981), by permission of Cambridge University Press; Conrad Aiken, extract article 'Murder in the Cathedral' in *The Collected Criticism of Conrad Aiken*, Oxford University Press, copyright © 1958 by Conrad Aiken. Reprinted by permission of Brandt & Brandt Literary Agents Inc. T. S. Eliot, extracts from 'A Dialogue on Dramatic Poetry' (1928) and 'John Marston' (1934) reprinted in *Selected Essays*; extract from 'The Need for Poetic Drama' in *The Listener* (1936); extract from Introduction to Charlotte Eliot's *Savonarola* (1926); extract from T. S. Eliot's Introduction to S. L. Bethell, *Shakespeare and the Popular Dramatic Tradition* (1944) from uncollected Eliot material; two extracts from 'The Three Voices of Poetry' from *On Poetry and Poets* (1953); four extracts from 'Poetry and Drama', from *On Poetry and Poets* (1957); extract from 'Conclusion' from *The Use of Poetry and the Use of Criticism* (1933); extract from *The Pound Era*. Reprinted by permission of Mrs Valerie Eliot and Faber and Faber Ltd. extract from *Writers at Work*, Vol II (1963) edited by Van Wyck Brooks, by permission of Martin Secker & Warburg Ltd; extract from 'The Possibility of a Poetic Drama' in *The Sacred Wood* (1920) by permission of Methuen, London. Extract from William Turner Levy and Victor Scherle, *Affectionately T. S. Eliot: The Story of a Friendship 1947–1965* (1968) by permission of Dent; Francis Fergusson, extract from *The Idea of a Theater* (1949), renewed by Princeton University Press, reprinted by permission of Princeton University Press; Northrop Frye, extract from *T. S. Eliot* by permission of The University of Chicago Press; Dame Helen Gardner, extracts from *The Art of T. S. Eliot* by permission of Cresset Press/Hutchinson Publishing Group, also 'The Comedies of T. S. Eliot' Royal Society of Literature Lecture 1965, reprinted in *T. S. Eliot: The Man and His Work* edited by Allen Tate, Chatto and Windus (1967) by permission of the author and the *Sewanee Review*; Ronald Gaskell, extract from *Drama and Reality in the European Theatre since Ibsen* (1972), by permission of Routledge & Kegan Paul Ltd; Ronald Hayman, extract from *British Theatre since 1955* (1979) by permission of Oxford University Press; Michael Goldman, extract from *Eliot in His Time: Essays on the Occasion of the Fiftieth Anniversary of 'The Waste Land'* (1973), edited by A. Walton Litz, by permission of Princeton University Press; Herbert Howarth, extracts from *Notes on Some Figures Behind T. S. Eliot* (1965), by permission of the author's Literary Estate and Chatto and Windus Ltd; Andrew Kennedy, extract from *Six Dramatists in Search of a Language* (1975) by permission of Cambridge University Press; Hugh Kenner, extracts from *The Invisible Poet* (1960) by permission of W. H. Allen & Co. Ltd; Rojer Kojecký, extract from *T. S. Eliot's Social Criticism* (1971) by permission of Farrar, Straus & Giroux, Inc; Gareth Lloyd Evans, extract from *The Language of Modern Drama* (1977), by permission of J. M. Dent & Sons Ltd; John Peter, extracts from *Scrutiny*, XVI (1949), XVII (1950) reprinted in F. R. Leavis (ed.), *A Selection from 'Scrutiny'* vol. 1, Cambridge University Press (1968); Carol H. Smith, extract from *T. S. Eliot's Dramatic Theory and Practice, from Sweeney Agonistes to the Elder Statesman* (1963) by permission of Princeton University Press; Stephen Spender, extracts from *Eliot* (1975) by permission of Fontana Paperbacks/Collins; Katharine J. Worth, article from *Revolutions in Modern English Drama* (1972) by permission of Bell & Hyman.

# INDEX

Page numbers in **bold type** denote essays or extracts in this casebook.

Ackroyd, Peter   9, 15
Aeschylus   13, 21, 74, 76, 78, 105, 122
Aiken, Conrad   **90–1**
Albee, Edward   14, 37
Aristotle   20, 23, 60, 77, 94
Arnold, Matthew   12
Arrowsmith, William   12, 15

Baudelaire, Charles   79, 82
Beckett, Samuel   10, 64, 78
Bennett, Arnold   9–10, 14
Bergonzi, Bernard   **77–9**
Bethell, S. L.   23–4
Bradbrook, Muriel C.   14, **31–42**
Browne, E. Martin   8, 10, 11, 60, 61, 68, 85, 91, 114, **171–2**, 181
Browning, Robert   9, 28, 29, 165

Canary, Robert H.   12, 15
*Cats*   14
Catullus   19
Chekhov, Anton   11, 20
*Cocktail Party, The*   10, 13, 31, 38–42, 46–52, 55, 59, 60, 61, 62, 67–9, 143–70, 175, 176
Cocteau, Jean   35, 41
*Confidential Clerk, The*   8, 10, 12, 40, 42, 46, 52–6, 59, 60, 69, 171–5, 176, 178
Congreve, William   25, 48
Cornford, Francis M.   10, 73, 76, 79
Coward, Noel   11, 14, 67, 68

Dickinson, Hugh   13, 15
Dryden, John   31, 47

*Elder Statesman, The*   8, 10, 14, 39, 40–1, 42, 45, 56–9, 60, 69–70, 176–83

Eliot, T. S. (Poetry) 'Ash Wednesday'   9, 79, 165; 'Coriolan'   9; *Four Quartets*   8, 9, 12, 44, 56–7, 79, 123, 124, 125, 137, 142; 'Gerontion'   77; *Old Possum's Book of Practical Cats*   14; 'Portrait of a Lady'   37; 'Prufrock'   37, 77; *Waste Land, The*   9, 10, 38, 75, 76, 78, 81, 82, 131, 159, 164, 166; (Prose) 'Beating of a Drum, The'   10, 163; 'Dialogue on Dramatic Poetry, A'   **21–2**; 'Five Points on Dramatic Writing'   **23**; 'Four Elizabethan Dramatists'   9; *Idea of a Christian Society, The*   12, 45, 169–70; 'John Marston'   12, **22**; 'Need for Poetic Drama, The'   **22–3**; 'Poetry and Drama'   11, **24–6, 88–90, 121–3, 143**, 160; 'Possibility of a Poetic Drama, The'   9, **19–21**; *Sacred Wood, The*   12, 136; 'Three Voices of Poetry, The'   9, **27–9, 83–4**; 'Ulysses, Order and Myth'   10
Euripides   20, 21, 32; *Alcestis*   13, 46, 47, 49, 143, 162, 163, 168; *Ion*   52, 172, 173–5
Evans, Gareth Lloyd   **108–15**

*Family Reunion, The*   8, 10, 11, 12, 13, 33–7, 39, 42, 44, 50, 61, 64–7, 70, 110, 121–42, 143, 144, 145, 146, 150, 151, 155, 162, 165, 166, 176, 178, 180, 181
Fergusson, Francis   12, **106–7**
Frazer, J. G.   10
Fry, Christopher   11, 37
Frye, Northrop   **172–3**

Gardner, Helen   14, **42–59**, **86–7**,
    **94–6**
Gaskell, Ronald   **137–42**
Gielgud, John   11, 64
Goethe, J. W. von   20
Goldman, Michael   **101–4**,
    **159–62**, **177–9**

Harrison, Jane E.   10
Hayman, Ronald   **81–2**
Hofmannsthal, Hugo von   93, 165
Howarth, Herbert   **92–3**, **162–5**

Ibsen, Henrik   11, 13, 20, 68, 133

Jones, D. E.   13
Jonson, Ben   37

Kennedy, Andrew   **79–80**
Kenner, Hugh   11, 12, 14, 77, 78,
    **104–6**, **123–5**, **165–8**
Kojecký, Roger   12, **84–6**, **168–70**

Levy, W. T. (with Scherle, V.)   30
*Look Back in Anger*   10, 14, 63, 171

Maeterlinck, Maurice   22
Molière (alias for Poquelin, J. B.)
    25
*Murder in the Cathedral*   8, 10, 11, 12,
    13, 31–3, 34, 37, 42, 44, 58, 82, 87,
    88–117, 122, 126, 144, 148, 150,
    155, 163, 172
Murry, Middleton   9, 128

Osborne, John   10
Ovid   19

*Paris Review, The* (interview)   **29–30**
Peter, John   **125–32**, **150–5**
Pinter, Harold   14, 37, 39, 60, 63,
    67, 70, 81

Pound, Ezra   15, 23, 29, 33, 105,
    165
Priestley, J. B.   64, 66–7
Propertius   19

*Rock, The*   9, 10, 11, 12, 13, 83–7,
    100, 106, 153, 163
Rougemont, Denis de   51

*Savonarola* (by Charlotte Eliot)   10,
    21
Shakespeare, William   21, 24, 25,
    26, 52, 79, 88, 105, 110, 155;
    *Hamlet*   131–3, 163; *Macbeth*   107,
    150; *Measure for Measure*   156;
    *Tempest, The*   29
Shaw, G. B.   20, 25, 126; *St Joan*
    90, 99
Smith, Carol H.   13, **73–6**, **173–5**,
    **179–83**
Smith, Dodie   64–5
Smith, Grover C.   13
Sophocles   181–3
Spender, Stephen   **96–101**, **156–9**
St John of the Cross   74, 75, 78, 79
Strindberg, August   62
*Sweeney Agonistes*   9, 10, 13, 31, 33–4,
    36, 39, 42, 44, 60, 62–4, 70, 73–82,
    86, 116, 134, 142, 145, 166, 176
Swift, Jonathan   130

Tynan, Kenneth   8, 11, 12, 14

*Waiting for Godot*   10, 77, 78
Weston, Jessie L.   10, 76, 163
Williams, Raymond   13, **115–17**,
    **133–7**, **144–9**, **176–7**
Worth, Katharine J.   13, 14,
    **60–70**, 77

Yeats, W. B.   31, 33, 34, 36, 41